Administrative Law for Public Managers

ADMINISTRATIVE LAW FOR PUBLIC MANAGERS

SECOND EDITION

David H. Rosenbloom
American University

Routledge
Taylor & Francis Group
New York London

First published 2015 by Westview Press

Published 2018 by Routledge
711 Third Avenue, New York, NY 10017, USA
2 Park Square, Milton Park, Abingdon, Oxon OX14 4RN

Routledge is an imprint of the Taylor & Francis Group, an informa business

Library of Congress Cataloging-in-Publication Data

Rosenbloom, David H., author.
   Administrative law for public managers / David H Rosenbloom. -- Second edition.
      pages cm
   ISBN 978-0-8133-4881-0 (paperback) -- ISBN 978-0-8133-4882-7 (e-book)   1.
Administrative law--United States. 2. Public administration--United States. I. Title.

KF5402.R669 2014
342.73'06--dc23
                                                                    2014015458

ISBN 13: 978-0-8133-4881-0 (pbk)

Contents

Preface to the Second Edition   *xiii*

1   What Is Administrative Law?   1

2   The Constitutional Context of US Public Administration   19

3   Administrative Rulemaking   63

4   Evidentiary Adjudication and Enforcement   89

5   Transparency   123

6   Judicial and Legislative Review of Administrative Action   151

7   Staying Current   185

References   *195*
Index   *209*

Detailed Table of Contents

Preface to the Second Edition   *xiii*

1   **What Is Administrative Law?**   1

     INTRODUCTION: WHAT IS ADMINISTRATIVE LAW? 1
     WHY WE HAVE ADMINISTRATIVE LAW STATUTES: DELEGATION AND
         DISCRETION, 4
         Delegation, 4
         Discretion, 7
     ADMINISTRATIVE DECISIONMAKING, 8
     PROCEDURAL AND SUBSTANTIVE REVIEW OF ADMINISTRATIVE
         DECISIONS, 10
     THE DEVELOPMENT OF US ADMINISTRATIVE LAW, 12
     CONCLUSION, 16
     ADDITIONAL READING, 16
     DISCUSSION QUESTIONS, 16

2   **The Constitutional Context of US Public Administration**   19

     THE SEPARATION OF POWERS, 22
         Congress, 22
         The President, 23
         The Judiciary, 32
     FEDERALISM, 35
         The Commerce Clause, 36
         The Tenth Amendment, 40
         The Spending Clause, 41
         The Eleventh Amendment, 41
     INDIVIDUALS' CONSTITUTIONAL RIGHTS IN ADMINISTRATIVE
         ENCOUNTERS, 43

Relationships with Clients and Customers, 43
   Equal Protection, 43
   New Property and Procedural Due Process, 46
   Unconstitutional Conditions, 47
Public Personnel Management, 48
   First Amendment Rights, 49
   Fourth Amendment Privacy, 51
   Procedural Due Process, 51
   Equal Protection, 52
   Substantive Due Process Rights, 52
Relationships with Contractors, 53
Public Mental Health Patients, 54
Prisoners' Constitutional Rights, 55
Street-Level Regulatory Encounters, 56
   Fourth Amendment Constraints, 56
   Equal Protection Constraints, 57
PUBLIC ADMINISTRATORS' LIABILITY FOR CONSTITUTIONAL TORTS, 58
CONCLUSION, 60
ADDITIONAL READING, 60
DISCUSSION QUESTIONS, 61

3   Administrative Rulemaking   63

INTRODUCTION: SMOKING WHITEFISH, 63
RULEMAKING: DEFINITIONS AND GENERAL CONCERNS, 64
RULEMAKING PROCESSES, 71
   Limited or No Procedural Requirements, 71
   Informal Rulemaking, 72
   Formal Rulemaking, 74
HYBRID AND NEGOTIATED RULEMAKING PROCESSES, 75
   Hybrid Rulemaking, 75
   Negotiated Rulemaking, 76
ADDITIONAL FEATURES OF THE IDEALIZED LEGISLATIVE MODEL FOR
   RULEMAKING, 78
   Representation: Advisory Committees, 78
   Protecting Specific Interests and Values, 79
EXECUTIVE EFFORTS TO INFLUENCE FEDERAL AGENCY RULEMAKING, 82
CONCLUSION: THE PHILOSOPHER'S STONE VERSUS THE BUBBLE EFFECT,
   85
ADDITIONAL READING, 86
DISCUSSION QUESTIONS, 86

4   Evidentiary Adjudication and Enforcement   89

   ADJUDICATING *CINDERELLA*: A CASE OF DECEIT, ABUSE, AND DUE
       PROCESS, 89
   WHAT IS EVIDENTIARY ADMINISTRATIVE ADJUDICATION? 91
   CRITICISMS OF ADJUDICATION, 93
       Legal Perspectives, 94
       Administrative Perspectives, 95
   WHY ADJUDICATE? 99
       Agency Convenience, 99
       Advantages Presented by Incrementalism, 100
       Conduct and Application Cases, 101
       Equity and Compassion, 102
       Procedural Due Process, 106
       Caveat Estoppel, 107
   ADJUDICATORY HEARINGS, 108
       Presiding Officers, 110
           Administrative Law Judges, 110
           Other Presiding Officers, 113
   DECISIONS AND APPEALS, 113
   ALTERNATIVE DISPUTE RESOLUTION, 115
   ENFORCEMENT, 117
   CONCLUSION: SHOULD ADJUDICATION BE REFORMED? 120
   ADDITIONAL READING, 121
   DISCUSSION QUESTIONS, 121

5   Transparency   123

   INTRODUCTION: THE CENTRAL INTELLIGENCE AGENCY'S BUDGET? WHAT
       BUDGET? 123
   THE ADMINISTRATIVE LAW FRAMEWORK FOR TRANSPARENT
       GOVERNMENT, 125
   PUBLIC REPORTING, 126
   FREEDOM OF INFORMATION, 128
       The Freedom of Information Act, 128
       The Presidential Records Act, 138
   PRIVACY, 139
   OPEN MEETINGS, 142
   WHISTLE-BLOWER PROTECTION, 145
       Qui Tam, 148
   CONCLUSION: AN OPAQUE FISHBOWL? 148

ADDITIONAL READING, 149
DISCUSSION QUESTIONS, 150

6   Judicial and Legislative Review of Administrative Action   151

INTRODUCTION: THE DRUG COMPANIES' ACETAMINOPHEN, SALICYLIC
    ACID, AND CAFFEINE HEADACHE, 151
JUDICIAL REVIEW OF ADMINISTRATIVE ACTION, 153
    The Court System, 154
    Reviewability, 159
        Standing to Sue, 160
        Mootness, 162
        Ripeness, 163
        Political Questions, 165
    Timing, 165
        Primary Jurisdiction, 165
        Exhaustion of Administrative Remedies, 166
        Finality, 167
        Deference to State Courts, 167
    The Scope of Judicial Review, 168
        Agency Rules, 169
        FOIA Requests, 172
        Rulemaking Procedures, 172
        Agencies' Statutory Interpretations, 173
        Agency Nonenforcement, 175
        Discretionary Actions, 177
        Adjudication, 178
LEGISLATIVE REVIEW OF ADMINISTRATION, 178
    Oversight by Committees and Subcommittees, 179
    Reporting Requirements, 179
    Research, Evaluation, Audit, and Investigation, 180
    Sunset Legislation, 181
    Casework, 181
    Strategic Planning and Performance Reports, 182
    Congressional Review Act, 182
CONCLUSION: CHECKS, BALANCES, AND FEDERAL ADMINISTRATION, 183
ADDITIONAL READING, 184
DISCUSSION QUESTIONS, 184

7   Staying Current   185

THE PRIMARY FUNCTION OF US ADMINISTRATIVE LAW, 186
    Constitutional Contractarianism, 186
    Public Administrative Instrumentalism, 187
PERIODICALS AND WEBSITES, 190
TALK ADMINISTRATIVE LAW TALK, 191
ADMINISTRATIVE LAW AUDITS, 192
THE NEXT LEVEL, 192
DISCUSSION QUESTIONS, 193

References   195
Index   209

Preface to the Second Edition

It may come as a surprise that the *Encyclopedia of Life Support Systems*, which is sponsored by United Nations Educational, Scientific, and Cultural Organization (UNESCO), contains an entry on administrative law. I was certainly surprised when asked to write it.[1] I immediately had a science fiction inspired vision of earthlings boarding a spacecraft clutching the *Encyclopedia* in hand as they went to off to colonize a distant planet. Administrative law? Life support? At first, the connection seemed dubious at best. On reflection, however, I realized that the inclusion of administrative law is, in fact, necessary for life as we know it in modern, complex political systems. All governments in developed countries have mature administrative components. Public administration is the institutional means through which contemporary governments deliver public services and regulate aspects of economic, social, and political life. Administrative law is the regulatory law of public administration. It regulates public administrative activity. Without administrative law, public agencies could go about their business as they saw fit, perhaps routinely emphasizing administrative convenience and self-interest over other values and the public interest. In the United States, administrative law infuses public administration with democratic-constitutional values, including stakeholder representation, participation, transparency, fairness, accountability, and limited government intrusion on private activity. Life was once, and still could be, supported without it. However, other than perhaps some administrators themselves, few, if any, who know the history of US public administration would want to return to the days before the federal Administrative Procedure Act of 1946 went into effect.

---

1. See David H. Rosenbloom, "Administrative Law," UNESCO-EOLSS, http://www.eolss.net/sample-chapters/c14/e1-34-05-07.pdf.

To appreciate the importance of administrative law, one has to bear in mind that although students and scholars in the field of public administration tend to view administration as providing valuable public services, the rest of the world doesn't necessarily see it this way. Many in legislatures, small businesses, the health, medicine, industrial, and research sectors, and myriad other walks of life think of administration as bureaucracy imposing red tape and unwanted, often unnecessary, and even seemingly bizarre regulations. This is why administrative law books may contain chapters on "getting into court" and "staying in court" (W. Fox 2000). Looking from the outside in, administrative law constrains public administration, guards against abuses, and enables chief executives, legislatures, and courts to keep administrators in check. From the inside looking out, administrative law seeks to guide administrators and agencies in achieving their objectives within the framework of the nation's democratic-constitutional values and practices.

A solid grounding in administrative law is a prerequisite for understanding a substantial amount about the internal administrative processes used on a daily basis by public agencies in the United States. As with other aspects of public administrative practice, it is better to learn administrative law in the classroom than to be bewildered by its pervasiveness upon entering a public-sector job. Students already working in the public sector will need no reminder of the importance of administrative law. Nevertheless, they will benefit from gaining a systematic understanding of how and why it developed as it did.

Administrative law has such a major impact on what administrators and agencies do on a daily basis that it cannot be treated as tangential or as a specialization best left to lawyers. It needs to be integrated into day-to-day practice. For some administrators, such as those engaged in rulemaking, adjudication, and processing freedom-of-information requests, administrative law defines the fundamental structure and activity of their jobs.

This book aims to make administrative law accessible to public administration students, both those new to the subject and those already in practice. The book focuses on the essentials that public managers should know about administrative law—why we have administrative law; the broad constitutional constraints on public administration; administrative law's frameworks for rulemaking, adjudication, enforcement, and transparency; and the parameters of internal executive and external judicial and legislative review of administrative action. The book views public administration from the perspectives of managing, organizing, and doing administration rather than lawyering. It is far more concerned with staying out of court than getting into it.

The discussion is organized around federal administrative law. Where appropriate, state approaches are noted as alternatives or parallels to federal designs and requirements. After reading this book and grappling with the discussion questions at the end of each chapter, readers should have a firm grasp of federal administrative law and no difficulty learning the administrative law of any state.

Unlike most administrative law texts, the book neither contains legal cases nor devotes much attention to the development of case law. Federal court decisions are readily available on the Internet, and instructors can select them flexibly to augment the text. Books dealing comprehensively with case law tend toward dysfunctional excess in general public administrative education, sometimes exceeding 1,000 pages of material that is apt to go largely unused and soon be forgotten. This book also differs from others by including a chapter on the constitutional context of US public administration, which explains the constitutional constructs and doctrines within which today's public administration and administrative law operate.

The book is intended for classroom use in three ways. First, as a supplement, it will efficiently cover the main dimensions of administrative law in introductory public administration classes and courses on bureaucratic politics or the political context of public management. Second, it can serve as a core text in public administration courses dealing with administrative law or the legal basis or environment of public administration. As a core text, it can be coupled with selected legal cases of the instructor's choice. Third, in constitutional law courses, it can serve as a supplement to explain how abstract constitutional concerns such as delegations of legislative authority and procedural due process are transformed in concrete action by administrative agencies. It is unlikely that the book will be used in law school classes, though law students may find it refreshingly concise and helpful in explaining the political and administrative contexts in which administrative law is applied and the larger purposes it serves.

The challenge in writing the first edition was to explain the essentials of administrative law clearly and accurately, in nontechnical terms, with sufficient depth to provide readers with a sophisticated, lasting understanding of the subject matter. That there is now a second edition is testament to the success of that effort. The new edition thoroughly updates the previous one, adding discussion of new statutes and law cases, as well as developments during the first five years of Barack Obama's presidency. It also fine-tunes the earlier discussion for clarity. I hope those familiar with the first edition will view this one as fresh and refreshing and those new to the text will find in it a welcome alternative to other treatments of administrative law.

This edition continues to benefit from those acknowledged in the earlier one. I continue to extend my thanks to them. I would also like to thank the reviewers who gave such thoughtful feedback on the first edition for this revision, including Bradley Bjelke (California Lutheran University), Lorenda Ann Naylor (University of Baltimore), Stephanie Newbold (American University), Cindy Pressley (Stephen F. Austin State University), Susan E. Zinner (Indiana University Northwest), and others who wished to remain anonymous. Special mention should go to my American University colleague Jeffrey Lubbers, who is always generous with his time and patient in sharing his encyclopedic knowledge to explain the finer points of US federal administrative law to me.

1

What Is Administrative Law?

Introduction: What Is Administrative Law?

Administrative law can be defined as the body of constitutional provisions, statutes, court decisions, executive orders, and other official directives that, first, (a) regulate the procedures agencies use in adjudicating, rulemaking, and adopting policies, (b) control the exercise of their authority to enforce laws and regulations, and (c) govern the extent to which administration is open to public scrutiny (i.e., transparent); and, second, provide for review of agency decisions, rules, orders, policies, actions, and other aspects of their operations. In short, administrative law is the regulatory law of public administration. It regulates how public administrative agencies do what they do and why, as well as their authority to do it. As such, it is among the most important aspects of modern government. We are all affected by administrative law in myriad ways in our daily lives.

Food may present the best example of why administrative law is so important. What did you eat today? Is that all? Well, probably not. The US Food and Drug Administration (FDA) regulates the "maximum levels of natural or unavoidable defects in food for human use that present no health hazard." Known as the FDA "Rat Hair List," these regulations specify the amount of rodent hair that can be in one hundred grams of various foods such as apple butter, oregano, and peanut butter. The list also regulates the number of insect fragments and eggs, milligrams of mammalian excreta, maggots, and other unappetizing impurities in the foods that Americans consume every day (FDA, periodic). Chocolate can have up to sixty insect fragments per hundred grams (about two bars) and one rodent hair. On average, Americans eat 1.2 pounds of spider eggs and 2.5 pounds of insect parts annually.[1]

The FDA is empowered to set such standards by law. It would have no power to do so without statutory authorization. However, it does have considerable discretion in deciding what levels are unavoidable and do not pose health hazards and what to do about products that exceed the specified limits. An initial question is whether "unavoidable" should be determined based on technology or economics. Although the agency maintains that some defects cannot be completely screened out, removing from pizza sauce more fly eggs and maggots than are allowed is probably technologically feasible. Some producers may already do so. But is it economically feasible for the entire industry of large and small, relatively financially strong and weak firms to do so? Determining unavoidability also involves economic feasibility, which is related to the cost of producing products, their market price, and consumer demand for them. Some balance between purity and cost must be struck. The FDA seeks a desirable trade-off by testing products nationwide and determining the levels of defects present under the best production processes in use. This approach assumes that requiring investment to make the best practices even better is economically infeasible, or at least undesirable, and ultimately unnecessary because, while unappetizing, the acceptable levels are deemed safe to consume.

Safety is a second issue. Clearly, if people are not getting sick from the allowable defect levels in regulated foods, then these product levels are probably safe. Yet it is possible that the cumulative effect of the permitted impurities over one's lifetime takes a toll on health, even though the harm may not be traceable to them. It is also possible that the defects affect people differently based on age, allergies, and other factors. No doubt, aside from looking at best production practices, the FDA takes the views of health experts and research into account in considering where to set and maintain defect levels.

A third issue is transparency. As a consumer you may wonder if the FDA's regulations provide adequate information and protection. We are all familiar with the nutrition labels on food products sold in the United States. Peanut butter lists calories, fat calories, total fat, saturated fat, trans fat, polyunsaturated fat, monounsaturated fat, cholesterol, vitamins A and C, sodium, total carbohydrates, fiber, sugars, protein, calcium, and iron. The average number of insect fragments and rodent hairs is missing.

---

1. Data from http://www.spydersden.worldpress.com/2010/page/78; www.chacha.com/question/does-the-average-american-really-consume-1.2-pounds-of-spider-eggs-a-year-and-eat-2.5-pounds-of-insect-parts-a-year.

Should this be identified? Who should decide—Congress, which is elected by "We the People"; an administrative agency like the FDA, which is not; or the food industry itself? If it were decided to require information about "unavoidable defects," would it be sufficient to indicate compliance with FDA allowable levels? Should that level be specified on the product? Should the average number of various impurities be indicated? If Congress makes such decisions, it will hold hearings and receive testimony from representatives of the food industry such as the Snack Food Association, Pizza Industry Council, US Potato Board, National Confectioners' Association, Whole Grains Council, and other groups. If an agency makes these decisions, how should its decisionmaking process be structured? Should it be open to input from the same kinds of stakeholders, and if so, how? Regardless of where the decision is made, what role, if any, should health experts, hospitals and other care providers, health insurance companies, and consumer advocates play?

Finally, how should the FDA's defect levels be enforced? Should the FDA test products already in the marketplace, inspect production facilities, or both? If a firm's product exceeds the allowable defect levels, what steps should be taken? What opportunities should the firm have to contest the FDA's finding? Such questions are the stuff of administrative law. Although they focus largely on process, as they suggest, process can affect substance.

Administrative policymaking often involves a wide range of considerations and complex trade-offs like those involved in establishing the FDA's Rat Hair List. Administrators make a great number of decisions that directly affect the health, safety, and welfare of the population or sections of it. They have to address difficult issues regarding transportation, environmental protection, economic practices, labor relations, and much, much more. Their decisions are of fundamental consequence to the nation's quality of life and attract a great deal of political and media attention. Equally important to our constitutional democracy, though generally less visible and interesting to the public, is how administrators should make and enforce their decisions.

The how rather than the what is the essence of administrative law. What steps should an administrator and an agency take before regulating impurities in food? What values should be weighed and how heavily? How much evidence should be adduced to support agencies' conclusions? How open to public scrutiny and participation should decisionmaking be? How should the costs and benefits of agency action be weighed? How can an agency assess the impact of greater transparency on consumers' behavior? Would including the FDA's allowable defect levels on nutrition labels change Americans' diets, and if so, how—toward more or less healthful diets?

Additional administrative law questions focus on accountability and review of agency decisionmaking. How should the FDA be held accountable for whatever levels it sets? Should its standards be subject to review by Congress and/or a unit within the executive branch, such as the Office of Management and Budget (OMB)? Presuming that one or more of its standards is challenged in court, should the FDA have to show statistically that its maximum levels are safe, that lower levels would not be safer, or that the defects are unavoidable? Should the data relied on to reach its decisions be available to the public? Concerns like these are the crux of administrative law, and they are of recurring importance.

For the most part, administrative law is generic in the sense that one size fits all. Although there are apt to be exceptions, it more or less applies across the board to administrative agencies within a government, as opposed to being tailored to match each agency's mission individually. The phrase "administrative law," as used in the United States, makes an imperfect distinction between the procedures agencies use to make rules, set standards, and adjudicate and the substantive content produced by those actions. In other words, how the FDA sets maximum defect levels is a matter of administrative law, whereas the levels themselves are not. Similarly, how the Environmental Protection Agency (EPA) makes rules for clean air and water is a matter of administrative law; the actual regulations, such as parts per billion of arsenic allowed in groundwater, are not. The distinction is imperfect because administrative law provides for judicial review of agencies' rules, standards, and adjudicatory decisions, which may be found unlawful if their content is irrational or their scope is beyond the law. Moreover, administrative law, with the exception of some forms of adjudication, is not concerned with agency decisions regarding internal personnel, organizational, budgetary, outsourcing, and similar administrative matters. All levels of government in the United States rely on some form of administrative law to regulate their administrative activities. In the absence of US Supreme Court constitutional law decisions applying to all jurisdictions, the requirements of federal, state, and local administrative law need not be uniform. In fact, there is substantial variation.

Why We Have Administrative Law Statutes: Delegation and Discretion

Delegation

Administrative law statutes regulate administrative procedures and the review of agency actions. In the United States such statutes were adopted largely to control agencies' use of delegated legislative authority and their exercise of discretion. Although administration is usually associated with the executive branch of government, administrative activities nowadays also involve legislative functions. Rulemaking is the preeminent example. Agencies' legislative rules (also called "substantive" rules) are the equivalent of statutes and are essentially a substitute for them. Administrative rulemaking is sometimes called "supplementary lawmaking." For instance, legal standards for clean air and water can be imposed by statute as well as by EPA rules. But at the federal level, where agencies have no independent constitutional authority, such rules can be issued only pursuant to a congressional delegation (i.e., grant) of legislative authority to an agency.

At first thought, it may seem odd that legislatures would relinquish their own lawmaking authority to public administrators. After all, bureaucrats are hardly popular among the American public. Legislators and the media often deride them for usurping power and issuing undesirable rules written in impenetrable gobbledygook. However, legislatures find it necessary or desirable to delegate legislative authority to administrative agencies for several reasons. First, as the scope and complexity of public policy increase, legislatures have difficulty keeping abreast of the need to adopt and amend legislation. Legislative processes are typically cumbersome, especially in bicameral legislatures such as the US Congress and those of forty-nine of the fifty states (Nebraska being the sole exception with a unicameral legislature). A bill typically has to work its way independently through each house. It has to win majority support in both before being submitted to the president or governor for approval or veto. Legislative procedure is intended to provide ample checks and balances, but where the workload is heavy, it can overwhelm a legislature's capacity to deal with all the demands it faces. By delegating legislative authority to administrative agencies, legislatures can shed some of the lawmaking burden onto administrators.

Second, legislatures cannot be expected to have the level of detailed technical expertise often required in contemporary public policymaking. Environmental, health, and safety regulation can involve setting standards based on elaborate scientific analysis. Trade-offs, such as balancing technology, economics, and health concerns in setting the FDA's maximum defect levels, are also complex. Available science and statistical evidence may be inconclusive. For example, it may take years of technical analysis to determine how many parts per million or billion of a substance can be considered safe in drinking water, in the ambient atmosphere at a factory, or in our bodies, for that matter. In time, new information may require re-evaluation of that determination. Expert administrators are in a better position than legislators and their staffs to deal with such matters. Moreover, the range of regulatory standards and related policy concerns is too broad for legislatures to address. It takes the attention of numerous, specialized, and frequently large agencies.

Third, legislators may find it politically advantageous to delegate legislative authority to administrative agencies in order to avoid taking firm stands on controversial issues. It is easier to maintain constituents' favor by supporting broad objectives that are widely shared, such as protecting the environment, than by setting regulatory standards that will raise prices or cause unemployment in one's home district. Legislators may even score points with voters by denouncing decisions made by the very agencies and administrators that their legislation has empowered (Fiorina 1977, 48–49).

As necessary and convenient as delegations of legislative authority are, they raise a number of political questions. Constitutionality is one. The separation of powers at the federal level and in the states is intended to establish checks and balances as a means of protecting the people against the aggregation of power in one branch of government. Parliamentary systems fuse legislative and executive powers, but the framers of the US Constitution thought such a combination could produce tyranny. Following their lead, Americans have preferred to keep these powers separate, though less so at the local government level. Consequently, when legislative authority is delegated to administrative agencies, even though voluntarily on the part of legislatures, this can be seen as a threat to the constitutional order. As the US Supreme Court once summarized the problem, "The Congress is not permitted to abdicate or to transfer to others the essential legislative functions with which it is . . . vested," and there must be "limitations of the authority to delegate, if our constitutional system is to be maintained" (*Schechter Poultry Corp. v. United States* 1935, 529–530). Yet modern government requires at least some delegation. Large-scale administration would be impossible without it.

At the federal level, the formal constitutional solution to the tension between the separation of powers and the vesting of legislative authority in administrative agencies requires delegations to be accompanied by "an intelligible principle to which [an agency] . . . is directed to conform" (*J. W. Hampton, Jr. & Co. v. United States* 1928, 409). In theory, this intelligible principle doctrine ensures that Congress will clearly establish the broad objectives of public policy, relying on the agencies, when necessary, only to fill in the details. In practice, however, finding an intelligible principle in some delegations may be impossible. For instance, the federal Occupational Safety and Health Act of 1970 provides that the secretary of labor, "in promulgating standards dealing with toxic materials or harmful physical agents . . . shall set the standard which most adequately assures, *to the extent feasible*, on the basis of the best available evidence, that no employee will suffer material impairment of health or functional capacity even if such employee has regular exposure to the hazard dealt with by such standard for the period of his working life" (*Industrial Union Department, AFL-CIO v. American Petroleum Institute* 1980, 612 [emphasis added]). With obvious frustration, Justice William Rehnquist parsed this language in an unsuccessful quest for an intelligible principle: "I believe that the legislative history demonstrates that the feasibility requirement . . . is a legislative mirage, appearing to some Members [of Congress] but not to others, and assuming any form desired by the beholder" (*Industrial Union Department, AFL-CIO v. American Petroleum Institute* 1980, 681).

Rehnquist called the feasibility requirement "precatory," meaning that it essentially entreated the secretary of labor to take a balanced approach (*Industrial Union Department, AFL-CIO v. American Petroleum Institute* 1980, 682). Such "legislative mirages" are not unusual. Statutes are loaded with key "standards," such as "'adequate,' 'advisable,' 'appropriate,' 'beneficial,' 'convenient,' 'detrimental,' 'expedient,' 'equitable,' 'fair,' 'fit,' 'necessary,' 'practicable,' 'proper,' 'reasonable,' 'reputable,' 'safe,' 'sufficient,' 'wholesome,' or their opposites" (Warren 1996, 370). The Federal Communications Commission (FCC) is charged with regulating communications by wire and radio in the "public interest"—a term with no fixed meaning that can accommodate any reasonable action (Office of the Federal Register 1999, 524). The greatest certainty regarding the meaning of the phrase "stationary source" in the Clean Air Act Amendments of 1977 is that such a source of pollutants is not mobile. The EPA has interpreted these same words very differently in different programs and at different times (*Chevron U.S.A., Inc. v. Natural Resources Defense Council, Inc.* 1984; see Chapter 6).

Discretion

Delegations of legislative authority call on administrators to use discretion in formulating standards and policies. The weaker the intelligible principle in the statutory delegation, the greater the potential range of administrative discretion. However, administrative discretion also goes well beyond the rulemaking function. Agencies may exercise a great deal of it in implementing or enforcing laws, rules, other regulations, and policies. They often lack the resources to do everything legally required of them. Universal enforcement may be impossible or impracticable. It is an uncomfortable fact that selective application of the law is often inevitable. Equally important, the legal acceptability of many matters is determined by the discretion of "street-level" administrators, such as safety and health inspectors, or weighed on a case-by-case basis through adjudication within administrative agencies.

The use of discretion by thoroughly trained, professional, expert administrators can be highly beneficial—society has come to depend on it. We have master's programs in public administration or policy to provide public managers and policy analysts with the tools and ethical and legal grounding to exercise discretion soundly. We rely on merit systems and career civil services to reduce the likelihood that discretion will be abused for political gain. From a public administrative perspective, discretion is essential to the implementation of laws and the successful achievement of a government's policy objectives.

There is also another view. The motto "Where law ends tyranny begins" is prominently engraved on the US Department of Justice's headquarters building in Washington, DC. From the vantage of US democratic constitutionalism, then, discretion is often at war with the bedrock principle of the rule of law (Warren 1996, 365). The Supreme Court has even called unconstrained discretion in law enforcement an "evil" (*Delaware v. Prouse* 1979).

Administrative law is a major means of checking the exercise of administrative discretion to ensure that its use is rational and fair. It does this primarily in two ways: by structuring administrative decisionmaking processes and by providing for procedural and substantive review of administrators' decisions.

Administrative Decisionmaking

The federal Administrative Procedure Act (APA) of 1946 is representative of US administrative law statutes in trying to promote rationality and lawfulness in agency decisionmaking without imposing overly encumbering procedural requirements. It specifically seeks to prevent decisions that are

> (A) arbitrary, capricious, an abuse of discretion, or otherwise not in accordance with law; (B) contrary to constitutional right, power, privilege, or immunity; (C) in excess of statutory jurisdiction, authority, or limitations, or short of statutory right; (D) without observance of procedure required by law; (E) unsupported by substantial evidence . . . ; (F) unwarranted by the facts. (sec. 706)[2]

---

2. Citations to codified statutes in the text are to their section number in the *United States Code* (U.S.C.). Rather than repeat the title number of the *Code* in which the statute is found in each citation, this information is provided in the References section at the end of the book. The full citation to this section of the APA is 5 U.S.C. 706.

These objectives are often augmented by other statutes and executive orders that require agencies to use the best science available, engage in cost-benefit analysis, prepare environmental and other impact statements, or promote substantive values such as vibrant federalism and environmental justice. (These matters are addressed in Chapter 3 on rulemaking.)

In administrative law, agency decisions may be either "formal" or "informal." Although the distinction is imperfect, decisions resulting from activities whose procedures are substantially regulated by administrative law, such as rulemaking and adjudication, are considered formal. Informal decisions are more likely to involve questions such as which firm to investigate or inspect, how carefully, when, and what enforcement actions, if any, to take. Except where constitutional law is involved (e.g., the Fourth Amendment's protection against unreasonable searches and seizures), informal decisions are overwhelmingly regulated by individual agency protocol rather than administrative law.

Administrative decisions can also be categorized as retrospective, prospective, or present tense. Administrative law uses a variety of processes to structure formal decisions of each type and to constrain the administrators making them. *Retrospective decisions* require assessing the past behavior of an individual, firm, group, governmental unit, or other entity. They involve questions such as whether a corporation has engaged in illegal false advertising or an unfair labor practice. Retrospective decisions are often made in an adjudicatory framework. The agency and the regulated party make their cases before a hearing examiner, an administrative law judge, or a commission or board of some kind. The process can take place in writing or involve the presentation of oral statements. It can range from an almost cursory review of the facts and issues by the decisionmaker to a full-fledged hearing that resembles courtroom procedure. It may also include a right to appeal adverse decisions to a higher unit within the agency. In all cases, however, the objective is to establish the facts, including motives where relevant, and to apply the law to them in an unbiased fashion. Consequently, administrative law may specify a great deal about the procedures required, the kind of information that can be considered, and the credentials and neutrality of the decisionmaker. (Adjudication is discussed in Chapter 4.)

Prospective decisions apply to events in the future. Rulemaking is the clearest example. Administrative law requirements are generally based on the assumption that prospective decisionmaking on complex matters will be more rational when it is open to public scrutiny and participation. Ideally, open rulemaking and related decisionmaking will bring a greater range of perspectives and information to the administrators' attention. Administrative law can require that the decisionmakers respond to public input, which often comes from stakeholders, and explain their evaluation of it. Upon judicial review, rules may also be subjected to a rationality standard, such as whether they are supported by substantial evidence (reasonableness).

Present tense decisions often involve questions of eligibility or immediate compliance with a regulatory requirement. Many licensing decisions are present tense and strongly regulated by administrative law statutes. However, much present tense decisionmaking is informal, and some is largely regulated by constitutional law decisions as opposed to administrative procedure acts. For example, the denial or termination of a welfare or other benefit may raise equal protection, due process, or other constitutional concerns. Many law enforcement decisions by police and health, safety, and housing inspectors are also present tense. Their discretion as to whether to issue citations is generally not regulated by administrative law and is constrained by constitutional law only within broad parameters (Lipsky 1980; Bardach and Kagan 1982).

It is often difficult to establish or maintain the balance that administrative law seeks to secure between constraining discretion and allowing administrators enough flexibility to carry out their legislative mandates cost-effectively. Administrators may complain that the procedural requirements for rulemaking and adjudication are counterproductive and too complex, whereas regulated entities may want even more elaborate procedures to protect their interests. The compromises reached in administrative law statutes upon their enactment can also become outdated or upset by future legislation. Finding and keeping a satisfactory balance between under- and overregulation of administrative decisionmaking is part of the challenge and vibrancy of administrative law.

Procedural and Substantive Review of Administrative Decisions

Administrative law provisions regarding the procedural and substantive review of agency decisions also seek a balance of competing concerns. On the one hand, the political system relies on administrators to bring a high level of specialized expertise to the formulation and implementation of public policies. Subjecting their decisions to review by generalists who know less about the specifics of these policy areas and enforcement can result in delay, expense, and poor decisions. On the other hand, administrators' judgments can be distorted by self-interest, untoward internal or external influences, a failure to recognize competing priorities, over- or underconfidence, and many other factors that negatively affect individual and group decisionmaking. It is easy to find excellent as well as shockingly bad examples of administrative decisionmaking. Administrators have sent astronauts to the moon and back; they have also allowed American children to play in highly toxic radioactive fallout (H. Ball 1986). The trick is to protect against the bad decisions while not upsetting the good ones or wasting time, effort, and money reviewing them.

Administrative law focuses on four venues for review of agency decisions. First, review may be available within the agency itself. For instance, decisions by administrative law judges (ALJs) in the federal government can be overturned by agency heads, boards, or commissions on procedural and substantive grounds. This allows political appointees, who are often generalists, to substitute their judgment for that of more specialized ALJs in the career civil service. They can correct decisions for failure to see public policies from a big picture perspective, as well as for simple errors of judgment. Of course, political appointees' decisions themselves may be subject to review by the courts, and so, before making them, appointees normally consult with agency attorneys and experts.

Second, administrative law may provide for review by specific units within the executive branch. Currently, the OMB plays this role with regard to aspects of rulemaking and information gathering by many federal agencies. Its Office of Information and Regulatory Affairs (OIRA) reviews agency proposals to engage in major rulemaking—that is, the creation of rules that will have an annual economic impact of $100 million or more. Agencies are also required to obtain OIRA's clearance to use forms and other instruments for collecting information from individuals and organizations outside the federal government (see Chapter 3). The primary purposes of executive review of this kind are to coordinate agency activity and to ensure that it is in keeping with the goals of a president, governor, or other elected executive.

Third, administrative law statutes can establish the scope of judicial review of agency decisions, though the courts retain independent authority under the federal and state constitutions to hear cases alleging violations of constitutional rights and powers. Judicial review has become so common at the federal level that for some agencies (e.g., the EPA), it can be considered part of the administrative process (Coglianese 1997, 1296–1309). (Judicial review is discussed in Chapter 6.)

Finally, there are procedures in Congress and some state legislatures for reviewing agency rulemaking decisions. Their logic is clear enough. The agencies' use of delegated legislative power ought to be reviewed by the legislature, which empowered them, in order to ensure conformance with legislative intent. (Legislative review is further discussed in Chapter 6.)

The Development of US Administrative Law

The United States began to develop a substantial administrative component in the 1870s and 1880s. In time, administrative agencies engaged in so much policy formulation and implementation that the term "administrative state" was adopted to convey their centrality to modern government. Against the background of industrialization, urbanization, and population growth, governments became increasingly involved in the economy and society and came to rely more heavily on administrative agencies to do much of their work. As noted earlier, the Congress and state legislatures were unable to keep up with the continual need for new legislation, often involving complex health, scientific, or technological issues. The courts, which once engaged in a good deal of regulation of economic practices under common law doctrines, were overwhelmed by the changes industrialization caused in production, employment, transportation, and marketing. Vesting rulemaking and adjudicatory functions in administrative agencies was the nation's response to the ever-expanding scope and complexity of governing. More government activity also meant more enforcement by the executive branch.

A key feature of the administrative state is that agencies perform legislative, judicial, and executive functions. In other words, the constitutional separation of powers, which largely places these functions in different branches, collapses in administrative agencies. Administrators make rules, adjudicate alleged violations of laws and rules, and execute and implement public policy. After the massive federal administrative growth during the New Deal (1933–1938) and US involvement in World War II (1941–1945), it was fair to say, along with Supreme Court Justice Robert Jackson, that the agencies "have become a veritable fourth branch of the Government, which has deranged our three-branch legal theories as much as the concept of a fourth dimension unsettles our three-dimensional thinking" (*Federal Trade Commission v. Ruberoid* 1952, 487). By 1946, Congress viewed the power and independence of administrative agencies as a threat to its own role in government and to the overall constitutional scheme (Rosenbloom 2000). In response, it enacted the APA, which still frames federal administrative law.

Several basic premises underlie the APA and state administrative law. One is that when agencies engage in legislative functions, they should be informed by legislative values; when they adjudicate, they should follow judicial procedure; and enforcement should be fair, relatively nonintrusive, and subject to review. Importantly, Congress was willing to sacrifice some administrative cost-effectiveness to promote these values. As the APA's chief sponsor in the Senate approvingly noted, the Senate Judiciary Committee had "taken the position that the bill must reasonably protect private parties even at the risk of some incidental or possible inconvenience to, or change in, present administrative operations" (US Congress 1946, 2150).

In terms of rulemaking, as another APA supporter explained, "day by day Congress takes account of the interests and desires of the people in framing legislation; and there is no reason why administrative agencies should not do so when they exercise legislative functions which the Congress has delegated to them" (US Congress 1946, 5756). Prior to the APA, administrative rulings might be made "in the form of letters, and nothing in the way of even an informal hearing [was] required. If the citizen [had] a hearing it [was] at the grace of the administrator or bureau chief" (US Congress 1940, 13668). From this perspective, the act could be seen as "a bill of rights for the hundreds of thousands of Americans whose affairs are controlled or regulated in one way or another by agencies of the Federal Government" (US Congress 1946, 2190). Its provisions for administrative adjudication model judicial procedure and constitutional procedural due process.

The APA did not provide for legislative or executive review, but it adopted a strong presumption of judicial review of enforcement and other actions: "Any person suffering legal wrong because of agency action, or adversely affected or aggrieved by agency action within the meaning of a relevant statute, is entitled to judicial review thereof" (sec. 702). The act also contained a number of transparency provisions, including the general expectation that agencies would publish information about their organization, rules, adjudicatory decisions, and methods of operation, as well as make their public records available to "persons properly and directly concerned" (sec. 3). (Transparency is the subject of Chapter 5.)

The APA continues to serve as a platform for requiring federal administrative processes to embrace the basic democratic-constitutional values of openness for accountability, representativeness and public participation in policy formulation, reviewability for adherence to the rule of law, procedural due process for the fair treatment of individuals, and rationality and limited intrusiveness when regulating private parties and other entities. Over the years the APA has been amended and augmented by several additional statutes. The following list provides a snapshot of the development and scope of federal administrative law:

1. The Freedom of Information Act (1966; significantly amended in 1974, 1986, 1996, and 2007) vastly expanded the provisions for transparency contained in the APA.
2. The Federal Advisory Committee Act (FACA; 1972) promotes representativeness and transparency in the agencies' use of advisory committees in policymaking.
3. The Privacy Act (1974) protects against unwarranted administrative invasions of personal privacy and the release of information on private individuals without their consent.
4. The Government in the Sunshine Act (1976) requires multiheaded federal boards and commissions to hold open meetings.
5. The Regulatory Flexibility Act (1980) requires agencies to consider the impact of potential rules on small businesses and entities.
6. The Paperwork Reduction Acts (1980, 1995) seek to reduce the intrusiveness and burdensome quality of agency efforts to collect information from individuals and organizations outside the federal government.
7. The Administrative Dispute Resolution Act (1990) provides for alternative dispute resolution of matters that might otherwise be adjudicated within federal agencies.
8. The Negotiated Rulemaking Act (1990) outlines the general process through which agencies may attempt to negotiate rules with parties whose interests will be directly affected by them.
9. The Government Performance and Results Act (1993) requires agencies to engage in strategic planning and annual performance measurement and reporting.
10. The Small Business Regulatory Enforcement Fairness Act (1996) requires the Occupational Safety and Health Administration and the EPA to solicit information from small entities when writing rules. It contains a title, known as the Congressional Review Act, that provides for congressional review of federal agency rules.
11. The Assessment of Federal Regulations and Policies on Families Act (1998) requires agencies to consider the impact of their policies and regulations on family stability, marital commitments, parental authority, autonomy, and economic well-being.
12. The Data Quality Act (2000), also known as the Information Quality Act, requires the OMB to issue guidelines to ensure and maximize the quality, objectivity, utility, and integrity of information released by federal agencies. To achieve this objective, OMB guidelines favored ensuring quality by relying on information that has been

peer-reviewed and is reproducible. Although the act and guidelines could be construed as a basis for challenging the studies on which rulemaking is based, to date, the federal courts have rejected this position (*Salt Institute v. Leavitt* 2006).

13. The Openness Promotes Effectiveness in Our National Government Act (OPEN Government Act; 2007) strengthens freedom of information by requiring agencies to designate chief information officers, establish public liaisons to resolve disputes between requestors and agencies, and promote timeliness in processing information requests.

14. The Government Performance and Results Act Modernization Act (2010; signed into law January 4, 2011) strengthens agency strategic planning and performance reporting, coordinates strategic plans with the presidential term of office, calls on the OMB to develop an overall federal government performance plan, and requires agencies to designate chief operating officers and performance-improvement officers.

15. Various executive orders provide for executive review of agency rulemaking and information gathering, as well as seek to promote substantive values, such as favorable benefit-cost ratios and use of plain English in agency rules and communication. These tend to change with different presidential administrations.

16. An extensive body of judicial decisions deals with constitutional constraints on agencies and the appropriate scope of judicial review of agencies' interpretation of statutes, rulemaking, adjudication, and other actions.

The subjects listed above are the focus of the remainder of this book. There are parallel administrative law provisions in the states, though with a good deal of variation. North Dakota and California adopted administrative procedure acts in the 1940s, prior to the federal APA. Many more states followed suit between the mid-1950s and 1980. At least half of the state acts are based on the 1961 Model State Administrative Procedure Act. Some include provisions incorporated into the Model State Administrative Procedure Act of 1981, which placed more emphasis on protecting individual rights against administrative abuse. The state APAs typically apply to state agencies but not to local governments. The discussion here centers on federal administrative law but highlights significant alternatives or differences found in the states, where equivalent values and approaches may be stronger, weaker, or even nonexistent (Bonfield 1986, ch. 1; Bonfield and Asimow 1989; Asimow, Bonfield, and Levin 1998).

Conclusion

Public administration courses and programs generally emphasize management and the political context in which administrators operate. They sometimes view administrative law as a dry, technical matter for lawyers and judges. It may even be seen as interfering with cost-effective professional public management. In legal education, administrative law is taught from the perspectives of protecting private parties from administrative abuse and suing agencies for some type of relief. Both of these approaches tend to consider administrative law from the outside in—that is, as something imposed on agencies that is external to their central missions, professional expertise, and administrative values. This book treats administrative law from the inside out. It explains how administrative law's underlying values, as well as typical requirements, are an integral part of contemporary public administration. It also emphasizes how administrative law helps make public administration comport more fully with the core values and processes of US democratic constitutionalism. Administrative law helps prevent the modern administrative state from "becoming a government by the government and not by the people" (US Congress 1940, 4648). Administrative law makes public bureaucracy safe for democracy.

Additional Reading

Warren, Kenneth. "The Growth of Administrative Power and Its Impact on the American System." *Administrative Law in the Political System*, 37–114. 5th ed. Boulder, CO: Westview, 2011.

Discussion Questions

1. The FDA's "Rat Hair List" can be disconcerting. Do you think (1) the FDA should not publish the list because the defect levels allowed do not pose a risk to human health and just make some of our favorite foods less appetizing (i.e., what you don't know won't hurt you)? (2) the allowable defect levels should be published on the nutrition labels of foods to which they apply? Why?

2. If you were in charge of determining the allowable defect levels in the "Rat Hair List," how would you define "unavoidable" defects—in terms of economics, technology, or both? Are there other considerations you would add?

3. Since the 1930s, Congress has been able to delegate an immense amount of legislative authority to administrative agencies without violating the intelligible principle doctrine despite the fact that many of the statutes it enacts use terms like those quoted in the chapter that have little or no inherent meaning. Do you think the Supreme Court should tighten the application of the intelligible principle doctrine to make it more restrictive? How would it affect Congress, federal administration, and government responsiveness to the public if the Court did so?

2

The Constitutional Context of US Public Administration

In 1887, Woodrow Wilson, who is often considered the founder of the academic field of public administration in the United States, could write that public administration "at most points stand[s] apart . . . from the debatable ground of constitutional study" ([1887] 1987, 18). Perhaps in Wilson's day, but no longer. Today public administrative processes and practices are infused with constitutional concerns—and as the following cases illustrate, sometimes in surprising ways.

- In 1952, President Harry Truman (1945–1953) issued an executive order authorizing his secretary of commerce to seize the nation's steel mills in order to resolve a labor dispute that threatened to harm the US military effort in the Korean War.
- President Richard Nixon (1969–1974) sent a budget message to Congress in 1973 that included no funds for the Office of Economic Opportunity (OEO). OEO's acting director, Howard Phillips, started closing down the agency. He wanted to prevent wasteful spending on activities he thought would come to a screeching halt at the end of the fiscal year.
- In 1987, a grand jury subpoenaed Theodore Olson, a former assistant attorney general in the Environmental Protection Agency, at the behest of an independent counsel who believed Olson had given false and misleading testimony to Congress. Olson, who later became solicitor general in the George W. Bush (2001–2009) administration,

challenged the subpoena on the ground that independent counsel's position violated the constitutional separation of powers. The independent counsel was appointed to the Department of Justice by a special federal court and could be dismissed by the attorney general only for very limited, performance-related causes.

- Seeking to make federal procurement more efficient and economical, President Bill Clinton (1993–2001) issued an executive order in 1995 authorizing the secretary of labor to bar purchases from firms that hired workers permanently to replace employees who were legally on strike. The National Labor Relations Act of 1935 protects an employer's right to utilize permanent replacements, but Clinton claimed the Procurement Act of 1949 and his position as chief executive empowered him to override federal labor law when establishing policies for federal contracting.

- In 1993, Mayor Reid Paxon of Northlake, Illinois, removed John Gratzianna's company from the town police's tow truck rotation list. Paxon's action deprived Gratzianna of the business generated by the town's enforcement of parking and other traffic regulations. Gratzianna had a preexisting commercial relationship with Northlake but no contract. The mayor was showing his displeasure with Gratzianna's refusal to contribute to his reelection bid and for supporting an opposition candidate instead.

- In 1995, Patricia Garrett, who had breast cancer, was forced to give up her position as director of nursing for OB-Gyn/Neonatal Services at the University of Alabama Hospital because her boss felt that her illness and the medical treatment she was receiving made her an undesirable employee. Garrett sued the hospital in federal court, claiming a violation of her rights under the Americans with Disabilities Act (ADA) of 1990.

- In 2002, the Sarbanes-Oxley Act created the Public Company Accounting Oversight Board. The five-member board is appointed by the Securities and Exchange Commission (SEC), an independent regulatory commission established in 1934. The board has executive functions, including oversight of accounting firms that audit companies issuing publicly traded stock. Board members could be removed from their positions by the SEC, but only for good cause and according to specified procedures.

Each of these cases raises a substantial constitutional issue. Presidents Truman and Clinton lacked constitutional and legal authority for their executive orders. The head of the OEO was bound to follow the law, not the chief executive's budget message. Olson overstated the extent to which the separation of powers compartmentalizes the branches of government or places federal administration under the president. Although Garrett could sue a private employer who did the same thing, the Eleventh Amendment bars such suits against states and their agencies and institutions. The mayor violated Gratzianna's constitutionally protected freedom of speech. The organizational design of the Public Company Accounting Oversight Board violated Article II of the Constitution because it twice insulated its members from direct presidential control—the president could remove SEC commissioners only for inefficiency and other maladministration, and the SEC, in turn, could remove board members only for similar reasons. (The offending good cause provision was severed from the Sarbanes-Oxley Act, and the board continues to operate as otherwise intended.)

These outcomes were not self-evident. Some made new law; others clarified or integrated existing principles. Together, they provide a sampling of how constitutional law frames many aspects of public administration in this country. The cases involving Truman, Nixon, Olson, Clinton, and the Public Company Accounting Oversight Board speak to the limits of executive authority. Garrett was done in by the doctrine of state sovereign immunity, which is an important component of contemporary US federalism. Paxon's action illustrates that administrative decisionmaking is constrained—sometimes in surprising ways—by individuals' constitutional rights. Constitutional law is ever changing, and even practices as old as the American republic itself, such as partisanship in hiring, firing, and contracting, can one day be ruled unconstitutional (*Rutan v. Republican Party of Illinois* 1990; *O'Hare Truck Service, Inc. v. City of Northlake* 1996).

This chapter explains four key aspects of public administration's constitutional framework: (1) the separation of powers, which places administrative agencies under executive, legislative, and judicial authority; (2) federalism, which affects the relationships between state and federal administrators; (3) individuals' rights in the context of different administrative encounters; and (4) public administrators' liabilities for violating individuals' constitutional rights. Together, these constitutional features define and confine US public administration. They make it clear that although politicians, reformers, and media pundits often call for running government like a business, constitutional law makes the public's business very different from others.

The Separation of Powers

The US Constitution's separation of powers has a tremendous impact on federal and state administration. It divides authority over public agencies and administrators. Legislatures and courts, as well as executives, are constitutionally mandated to play substantial roles in public administration. Each branch brings a somewhat different value set to administration. Almost everybody wants the efficient, economical, and effective government associated with good public management. But at what cost to other concerns? Legislatures write administrative law to promote representativeness, public participation, transparency, and fairness in public administration. These values are also widely shared by Americans. The same is true of the courts' efforts to protect the integrity of constitutional structure and individual rights. Maximizing all these values simultaneously is often impossible. One person's open, participatory public administration is another's delay and hurdle to achieving programmatic results; a judge's procedural due process is an executive's red tape; and so on and so forth. Yet the separation of powers is not merely about executive, legislative, and judicial controls over public administration; it goes directly to the matter of what public administration should be.

The US Constitution's design for the separation of powers is extreme in its impact on federal administration. Its main provisions were written at a time when no one could have possibly foreseen the development of the modern administrative state. The number of civilian federal employees at its historical highpoint—4 million in 1945—was just about equal to the entire US population when the Constitution took effect in 1789. Although the framers' provisions for public administration were rudimentary at best, they remain largely in place today. By contrast, the states have found it easier to amend their constitutions or even adopt new ones in order to keep pace with political change, including administrative growth. They have been in a better position to clarify powers over public administration, especially those of the governor. By and large, local governments avoid the separation of powers altogether or rely on a much weaker version than the federal government. The following discussion focuses on Congress, the president, and the federal judiciary because the division of authority among them provides the clearest example of the impact of separation of powers on public administration.

Congress

It is fair to say that the Constitution makes Congress the source or author of federal administration (Willoughby 1927, 1934). Legislation is required to establish, empower, structure, staff, and fund federal agencies. Article I, section 9, clause 7 is unequivocal in providing, "No Money shall be drawn from the Treasury, but in Consequence of Appropriations made by Law." Article II, section 2, clause 2 requires that all federal positions not specifically established by the Constitution "shall be established by Law." These provisions were written to check presidential power. In the absence of an appropriations statute, the president cannot constitutionally draw even a penny from the US Treasury; without delegated legislative authority, the president cannot create and legally empower a single administrative office.

Relying on its constitutional powers, Congress has substantially enhanced its role in federal administration. Since 1946, it has reorganized and staffed itself for continuous oversight of the agencies. It also created the Congressional Research Service (CRS) and the Congressional Budget Office to obtain better information regarding federal administration and public policy. Additionally, the Government Accountability Office (GAO; originally General Accounting Office), another legislative agency, gained greater capacity to investigate and evaluate federal administrative operations. Congress has also relied on inspectors general, who have been dubbed "congressional moles," and chief financial officers in the agencies to keep it informed about administrative activities (Moore and Gates 1986, 10). The Congressional Review Act (1996) enables Congress to permanently block agency rules (see Chapter 6). The Government Performance and Results Act of 1993 and the Government Performance and Results Act Modernization Act of 2010 require agencies to consult with Congress when formulating strategic plans and to issue performance reports.

The President

Some political scientists maintain that Congress, as a result of its constitutional authority and oversight activity, has gained dominance over federal agencies (see Wood and Waterman 1994, ch. 3). That may sound strange to the many Americans who look to the president to control and manage the executive branch. However, it is in keeping with what several presidents and high-ranking federal executives have had to say. When former vice president Dick Cheney (2001–2009) was White House chief of staff in the Gerald Ford (1974–1977) administration, he commented, "There's a tendency before you get to the White House or when you're just observing it from outside to say, 'Gee, that's a powerful position that person has.' The fact of the matter is that while you're here trying to do things, you are far more aware of the constraints than you are of the power. You spend most of your time trying to overcome obstacles getting what the President wants done" (Edwards and Wayne 1985, 351). President Jimmy Carter (1977–1981) may not have been the most effective president, but presidential power over federal administration may have hit its nadir when he complained, "I can't even get a damn mouse out of my office," due to a bureaucratic jurisdictional dispute between the Department of the Interior (White House grounds) and the General Services Administration (White House building) (Barger 1984, 145).

Carter's successors have done better, but both President Ronald Reagan (1981–1989) and President Bill Clinton met with considerable frustration in trying to promote fundamental administrative change. Reagan vowed to make the federal government smaller. When he left office, it was larger in terms of the number of cabinet departments, civilian employees, budget deficit, and spending as a percentage of the nation's gross domestic product (GDP). With Vice President Al Gore leading Clinton's Reinventing Government initiative, various reforms were implemented, including downsizing, outsourcing, deregulating and decentralizing the personnel system, streamlining procurement, and setting customer service standards (Gore 1993, 1995). Yet surveys of federal employees indicated that the reform effort had only a modest overall impact. Although 72 percent of the civil service knew about the reinvention effort, just 35 percent thought their own agencies made it a priority (Barr 2000, A27). It seems noteworthy that Gore barely mentioned the reinvention effort during his unsuccessful 2000 presidential campaign.

The president's problem is that the Constitution's provisions regarding the scope of executive authority over federal administration are very general. Article II, section 1 vests "The executive Power" in the president without specifying its content. President Theodore Roosevelt (1901–1909) declared that this gave him the "duty to do anything that the needs of the Nation demanded unless such action was forbidden by the Constitution or by the laws" (Olson and Woll 1999, 15). On more than one occasion, President Barack Obama (2009–) has echoed the same sentiment in indicating that if Congress doesn't take action on issues such as climate change and creating jobs he will use executive power to accomplish what he believes is necessary in the public interest (Associated Press 2011; Marks 2013). In terms of federal administration, one wonders just what this power might be without preexisting legal authority congressionally delegated to the president or executive agencies to implement a public policy, spend money, hire staff, or establish new administrative organizations. Congress is often called "the first branch," because very little can happen in terms of domestic administration until it provides statutory authority and funding.

Article II, section 3 is even more abstruse in authorizing the president to "take Care that the Laws be faithfully executed." Notice the "be." The framers charged the president not with faithfully executing the laws but apparently with overseeing and coordinating their execution—and not necessarily on an exclusive basis. In so doing the president "may require the Opinion, in writing, of the principal Officer of each of the executive Departments, upon any Subject relating to the Duties of their respective Offices" (Art. II, sec. 2, cl. 1). The president also has "the Power to fill up all Vacancies that may happen during the Recess of the Senate, by granting Commissions which shall expire at the End of their next Session" (Art. II, sec. 2, cl. 3). This alternatively suggests that the president is either in charge of federal administration or merely a caretaker when Congress is not in session.

When federal administrators are caught between competing congressional and presidential commands, they are constitutionally required to take refuge in the law. A Supreme Court decision issued in 1838 remains good constitutional principle today: "It would be an alarming doctrine, that [C]ongress cannot impose upon any executive officer any duty they may think proper, which is not repugnant to any rights secured and protected by the [C]onstitution; and in such cases, the duty and responsibility grow out of and are subject to the control of the law, and not to the direction of the President" (*Kendall v. United States* 1838, 610).

Howard Phillips's mistake, as acting director of the OEO, was precisely listening to the president rather than the law. He believed it was his "duty to terminate that agency's functions to effect the least 'waste' of funds" (*Local 2677, American Federation of Government Employees* [AFGE] *v. Phillips* 1973, 73). To the contrary, ruled the district court, "No budget message of the President can . . . force the Congress to act to preserve legislative programs from extinction prior to the time Congress has declared they shall terminate, either by its action or inaction. . . . An administrator's responsibility to carry out the Congressional objectives of a program does not give him the power to discontinue that program, especially in the face of a Congressional mandate that it shall go on" (*Local 2677, AFGE v. Phillips* 1973, 75, 77–78). (In the end, some of the OEO's functions were transferred to other agencies, and it was disbanded.)

Clinton's executive order barring federal contracting with firms that permanently replace lawful strikers ran into a similar problem. Clinton claimed that the order's purpose was "to ensure the economical and efficient administration and completion of Federal Government contracts" (Executive Order 12,954 1995, sec. 1) and that it was congruent with the purposes of the Procurement Act of 1949. Again, a federal court saw things differently:

> It does not seem possible to deny that the President's Executive Order seeks to set a broad policy governing the behavior of thousands of American companies and affecting millions of American workers. The President has, of course, acted to set a procurement policy rather than a labor policy. But the former is quite explicitly based—and would have to be based—on his views of the latter. . . .
>
> No state or federal official or government entity can alter the delicate balance of bargaining and economic power that the NLRA [National Labor Relations Act of 1935] establishes, whatever his or its purpose may be.
>
> *If the government were correct [in its arguments supporting Clinton], it follows . . . that another President could not only revoke the Executive Order, but could issue a new order that actually* required *government contractors to permanently replace strikers, premised on a finding that this would minimize unions' bargaining power and thereby reduce procurement costs.* (*Chamber of Commerce of the United States et al. v. Reich* 1996, 1324 [emphasis added])

In short, the executive power does not give the president authority to use administrative processes, such as procurement, to contravene or circumvent federal statutes—even in the name of efficiency, economy, or effectiveness. If it did, as the court suggests, national policy could become unstable, and the rule of law might dissolve. Moreover, the president's de facto lawmaking power would be vast: in the mid-1990s, federal contracts accounted for 6.5 percent of the nation's GDP and 22 percent of its employment (*Chamber of Commerce et al. v. Reich* 1996, 1338).

Morrison v. Olson (1988), the independent counsel case, limits presidential power over federal administration from another angle. It essentially holds that the executive branch does not belong to the president but rather is subordinate to Congress and the federal courts as well. In a sense, the agencies are under the "joint custody" of all three branches, though *Morrison v. Olson* does not use that term specifically (Rourke 1993). The Ethics in Government Act of 1978 provided for the appointment of independent counsels by a federal court, called the Special Division. Independent counsels were vested with the "full power and independent authority to exercise all investigative and prosecutorial functions and powers of the Department of Justice, the Attorney General, and any other officer or employee of the Department of Justice" (*Morrison v. Olson* 1988, 662). They could be dismissed only by impeachment and conviction or by the *"personal action"* of the attorney general "for good cause, physical disability, mental incapacity, or any other condition that substantially impairs the performance of such independent counsel's duties" (*Morrison v. Olson* 1988, 663 [emphasis added]). No wonder Theodore Olson thought that Alexia Morrison, the independent counsel, was vexing him unconstitutionally. She was engaged in a core executive function—execution/enforcement of the law—and able to draw on the resources of the Department of Justice. Yet she was appointed by a court and provided by Congress with substantial legal protection from dismissal by her nominal superior, the attorney general, and she could not be fired directly by the nation's chief executive, the president, at all.

The Supreme Court found this arrangement perfectly acceptable. The Constitution's Appointment Clause specifically provides that "Congress may by Law vest the Appointment of . . . inferior Officers, as they think proper, in the President alone, in the Courts of Law, or in the Heads of Departments" (Art. II, sec. 2, cl. 2). Its wording left three main questions open:

- Was Morrison an "inferior officer" (as opposed to a principal officer, such as a department head, who must be appointed by the president with the advice and consent of the Senate, except when the latter is in recess)? Yes.
- Was there "some 'incongruity' between the functions normally performed by the courts and the performance of their duty to appoint" independent counsels? No.
- Did the independent counsel provisions "interfere impermissibly" with the president's "constitutional obligation to ensure the faithful execution of the laws"? No. (*Morrison v. Olson* 1988, 676, 693)

In a lone dissent, Justice Antonin Scalia protested, "There are now no lines. If the removal of a prosecutor, the virtual embodiment of the power to 'take care that the laws be faithfully executed,' can be restricted, what officer's removal cannot? This is an open invitation for Congress to experiment" (*Morrison v. Olson* 1988, 726). Precisely—that is the nature of joint custody. In the context of some administrative processes, such as dismissals and rulemaking, whole units—the independent regulatory commissions— may be beyond the direct reach of presidential executive powers (Moreno 1994). In *Humphrey's Executor v. United States* (1935, 628), the Supreme Court held that members of the Federal Trade Commission, which has quasi-legislative and quasi-judicial functions, occupy "no place in the executive department" and exercise "no part of the executive power vested by the Constitution in the President." By implication, the independent regulatory commissions are sometimes considered a "headless fourth branch" of the government.

The Sarbanes-Oxley Act's provision for removing members of the Public Company Accounting Oversight Board was unconstitutional because it doubly insulated them from direct presidential control. The president's power to remove SEC commissioners is limited to reasons of inefficiency and other maladministration. The SEC, in turn, could remove members of the board only for similar "good cause" reasons. The Supreme Court held that

> such multilevel protection from removal is contrary to Article II's vesting of the executive power in the President. The President cannot "take Care that the Laws be faithfully executed" if he cannot oversee the faithfulness of the officers who execute them. Here the President cannot remove an officer who enjoys more than one level of good-cause protection, even if the President determines that the officer is neglecting his duties or discharging them improperly. That judgment is instead committed to another officer, who may or may not agree with the President's determination, and whom the President cannot remove simply because that officer disagrees with him. This contravenes the President's "constitutional obligation to ensure the faithful execution of the laws." (*Free Enterprise Fund v. Public Company Accounting Oversight Board* 2010, 3147)

The Court went on to note that this two-level insulation also impairs "the public's ability to pass judgment on [the president's] efforts," is "incompatible with the Constitution's separation of powers," and would reduce the president to "cajoler-in-chief" (*Free Enterprise Fund v. Public Company Accounting Oversight Board* 2010, 3155, 3157).

Constitutional joint custody of administration hardly renders the president powerless. President Truman's effort to take over the steel mills was beyond his constitutional authority—even as commander in chief during a major war. However, his action yielded an important formula for assessing presidential powers that continues to inform analysis of the scope of executive authority today. As explained by Justice Robert Jackson in a concurring opinion,

> 1. When the President acts pursuant to an express or implied authorization of Congress, his authority is at its maximum, for it includes all that he possesses in his own right plus all that Congress can delegate. . . .
> 2. When the President acts in the absence of either a congressional grant or denial of authority, he can only rely upon his own independent

powers, but there is a zone of twilight in which he and Congress may have concurrent authority, or in which its distribution is uncertain. . . .

3. When the President takes measures incompatible with the expressed or implied will of Congress, his power is at its lowest ebb, for then he can rely only upon his own constitutional powers minus any constitutional powers of Congress over the matter. (*Youngstown Sheet & Tube Co. v. Sawyer* 1952, 636–637)

The president's large role in federal administration is primarily a product of the circumstances in Jackson's first category. Congress delegates a great deal of initiative and authority over administration to the president. It looks to presidents for faithful execution of the laws it enacts, cost-effective day-to-day management, and coordination of the agencies' activities. Through legislation, Congress has given the president leadership roles in federal budgeting, personnel administration, and, to a lesser extent, agency organizational design. Within this framework, presidential power is exercised with a tool kit of sorts, consisting largely of the Executive Office of the President (EOP), political appointees, and executive orders.

The EOP was created in 1939 in response to massive administrative expansion under President Franklin D. Roosevelt (1933–1945) and the New Deal, which resulted in some one hundred agencies reporting directly to the president. Its primary purpose was to give the presidency the organizational capability to direct, coordinate, and monitor federal administrative activity. Today, its main units of importance to the agencies are as follows:

1. The White House Office, which promotes the president's policy agenda within the agencies, coordinates their activities, generates solutions to administrative and policy problems, and resolves conflicts among the president's appointees. It also includes the president's top advisers, the press secretary, legal advisers, and others who assist the president on a day-to-day basis. The White House Office has generally had more than four hundred employees under recent presidents. (It had 468 in 2012 [White House 2012].)

2. The Office of Management and Budget is perhaps the president's major source of control over contemporary federal administration. In 1970, the OMB replaced and expanded on the activities of the Bureau of the Budget, a unit first created in the Treasury Department in 1921 and later moved to the EOP in 1939. OMB plays a major role in formulating the federal budget for submission by the president to Congress; supervising agencies' spending, rulemaking, policy, and regulatory initiatives; and coordinating administrative activity. Its

Office of Information and Regulatory Affairs is especially important in overseeing and coordinating agencies' rulemaking and their use of forms and similar instruments for collecting information. It is characteristic of the separation of powers that although OMB is a quintessential presidential agency, the director, deputy directors, and head of OIRA require Senate confirmation. In recent years OMB has housed approximately five hundred employees.

3. The National Security Council, established in 1947, advises the president on the coordination and integration of domestic, foreign, and military policy as it relates to national security. Its leadership comprises mainly federal officials with other responsibilities, including the president, vice president, secretaries of the Departments of State and Defense, director of central intelligence, and chair of the Joint Chiefs of Staff.

4. The Office of Policy Development and similarly named units have had a checkered history since 1970, when first established. Their basic purpose is to help formulate, coordinate, and implement the president's domestic policy agenda. By and large, domestic policy units have been overshadowed by OMB.

Other EOP units include the Office of the Vice President, the Council of Economic Advisers, the Council on Environmental Quality, and offices for drug control, science and technology policy, and foreign trade. Presidents have considerable flexibility in using these units to promote their policies, although several of the top EOP appointees outside the White House Office require confirmation by the Senate. In 2001, President George W. Bush (who took office that year) established the Office of Homeland Security (OHS) to coordinate the nation's defense against terrorism. However, because OHS was carved out of existing presidential authority and budget, rather than based on new legislation, its role was largely advisory. The federal budget for homeland security was spread across 2,000 separate agency and department accounts (Miller 2002). The inherent problems in this arrangement were a direct outgrowth of the constitutional limits on presidential power. In mid-2002, Bush called on Congress to enact a statute establishing the cabinet-level Department of Homeland Security to supersede the OHS.

Political appointees to the departments and agencies also help the president direct and coordinate federal administration. Presidents rely on them to implement policy initiatives and to manage and monitor the career civil service on a day-to-day basis. There are several types of political appointees of varying importance. Top-level appointees, such as department and agency heads or commissioners, require Senate confirmation, whereas most others do not. In recent years, the overall number of political appointees has reached approximately 7,000, some of whom are part-time. About 800 are appointed by the president contingent on Senate confirmation,[1] 800 others are in the Senior Executive Service, and 1,400 are known as Schedule C appointees in the mid-range grades of federal agencies (Pfiffner, n.d.). Most of these appointees have policy-related functions, though perhaps limited at the Schedule C levels. Scholars consider this number so large as to impede efficiency and effectiveness (Light 1995; Cohen 1996). In practice, all but a few department and agency heads have limited access to the president. They basically receive presidential direction through the White House Office and OMB. In terms of administration, the relatively short tenure of political appointees—often about two years or less in several presidential administrations—can be destabilizing or even disruptive to program implementation by the career civil service (Heclo 1977; Aberbach and Rockman 2000).

Executive orders are often a highly effective means of directing and controlling administrative activity. Presidents have issued more than 13,650 of them since 1862, when the term "executive order" was first used. They are a staple of presidential efforts to exercise authority over administrative agencies and processes. The executive order is one of the tools President Obama, who issued thirty-eight in 2012 and eighteen in 2013, has in mind when he says he will take action without Congress (National Archives 2012, 2013). Executive orders have been used, among other matters, to reorganize agencies, to require agencies to pay attention to particular values such as vibrant federalism and customer service, to regulate agencies' rulemaking processes, and to deal with federal personnel matters. They are often issued pursuant to congressional delegations of legislative authority, though they may be based on the president's assertion of Article II authority alone. To be valid, their implementation cannot contravene the Constitution or statutory law. They can be challenged in federal court, as were Truman's order dealing with the steel mills and Clinton's regarding permanent replacements for striking employees. Unless they fall into an area of exclusive presidential authority under the Constitution, Congress can negate them by statute (which is subject to presidential veto and override by a two-thirds vote in both the House of Representatives and the Senate).

To regulate the behavior of ordinary private citizens or businesses, an executive order must be based on a statute or a special connection to the

---

1. This figure excludes approximately 90 US attorneys, 94 marshals, and 180 ambassadors who also require Senate confirmation.

government, such as being a government contractor. For example, Executive Order 8,802 (1941) declared that "there shall be no discrimination in the employment of workers in defense industries or Government because of race, creed, color, or national origin." However, the prohibition of such discrimination in most private-sector employment had to wait several years for congressional legislation, namely, the Civil Rights Act of 1964. Overall, and perhaps by legislative default, executive orders have become a very powerful tool for regulating administrative processes and activity (Olson and Woll 1999).

Taken as a whole, then, Article II, delegations of legislative authority, and the tool kit put the president at the center of federal administration. Nevertheless, it is a mistake to assume that the executive branch is solely the president's. On most administrative matters, presidential power is shared with Congress—and sometimes with the courts as well.

The Judiciary

The judiciary is central to public administration and administrative law in the United States. At the federal level, and perhaps in many states, litigation is a normal rather than extraordinary feature of the administrative process. Individuals and other entities often sue the agencies that regulate them, fail to satisfy requests under the Freedom of Information Act, or are otherwise thought to be in violation of their rights. Agencies use litigation to enforce statutes and administrative rules. Perhaps to taxpayers' disbelief, sometimes federal agencies even sue each other (e.g., *U.S. Department of Defense v. Federal Labor Relations Authority*, discussed in Chapter 5). Litigation is so institutionalized that there is a specialized US Court of Appeals for the Federal Circuit that hears appeals dealing with patents, federal contracts, international trade, claims against the United States, federal personnel matters, and veterans' affairs. Through hundreds, if not thousands, of suits, federal and state judges define the constitutionality and legality of administrative procedures, decisions, and enforcement activities. Court decisions are part of the overall fabric of US administrative law. Consequently, their substantive holdings and requirements are fully integrated into this book's discussion of rulemaking, adjudication, and transparency. However, because it is easy to get lost in the details of myriad judicial rulings and doctrines, the discussion here explains the overall framework and coherence of the judiciary's impact on contemporary public administration.

Since the 1950s, the federal judiciary has responded to the post–New Deal and post–World War II role of public administration in the society, economy, and governmental structure primarily in four ways. First, it declared (or "created") a vast array of new constitutional rights for individuals in their encounters with public administrators. Prior to the 1950s, agencies' clients or customers, employees, contractors, and those confined to prisons and public mental health facilities had very few constitutional protections against abusive administrative action. The same was true of individuals involved in street-level interaction with enforcement officers, such as police and health and safety inspectors. Since then, however, there has been a dramatic turnabout (discussed below in the section "Individuals' Constitutional Rights in Administrative Encounters").

Second, the courts made it easier for individuals to gain *standing* (see Chapter 6) to sue administrators for violations of their newfound rights. Under Article III of the Constitution, the judicial power extends only to "cases and controversies." Consequently, the federal district courts, circuit courts of appeals, US Supreme Court, and other Article III courts do not give advisory opinions. To bring a case against an administrative agency— that is, to have standing to sue the agency—the plaintiff must show that he or she has been, or will imminently be, injured by the agency in some concrete and particular way that can be redressed appropriately through a lawsuit. The courts can tighten or loosen the standards for standing when assessing the nature of the injury, its cause, the extent to which it is borne by particular individuals or an identifiable class of persons, and whether the remedy sought is appropriate. Merely being a taxpayer whose taxes increase due to an agency's action is insufficient to create standing to sue a federal agency unless one is challenging Congress's authority under its Article I, section 8 taxing and spending power (*Flast v. Cohen* 1968). Such an injury is shared with millions of other individuals and therefore is not particularized. One may also lack standing because the injury is too limited to create a sufficient stake in the outcome of a suit, the injury was not caused by the party being sued, or the requested relief will not remedy the injury. At one point in the mid-1970s, the threshold for suing an agency in federal court was reduced "to the simple proposition that one who is hurt by governmental action has standing to challenge it" (Davis 1975, 72). That opened the door to more suits and, consequently, more judicial involvement in administration. Today, the door remains open wider than throughout most of US history (but somewhat less so than in the 1970s).

Third, the federal judiciary developed a new type of lawsuit that facilitates its direct intervention in public administration as a means of protecting the constitutional rights of discrete categories of people, such as prisoners or applicants for employment in a government agency. These suits, called remedial lawsuits, are aimed at creating thoroughgoing reforms in administrative institutions and processes. Public school desegregation suits are a familiar example, in which judges become deeply involved in the operation of school systems in order to remedy previous violations of some students' constitutional right to equal protection of the laws. Courts sometimes retain jurisdiction for years and may make decisions about neighborhood school boundaries, teachers' salaries, curricula, the location of new schools and the closing of older ones, and even the architecture of school buildings. Prisons, jails, public mental hospitals, and public personnel systems have also been subject to such judicial oversight (Rosenbloom, O'Leary, and Chanin 2010; see also *Missouri v. Jenkins* 1995).

Fourth, as is discussed later in this chapter, the federal courts greatly increased the personal liability for monetary compensation and punitive or exemplary damages that most public administrators face for violating individuals' constitutional rights. The administrators' best defense against suits alleging an injury to someone's constitutional rights is not to violate these rights in the first place. Because constitutional law "is what the courts say it is," as Justice Lewis Powell once remarked, potential liability provides a strong incentive for administrators to follow judicial decisions affecting the rights of their clients, customers, subordinates, contractors, or inmates, along with any others upon whom they may act in their official capacities (*Owen v. City of Independence* 1980, 669). Public administrators also need to integrate into their daily practices the constitutional values that underlie those decisions.

These four developments amount to a judicial response to the modern administrative state. Judges have declared new constitutional rights to protect individuals against administrative abuses, made it easier for them to sue agencies and administrators, developed a type of lawsuit that enables judges to intervene directly in administrative operations, and made administrators who ignore the constitutional rights of others far more vulnerable to personal liability. Much of their reasoning has been premised on the concern that "today's mounting bureaucracy, both at the state and federal levels, promises to be suffocating and repressive unless it is put into the harness of procedural due process" (*Spady v. Mount Vernon* 1974, 985). It is also based on a desire to ensure that "where an official could be expected to know that certain conduct would violate statutory or constitutional rights, he should be made to hesitate" (*Harlow v. Fitzgerald* 1982, 819). Taken as a whole, the judiciary has "constitutionalized" public administration throughout the United States by establishing constitutional law as a basis for constraining administrative activity and defining its processes, values, and ethical requirements (Rosenbloom, Carroll, and Carroll 2000; Rosenbloom, O'Leary, and Chanin 2010; Rohr 1989).

Federalism

Federalism—the division of power and sovereignty between the federal government and the states—is another constitutional arrangement of great importance to US public administration. The constitutional law of federalism is defined by the Commerce and Spending clauses in Article I, as well as by the Tenth and Eleventh amendments. The Tenth Amendment most succinctly underscores the basic theory of federalism in this country. The federal government is one of limited, enumerated powers, whereas the states have largely open-ended residuary sovereignty over a very broad range of policy areas: "The powers not delegated to the United States by the Constitution, nor prohibited by it to the States, are reserved to the States respectively, or to the people." The key issue in assessing federalism is determining which powers are denied to the states and which are vested in the federal government.

Because the states' powers are open-ended, it is easier to say what they cannot do (as opposed to what they can do) under the Constitution. Prohibitions on state activity in Article I, section 10 include entering into treaties, alliances, and confederations; coining money; passing ex post facto laws, bills of attainder, and laws impairing the obligation of contracts; and granting titles of nobility. The section permits the states to do the following, but only with congressional consent: levy duties on imports and exports (except those that are "absolutely necessary" for executing state inspection laws); keep troops or warships during peacetime; enter into compacts with other states or foreign powers; and engage in war, except if imminently threatened by invasion or actually invaded.

In addition to these limitations, the states are directly constrained by several constitutional amendments. In terms of contemporary administration, the Fourteenth Amendment is most important. It reads, in part, "Nor shall any State deprive any person of life, liberty, or property, without due process of law; nor deny to any person within its jurisdiction the equal protection of the laws" (sec. 1). The federal courts have interpreted the word "liberty" to "incorporate" much of the Bill of Rights (i.e., the first ten amendments) and to apply their restrictions, which originally pertained to the federal government, to the states. For example, the First Amendment's provision that "Congress shall make no law respecting an establishment of religion, or prohibiting the free exercise thereof; or abridging the freedom of speech, or of the press" applies to the states through the Fourteenth Amendment. As a consequence, the US Constitution and federal courts now play a much greater role in protecting individuals' fundamental rights from infringement by the states than the framers anticipated in 1787. Several other amendments also directly limit the states. The Thirteenth (1865) bans slavery and involuntary servitude (except as punishment for convicted criminals); the Fifteenth (1870), Nineteenth (1920), Twenty-Fourth (1964), and Twenty-Sixth (1971), respectively, prohibit abridgment of the right to vote on account of race, sex, failure to pay a poll tax, or age (for those eighteen and older). The Twenty-First (1933), by contrast, empowers the states to regulate the delivery and use of intoxicating liquors.

The Commerce Clause

Federalism is more complicated when the states are denied powers because they are constitutionally vested in the federal government. The Commerce Clause, in particular, has been central to defining the scope of federal and state powers. It authorizes Congress "to regulate Commerce with foreign Nations, and among the several States, and with the Indian Tribes" (Art. I, sec. 8, cl. 3). However, it does not define "commerce" or "among." The Supreme Court's interpretation of these words changes over time and thereby alters the balance of federal and state power.

At the low point of federal power, "commerce," defined as buying, selling, bartering, and transporting, did not include production, manufacturing, and mining. Regulation of these activities, including working conditions within them, was a matter for the states. The federal government could regulate commerce if it was interstate or had a direct effect on interstate trade. In the 1930s, the New Deal effort to overcome the Great Depression was frustrated by such a narrow Commerce Clause interpretation, which put a great deal of economic activity beyond the reach of federal regulation. For example, in 1936 the Supreme Court strongly rebuffed Congress's attempt to regulate labor practices, wages, and other working conditions in coal mining: "The distinction between a direct and an indirect effect turns, not upon the magnitude of either the cause or the effect, but entirely upon the manner in which the effect has been brought about. If the production by one man of a single ton of coal intended for interstate sale and shipment . . . affects interstate commerce indirectly, the effect does not become direct by multiplying the tonnage, or increasing the number of men employed, or adding to the expense or complexities of the business, or by all combined" (*Carter v. Carter Coal Co.* 1936, 308). Under this approach, if production was local, there was no difference between one ton and a million tons, and a "production crisis in every part of the country simultaneously could never add up to a national problem with which Congress could deal" (Pritchett 1977, 193). Regulation would have to come from the states, which for economic reasons might want to be more lax, or at least not significantly more stringent than their neighbors.

The Supreme Court's constricted reading of the Commerce Clause in the 1930s triggered a great deal of criticism. President Roosevelt sought to "pack" the Court (i.e., expand its size in order to appoint up to six new justices, who presumably would be more amenable to New Deal measures). The court-packing plan proved unnecessary. In 1937, the Court began to accept a broader role for the federal government in regulating the economy. By 1942, the Commerce Clause could be used to regulate a farmer's production of wheat on his farm in one state, even though almost all of it was consumed there and only a trivial amount ever entered any market. In the Court's new and expansive interpretation of the Commerce Clause, "even if [the] activity be local, and though it may not be regarded as commerce, it may still, whatever its nature, be reached by Congress if it exerts a substantial economic effect on interstate commerce, and this irrespective of whether such effect is what might at some earlier time have been defined as 'direct' or 'indirect'" (*Wickard v. Filburn* 1942, 125). The Court's underlying theory was that if a large number of farmers grew and consumed wheat on their farms in excess of federal crop quotas, it would have a substantial effect on the national market for wheat.

In addressing the current scope of the Commerce Clause, the Supreme Court explained,

> [W]e have identified three broad categories of activity that Congress may regulate under its commerce power. . . . First, Congress may regulate the use of the channels of interstate commerce. . . . "'[T]he authority of Congress to keep the channels of interstate commerce free from immoral and injurious uses has been frequently sustained, and is no longer open to question.'" . . . Second, Congress is empowered to regulate and protect the instrumentalities of interstate commerce, or persons or things in interstate commerce, even though the threat may come only from intrastate activities. . . . ("[F]or example, the destruction of an aircraft . . . or . . . thefts from interstate shipments. . . . "). Finally, Congress' commerce authority includes the power to regulate those activities having a substantial relation to interstate commerce. (*United States v. Lopez* 1995, 558–559)

Based on these principles, the Commerce Clause gives Congress power to enact such landmark legislation as the Civil Rights Act of 1964, which prohibits discrimination based on sex and the factors mentioned earlier in most employment, by labor unions, and in public accommodations and transportation. The clause also supports federal law against discrimination based on age or disability, as well as regulations for crop quotas, as in *Wickard v. Filburn,* noted above.

The breadth of the post–New Deal Commerce Clause raised two main questions. First, are there any limits to what Congress can regulate? After all, if sufficiently repeated or aggregated, almost any behavior Congress might reasonably want to control could have a substantial effect on interstate commerce. Second, when does congressional legislation entirely preempt the states from regulating in the same policy area?

Until the 1990s, there appeared to be no clear limits to the federal government's Commerce Clause powers. However, in *United States v. Lopez* (1995) and *United States v. Morrison* (2000), the Supreme Court emphasized that the act regulated must be economic in character. In *Lopez* the Court held that the Commerce Clause could not sustain a federal statute banning the possession of a gun in any school zone in the United States. The Court's majority contended that if the statute were valid, "we are hard-pressed to posit any activity by an individual that Congress is without power to regulate," and federal powers would therefore endlessly overlap those of the states (*United States v. Lopez* 1995, 564). Similarly, in *Morrison* the Court found a section of the 1994 Violence Against Women Act unconstitutional because Congress may not regulate "noneconomic, violent criminal conduct based solely on that conduct's aggregate effect on interstate commerce" (*United States v. Morrison* 2000, 617).

In *Gonzales v. Raich* (2005), however, the Supreme Court held that marijuana used for medicinal purposes under California law could be regulated under the federal Controlled Substances Act even though it was locally cultivated and never bought or sold. The Court reasoned that the marijuana involved was part of a subset of economic activities that Congress could regulate, because

> one need not have a degree in economics to understand why a nationwide exemption for the vast quantity of marijuana (or other drugs) locally cultivated for personal use (which presumably would include use by friends, neighbors, and family members) may have a substantial impact on the interstate market for this extraordinarily popular substance. The congressional judgment that an exemption for such a significant segment of the total market would undermine the orderly enforcement of the entire regulatory scheme is entitled to a strong presumption of validity. Indeed, that judgment is not only rational, but "visible to the naked eye," . . . under any commonsense appraisal of the probable consequences of such an open-ended exemption. (*Gonzales v. Raich* 2005, 28–29)

In dissent, Justice Sandra Day O'Connor contended that the majority's decision was inconsistent with *Lopez* and *Morrison*. She noted, "Most commercial goods or services have some sort of privately producible analogue. Home care substitutes for daycare. Charades games substitute for movie tickets. Backyard or windowsill gardening substitutes for going to the supermarket. To draw the line wherever private activity affects the demand for market goods is to draw no line at all, and to declare everything economic. We have already rejected the result that would follow—a federal police power [in *Lopez*]" (*Gonzales v. Raich* 2005, 49–50).

As O'Connor's dissent points out, it is fair to say that the majority's ruling in *Gonzales* adds confusion to determining what constitutes an economic activity subject to regulation under *Lopez* and *Morrison*. In *National Federation of Independent Business v. Sebelius* (2012), which upheld the constitutionality of the Patient Protection and Affordable Care Act ("Obamacare"), the Supreme Court set what seems to be a clear and indelible limit to congressional Commerce Clause authority. It held that Congress lacks the power to compel individuals to engage in commerce: "Construing the *Commerce Clause* to permit Congress to regulate individuals precisely because they are doing nothing would open a new and potentially vast domain to congressional authority" (*National Federation of Independent Business v. Sebelius* 2012, 2587).

Preemption doctrine is also complex. The fact that Congress regulates something, such as the environment, does not automatically mean that the states lose all power to address the same policy area. For instance, a state might want its groundwater to be even freer of toxins than EPA standards require. However, when federal legislation comprehensively occupies a policy field, the states are preempted—that is, excluded—from asserting jurisdiction over it. In general, states are more likely to be preempted by federal legislation when (1) the policy area requires uniform national regulation, (2) the policy area has not historically been dominated by the states (e.g., nuclear energy), (3) dual regulation will promote conflict, and (4) a federal agency has been created to regulate the policy area. Business interests often favor national regulation that preempts the states from setting a variety of separate standards, but both the federal and state governments are active in regulating health, safety, labor, the environment, transportation, and other matters.

Federal preemption can also be based on the Commerce Clause alone. A judicial construct called the "negative" or "dormant" Commerce Clause prohibits state and local governments from passing regulations that discriminate against interstate commerce or impose burdens on interstate commerce that are "clearly excessive in relation to the putative local benefits"

(*C & A Carbone, Inc. v. Town of Clarkstown* 1994, 390). The usual motive for discrimination is to retain as much economic activity as possible within a state. For instance, a state might try (probably unsuccessfully) to require that all timber or shrimp harvested within its borders be processed there as well. The excessive burden test requires a subjective balancing by the courts. In one example, Arizona sought to enhance its reputation for fine agricultural produce by requiring that cantaloupes grown there be packed in boxes clearly showing their origin. In order to ensure effective enforcement, the packaging would have to be done in Arizona as well. The Supreme Court found the regulation excessively burdensome to a grower who, lacking a packing facility in Arizona, shipped his cantaloupes to a nearby one in California and would have had to make a $200,000 capital investment to comply (*Pike v. Bruce Church, Inc.* 1970).

The Tenth Amendment

The Tenth Amendment ratifies the concept of dual sovereignty, whereby the federal government is sovereign in some areas and the states in others. The residuary state powers it protects necessarily vary with judicial interpretation of the Commerce Clause. As Justice O'Connor explained, "If a power is delegated to Congress in the Constitution, the Tenth Amendment expressly disclaims any reservation of that power to the States; if a power is an attribute of state sovereignty reserved by the Tenth Amendment, it is necessarily a power the Constitution has not conferred on Congress" (*New York v. United States* 1992, 156). The broader state sovereignty under the Tenth Amendment, the narrower the Commerce Clause, and vice versa.

State sovereignty under Tenth Amendment interpretation waned in the wake of the New Deal. In 1985, the Supreme Court came close to holding that the amendment was no longer judicially enforceable. Rather, the states should look to their representation in Congress—the Senate, in particular—for protection against federal encroachment: "The Framers chose to rely on a federal system in which special restraints on federal power over the States inhered principally in the workings of the National Government itself, rather than in discrete limitations on the objects of federal authority" (*Garcia v. San Antonio Metropolitan Transit Authority* 1985, 552).

Tenth Amendment jurisprudence was resuscitated by the Supreme Court in the 1990s. Today, the amendment's main ramification for public administration is to prohibit the federal government from compelling "the States to enact or administer a federal regulatory program" (*New York v. United States* 1992, 188). This means Congress cannot conscript or press state officers to implement federal laws (other than those statutes regulating the states themselves). For example, Congress cannot compel state law enforcement officers to perform the background checks required by federal gun-control legislation. Rather, the federal government must either gain the states' cooperation or administer such a law through its own employees or agents. Even though the benefits of requiring state employees to administer federal laws might far outweigh the costs, the Supreme Court rejected a "balancing analysis" where "the very *principle* of state sovereignty" is offended (*Printz v. United States* 1997, 932). This interpretation of the Tenth Amendment highlights the importance of the Spending Clause as a vehicle for exercising federal power.

The Spending Clause

The Spending Clause (Art. I, sec. 8, cl. 1) authorizes Congress to "lay and collect Taxes, Duties, Imposts and Excises, to pay the Debts and provide for the common Defence and general Welfare of the United States." The clause has been interpreted expansively to permit Congress to use conditional grants to the states to achieve indirectly purposes it could not pursue directly under the Commerce Clause or its other enumerated powers. For example, even if Congress cannot constitutionally set a national drinking age (something that is probable under the Twenty-First Amendment), it can induce the states to set the age at twenty-one by withholding federal highway funds from those declining to do so (*South Dakota v. Dole* 1987). The key restrictions are that (1) the spending must be in pursuit of a general public purpose, (2) the conditions must be unambiguous so that the states clearly understand their obligations, (3) the conditions must be related to a "federal interest in particular national projects or programs," and (4) the conditions cannot be prohibited by other constitutional provisions, such as the Fourteenth Amendment's guarantee of equal protection of the laws (*South Dakota v. Dole* 1987, 207). It is also important for congressional use of the Spending Clause to buy, rather than effectively extort or coerce, state compliance (see *National Federation of Independent Business v. Sebelius* 2012). However, within these limits Congress has very broad power to influence state policy and administrative operations through conditional grants.

The Eleventh Amendment

The Eleventh Amendment (1795) protects the states' sovereign immunity by preventing suits against them in federal court. It provides that "the Judicial power of the United States shall not be construed to extend to any suit in law or equity, commenced or prosecuted against one of the United

States by Citizens of another State, or by Citizens or Subjects of any Foreign State." The Supreme Court has reasoned that "the preeminent purpose of state sovereign immunity is to accord States the dignity that is consistent with their status as sovereign entities"; consequently, the scope of immunity exceeds the letter of the Eleventh Amendment (*Federal Maritime Commission v. South Carolina State Ports Authority* 2002, 760). The Court has expanded this immunity to cover suits by the states' own citizens as well as actions by private parties seeking adjudication of claims against state agencies in federal regulatory commissions, such as the Federal Maritime Commission.

There are several exceptions to the states' immunity from suits in federal court: (1) suits may be brought in federal court against named state officials for their violations of rights protected by the US Constitution, (2) a state court decision involving a constitutional issue or question of federal law can be appealed to the US Supreme Court, (3) the states may voluntarily waive their immunity, and (4) Congress can override state sovereign immunity via the enforcement clauses of the Thirteenth, Fourteenth, and Fifteenth amendments.

This framework contains some additional qualifications. State officers and administrators cannot be sued in their official capacities in federal court for constitutional violations if the relief requested would require the state to pay money damages for past conduct. (As noted later in this chapter, state officers and administrators can be sued in their personal capacities for such damages in federal court.) Suits are not barred if the remedy sought could require prospective state spending, as in remedial law decisions requiring prison reform.

Another complication involves congressional legislation under the enforcement clauses mentioned above. These specifically give Congress the power to enforce the amendments "by appropriate legislation." One means of enforcement is to authorize private individuals to sue a state in federal court for money damages for violations of their rights under any of the three amendments. However, in nurse Garrett's case, the Supreme Court emphasized that for enforcement clause legislation to be "appropriate," there must be "congruence and proportionality between the injury to be prevented or remedied and the means adopted to that end" (*Board of Trustees of the University of Alabama v. Garrett* 2001, 963). In applying this standard, the Court concluded that the Americans with Disabilities Act was constitutionally defective in authorizing state employees like Garrett to sue their states in federal court. In developing the ADA, Congress failed to show a pattern of discrimination in state employment that would violate the Equal Protection Clause. Consequently, the ADA's override of the Eleventh Amendment was not congruent with and proportional to the harm it was trying to stem.

By preventing private individuals from vindicating their rights in federal court under statutes like the ADA, the Eleventh Amendment complicates public administration in the United States (Rosenbloom 2013a). Enforcement of such federal laws may require a federal agency to sue a recalcitrant state or attempt to gain compliance through conditional grants. Either approach requires a greater federal administrative presence. Both are more costly and probably less efficacious than authorizing injured parties to sue the states directly. Furthermore, Eleventh Amendment immunity creates an incongruity of its own. It applies only to the states and affords no protection to local governments. Consequently, the means available for safeguarding individuals' federally protected rights depends on which level of government has violated them. If a state wanted to reduce the overall vulnerability of its public sector to suits for money damages, it could put a higher proportion of local-level administrators on its payroll (*McMillian v. Monroe County, Alabama* 1997).

Individuals' Constitutional Rights in Administrative Encounters

Constitutional law currently affords individuals broad rights in the context of their interactions with public administrators. At all levels of government, public administrators' encounters with clients and customers, coworkers, contractors, patients confined to public mental health facilities, prisoners, and individuals involved in street-level administrative regulation are significantly bounded by constitutional law (Rosenbloom, O'Leary, and Chanin 2010; Rosenbloom, Carroll, and Carroll 2000).

Relationships with Clients and Customers

Public administrative relationships with clients and customers are governed by the constitutional doctrines of equal protection, "new property," and unconstitutional conditions. Each of these was developed or substantially strengthened between the 1950s and the 1970s and continues to apply today.

Equal Protection. Contemporary equal protection doctrine has a three-tiered structure. The threshold issue is whether a government is classifying people by some characteristic such as race, sex, wealth, residency, or age. The classification may be implicit in a policy or its implementation rather than explicitly stated in legislation or formal regulations. However, if there is no classification, there is no equal protection issue. A "classification of one" is possible under equal protection, but unfair treatment of particular individuals is typically litigated under procedural due process protection against arbitrary or capricious administrative decisionmaking (*Village of Willowbrook v. Olech* 2000; *Engquist v. Oregon Department of Agriculture* 2008).

Classifications based on race or ethnicity are considered suspect. In view of the nation's history, it is likely that they will be used to disadvantage minorities. They are subject to *strict scrutiny* (the courts' most exacting level of judicial review) and are constitutional only when narrowly tailored to promote a compelling governmental interest. A heavy burden of persuasion rests on the government, and the courts will not be deferential to its claims. These requirements apply whether the purpose of the classification is benign, as in the case of affirmative action, or invidious, as in the case of racial segregation.[2] Classifications based on noncitizenship at the state and local levels may also trigger strict scrutiny.

Narrow tailoring is intended to ensure that a classification does not do significantly more damage to equal protection rights than is necessary to serve a compelling governmental interest. It is somewhat more flexible than a similar test, the *least restrictive alternative* analysis, which is sometimes applied to abridgements of First Amendment rights and requires government to use the least invasive means of achieving its compelling interests. Neither narrow tailoring nor the least restrictive alternative places much emphasis on the financial cost to government of finding ways to promote its interests that are less harmful to constitutional rights. Narrow tailoring generally requires that the use of a classification (1) be efficacious relative to other policy approaches that a governmental entity can reasonably be expected to consider; (2) have a fixed stopping point, either in terms of time or the achievement of a specific policy goal; (3) be sufficiently flexible so that irrational outcomes can be avoided; (4) in the case of affirmative action, be proportionate to the beneficiaries' representation in the relevant population, not excessively harm the interests of nonbeneficiaries, provide individualized consideration of all applicants so that race or ethnicity is a contributing factor rather than a determinative one, and not insulate minority applicants from competition with nonminorities (*Grutter v. Bollinger* 2003; *Gratz v. Bollinger* 2003; *Fisher v. University of Texas at Austin* 2013).

---

2. *Benign* and *invidious* are terms used in equal protection law. Justice Clarence Thomas is among others who maintain that no such distinction exists. See his opinions in *Adarand Constructors v. Peña* (1995) and *Fisher v. University of Texas at Austin* (2013).

Classifications based on factors that are considered somewhat remote from the Fourteenth Amendment's central purpose of extending equal protection of the laws to racial and ethnic minorities, such as wealth and residency, are constitutional when they are rationally related to the achievement of a legitimate governmental purpose. The burden of persuasion is typically on the challenger, and the courts grant considerable deference to the government's claims. This analysis turns on *mere rationality* or *rational basis*. It also applies to classifications based on age and noncitizenship at the federal level. An exception occurs if a nonsuspect classification directly interferes with the exercise of a protected constitutional right. For example, a residency requirement for welfare eligibility might abridge the constitutional right of indigents to travel and relocate across state lines. In such a case, the classification is subject to strict judicial scrutiny and must serve a compelling governmental interest in a way that is narrowly tailored or, possibly, the least restrictive of the protected constitutional rights involved (*Shapiro v. Thompson* 1969).

Classifications based on biological sex are quasi-suspect and face an intermediate test. They must be substantially related to the achievement of important governmental objectives. The courts may ask the government to provide an "exceedingly persuasive justification" for such classifications, many of which are legacies of earlier practices and beliefs about gender differences that society no longer supports (*United States v. Virginia* 1996, 531). For instance, women were once excluded from juries in order to shield them from hearing about the grisly acts of depraved criminals.

Contemporary equal protection interpretation constrains administrative behavior with respect to clients and customers in a range of circumstances. Most obviously, it prohibits racial and ethnic discrimination in public education, housing, welfare, health, recreation, occupational licensing, and other programs, except where the government can meet the compelling governmental interest and narrow tailoring tests under strict judicial scrutiny. Invidious discrimination is likely to be justified, if ever, under only the most extraordinary circumstances. Benign or remedial racial and ethnic classifications, as in affirmative action and minority business set-asides, face the same test, but some may serve a compelling governmental interest in a narrowly tailored fashion. Even though classifications based on gender do not require a compelling governmental interest and narrow tailoring, it is highly unlikely that invidious discrimination against females or males will be constitutional in client and customer relationships.

Theoretically, the weaker standard for gender classifications makes it easier to justify affirmative action programs for women and girls than for minorities. However, in practice there may be no real difference. Allowing affirmative action on the basis of gender, which would substantially benefit white women, but not on the basis of race would run counter to the historical purpose of the Fourteenth Amendment. By contrast, the weaker standard might permit single-sex public schools or classes even though racially segregated ones would be unconstitutional. Classifications based on other factors, such as age, will most likely be constitutional unless they are clearly irrational or interfere with the exercise of another protected constitutional right.

New Property and Procedural Due Process. New property theory treats an individual's governmental benefits as his or her own property, rather than as a privilege or gratuity (Reich 1964). As such, the benefits are covered by the Due Process clauses of the Fifth and Fourteenth amendments, which protect against the deprivation of "life, liberty, or property, without due process of law." Consequently, welfare benefits, public housing, public education, a variety of occupational and other licenses, and similar benefits cannot be withheld or terminated (during the period for which they have been offered) without a fair procedure.

Procedural due process requires a balancing of three factors: (1) the individual's interest in the benefit and/or severity of the deprivation at issue; (2) the risk, if any, that the procedure in place will result in erroneous decisions, as well as the probable value of additional procedures in reducing errors; and (3) the government's administrative and financial interests in avoiding additional or alternative procedures. The underlying assumption in this formula is that, in general, the more elaborate the procedures, the more costly they will be but the lower the risk of error. Once a statute or administrative regulation establishes a continuing new property interest, it can be withheld or terminated only in accordance with constitutional due process. In other words, statutory procedures for terminating a benefit, such as public housing, will be inadequate if they do not afford sufficient procedural due process.

The application of procedural due process is subjective. One must weigh both the individual's and the government's interests. Typically, two issues arise. First, is the client entitled to procedural due process prior to the termination of a benefit during the term for which it is offered? Recipients of means-tested welfare benefits, which may be vital to their survival or ability to use post-termination procedures, generally enjoy a procedural due process right to some pretermination protection against erroneous administrative decisions. An exception exists when there is no factual dispute about their continuing eligibility.

Second, how elaborate must the due process be? Procedures can range from highly informal notice and opportunity to respond, to a formal response in writing only, to the rudiments of a nonjury judicial trial with a right to counsel, presentation of evidence and witnesses, confrontation and cross-examination of adverse witnesses, a written transcript, a decision by an impartial decisionmaker, and a right to appeal (*Goldberg v. Kelly* 1970; *Goss v. Lopez* 1975; *Mathews v. Eldridge* 1976; *Board of Curators of the University of Missouri v. Horowitz* 1978). Impartiality prevents biased officials or those who have investigated or prosecuted the case from making adjudicatory decisions (see Chapter 4). Sometimes pre- and post-termination requirements are linked. For example, because elaborate post-termination procedures are available to Social Security disability recipients, only limited procedure is required before these non-means-tested benefits are cut off.

The impact of new property doctrine on administration depends on the specific context. Pre- or post-termination hearings are common in decisions to terminate welfare, disability benefits, and occupational licenses. Suspensions and expulsions from public schools are also controlled by procedural due process. It is important to remember that when benefits expire because they were offered for a fixed term or terminate because the recipients have aged, moved, married, or otherwise changed their eligibility status, procedural due process may require nothing more than notice, if that (procedural due process is discussed at greater length in Chapter 4).

Unconstitutional Conditions.   The conditions attached to governmental benefits sometimes interfere with clients' and customers' constitutional rights. For instance, a state might mandate that applicants for unemployment compensation be available for work on Saturday despite their Sabbatarian religious beliefs or that public school students recite prayers or pledge allegiance to the flag. The unconstitutional conditions doctrine seeks to limit a government's ability to use client and customer relationships as leverage for regulating behavior that it could not reach directly without violating individuals' constitutional rights.

The problem public administrators and lawmakers face is knowing which conditions imposed on clients or customers will be adjudged unconstitutional. Essentially, the courts apply a two-part test, but as in the case of procedural due process, a good deal of subjectivity is involved. Specific requirements vary with the nature of the benefit and type of condition. Conditions that gratuitously infringe on protected rights by failing to serve a significant governmental purpose or by prohibiting more than necessary in order to achieve a legitimate or compelling public interest are very likely to be unconstitutional. Conditions involving freedom of speech, association, religion, or protection from unreasonable searches must generally promote at least an important, if not compelling, governmental interest. Conditions attached to building permits that constitute a Fifth Amendment taking of private property must be roughly proportional to the impact that the proposed development will have on legitimate governmental interests, such as traffic congestion (*Dolan v. City of Tigard* 1994).

Together, contemporary equal protection, new property, and unconstitutional conditions doctrines bring constitutional law directly into the relationships between public administrators and their clients and customers. This complicates public administration by expanding the set of values that administrators and programs must protect and, sometimes, by requiring elaborate procedure. It also broadens the role of courts and judges in public administration.

Public Personnel Management

Public employees first began to gain significant constitutional rights in the context of their employment during the period from the 1950s to the 1970s as equal protection was applied to public employment, civil service jobs were considered part of the new property, and the unconstitutional conditions doctrine was invoked to protect public employees' First Amendment rights. However, the constitutional doctrine that regulates public personnel management differs from that affecting relationships with clients and customers.

Constitutional rights within the framework of public employment are assessed through a *public service model*. Its core premise is that the administrative values of efficiency and effectiveness are more important to governments when they act as employers than when they seek to regulate the behavior of ordinary citizens. Government, like any employer, needs greater authority over its employees than it can exercise over its clients, customers, or the general public. But there are also limits to that authority.

The public service model balances four considerations: (1) the interest of the employee in exercising his or her constitutional rights, that is, in being free of governmental controls; (2) the government's interest in achieving some important purpose as an employer; (3) the public's interest in the way government and public administration operate; and (4) avoidance of overly intrusive judicial involvement in public management. The crux of the public service model is that the public's interest may coincide with that of either the employee or the government. For example, in the realm of free speech, the public has a very clear interest in strong constitutional protection of whistle-blowing by public employees. The public is better able to assess governmental performance when public employees can freely expose illegality, gross waste, fraud, abuse, and specific and immediate dangers to public health and safety. By contrast, the public has only a minimal interest, if any, in public employees' partisan campaign speeches, routine office gossiping, and grousing about political bosses and administrative higher-ups. Under the public service model, whistle-blower speech is constitutionally protected, whereas partisan speech and speech that is of minimal or no public concern are not. (Whistle-blowing is discussed in Chapter 5.) Although the public might be interested in the reports, memos, and other work produced by public employees, such "work-product" speech does not enjoy constitutional protection. This is largely because protecting it would "commit state and federal courts to a new, permanent, and intrusive role, mandating judicial oversight of communications between and among government employees and their superiors in the course of official business" (*Garcetti v. Ceballos* 2006, 423).

The same kind of public service model balancing applies to public employees' free exercise of religion and association as well as to their Fourth Amendment privacy rights and equal protection guarantees. In constitutionally evaluating constraints on personnel management in these contexts, one always considers the individual's interest in exercising or retaining protected rights, government interests that could justify abridgments, and the public's interest. The judiciary's interest in avoiding undue intrusion into public management sometimes also comes into play. It is important that public personnelists, managers, and employees bear in mind that the government's interest, though often stated as serving the taxpayers, is not necessarily synonymous with the public interest. Even in the context of public employment, a governmental interest in cost-effective administration may not justify infringements on constitutionally protected rights. If there is no clear public or judiciary interest one way or the other, then the balance is simply between the interests of the employee and the government. The employee will sometimes win because judges may place a higher value on protecting the robustness of constitutional rights than on obtaining administrative results or maximizing values such as efficiency and economy (*Stanley v. Illinois* 1972).

First Amendment Rights.   Public employees enjoy broad First Amendment rights to speak openly on matters of policy, politics, administration, and public affairs. Under the public service model, the major limitations on their freedom of speech are as follows: (1) in order to enjoy constitutional protection, expressive activity must be on a matter of public concern (that is, public interest); (2) speech as part of a partisan political campaign may be banned; and (3) speech, including written documents, produced pursuant to work assignments (i.e., work-product speech) may be the basis of adverse personnel actions such as demotion or dismissal. Disruptive remarks on matters only of private concern are not protected because they serve no public interest. Restrictions on the partisan political activity of public employees are constitutionally justified by the public interest in administrative impartiality and efficiency, as well as by the protection they afford government workers against being coerced by political appointees and supervisors to support political parties and partisan candidates.

In general, public employees' non-work-product speech on matters of public concern is most vulnerable to forming the basis for a successful adverse action when it impairs discipline or harmony in the workplace, jeopardizes close working relationships, interferes with normal operations, or detracts from the employee's ability to do his or her job. In balancing the interests of government, employee, public, and judiciary, attention must be paid to the nature of the employee's position in the organization (*Rankin v. McPherson* 1987). Identical remarks by those at the top and bottom of an organizational hierarchy may be treated differently. When disciplining employees for their off-the-job remarks or other protected activities, the government should be able to show a nexus between its significant interests as an employer and the conduct involved (*United States v. National Treasury Employees Union* 1995; *San Diego v. Roe* 2004).

The public service model also broadly protects employees' freedom of association and religion. Restrictions on these freedoms have to be justified by the balance among the interests of employee, public employer, public, and judiciary. Constitutional law extends extensive protection to employees' freedom of association on the premise that membership alone is not a proxy for behavior. Consequently, employees may join labor unions (though there is no constitutional right to collective bargaining), employee associations, hate groups such as white or black nationalist, and even subversive organizations. Exceptions are permissible for categories of employees whose membership in particular organizations would significantly harm the employer's or the public's interests. For instance, supervisors and managers can be banned from joining labor unions representing rank-and-file employees because such membership might conflict with their hierarchical responsibilities. Employees also have the right not to join organizations; consequently union-shop labor agreements are unconstitutional in the public sector (*Abood v. Detroit Board of Education* 1977; *Chicago Teachers Union v. Hudson* 1986). Since the late 1970s, public employees' freedom of association has been interpreted to make job actions based on political partisanship unconstitutional unless the government can show that relying on party affiliation is the means of ensuring effective job performance that is least restrictive of constitutional rights or narrowly tailored to avoid excessive intrusion on those rights (*Rutan v. Republican Party of Illinois* 1990).

The parameters of public employees' religious freedom are less clear. A government employer cannot coerce employees to engage in prayer or other religious activity. Neither can it gratuitously restrict their religious expression or behavior. Because federal equal employment opportunity law prohibits discrimination based on religion, civilian public employees at all levels of government ordinarily are permitted to wear religious jewelry or headgear, even if other workers find it objectionable. Restrictions on religious activity might be justified when overt religious proselytizing or vocal praying at work is disruptive or otherwise interferes with the employer's legitimate interests in workplace harmony and cost-effectiveness.

Fourth Amendment Privacy. Public employees retain protections against unreasonable searches and seizures even while at work in public buildings. The threshold question is whether the employee has a reasonable expectation of privacy under the circumstances, that is, an expectation of privacy that society is prepared to support (according to judges). Absent such an expectation, public employers are free to search an employee's workspace, desk, files, computer, and so forth. Where there is a reasonable expectation of privacy, the governmental search must be reasonable in its inception and scope. Employees have a reasonable expectation of privacy in their bodily fluids, but suspicionless drug testing is constitutionally permissible when it reasonably promotes national security, law enforcement, or public safety (see *City of Ontario, California v. Quon* 2010).

Procedural Due Process. Civil service systems typically provide public employees with new property rights in their jobs. Consequently, procedural due process protects them against arbitrary, capricious, or abusive dismissal or demotion. Pretermination notice and opportunity to respond are generally required, as are more elaborate post-termination procedures (*Cleveland Board of Education v. Loudermill* 1985). Depending on the circumstances, a public employee may not have a right to procedural due process prior to suspension without pay for wrongdoing. However, the employee should be offered a hearing of some kind within a reasonable time after the suspension takes effect (*Gilbert v. Homar* 1997).

For the most part, the constitutional requirements for public employees' procedural due process are now written into civil service laws and regulations. However, once the government creates a new property right in public employment, its termination or diminution is controlled by constitutional rather than statutory law. Where public employees do not have civil service or tenured status, adverse actions may be at will only insofar as they do not violate First or Fourth Amendment, equal protection, or other constitutional rights.

Equal Protection. The three-tiered equal protection analysis previously discussed applies to public employees as well as to clients and customers. Racial and ethnic classifications, whether benign or invidious, are subject to strict scrutiny. To date, the Supreme Court has not held that promoting workforce diversity is a compelling governmental interest. It has permitted benign racial classifications only as a remedy for past, proven, egregious violations of equal protection. These and other racial/ethnic classifications must be narrowly tailored. For instance, the public service model does not generally permit personnel assignments based on race or ethnicity, but such criteria might be acceptable when necessary for the achievement of a specific and important governmental purpose, as in undercover police work (see *Baker v. City of St. Petersburg* 1968).

Residency and age requirements are subject to rational basis analysis. They will be constitutional if they are rationally related to the achievement of a legitimate governmental purpose. Gender-based classifications face a higher standard—they must be substantially related to the achievement of important governmental purposes.

Substantive Due Process Rights. The Fifth and Fourteenth amendments protect individuals against governmental deprivations of "life, liberty, or property, without due process of law." The body of constitutional interpretation defining "liberty" in this context is *substantive due process*. It enables the courts to identify and protect fundamental rights that are not specifically mentioned elsewhere in the Constitution. Consequently, substantive due process is open-ended, and specific decisions under it are often controversial. In the context of public personnel management, the Supreme Court invalidated overly restrictive maternity leave policies on the grounds that the "Court has long recognized that freedom of personal choice in matters of marriage and family life is one of the liberties protected by the Due Process Clause of the Fourteenth Amendment. . . . [T]here is a right 'to be free from unwarranted governmental intrusion into matters so fundamentally affecting a person as the decision whether to bear or beget a child'" (*Cleveland Board of Education v. La Fleur* 1974, 639–640). In another case, the Court found no substantive due process barrier to short-hair and clean-shave grooming regulations for police (*Kelley v. Johnson* 1976). There is little judicial guidance on how to analyze substantive due process claims within the public service model. As a threshold matter, the government should be able to demonstrate a reasonable connection between its interests and the prohibited behavior.

Relationships with Contractors

Contractors also have constitutional protections against governmental infringements on their rights. Some of these are well settled. Governments cannot engage in invidious racial, ethnic, or gender discrimination when contracting out. Contracts that establish new property interests cannot be terminated without procedural due process. Since the late 1980s, the Supreme Court strengthened the Constitution's application to contractor relationships in three ways.

First, the Court unequivocally held that benign racial and ethnic classifications in governmental contracting are subject to strict scrutiny (*Adarand Constructors v. Pena* 1995). They must serve a compelling governmental interest in a narrowly tailored fashion. This severely restricted the use of minority business set-asides and other preferences. Even though the constitutional test for gender classifications is weaker, preferences for women-owned businesses will also be difficult to sustain.

Second, the Court made it clear that contractors and those engaged in preexisting commercial relationships with governments, such as Gratzianna's with the city of Northlake, retain First Amendment rights. Using unconstitutional conditions analysis, the Court held that the Constitution protects contractors' public criticism of a government and their political campaigning against its officials. Essentially, the same constitutional test that applies to public employees' speech is used to determine the free speech rights of contractors and others engaged in ongoing business relationships with government. A government can terminate its commercial relationship with such parties in response to their speech only if it can show that, on balance, such action is justified by the speech's detrimental impact on the government's ability to deliver public services.

Third, the Court clarified the application of state action doctrine to contractors. With the exception of the Thirteenth Amendment, the Constitution ordinarily does not govern relationships among purely private parties. However, under some circumstances, contractors may be considered *state actors* (i.e., governmental actors, regardless of whether at the state, local, or federal level) and are thereby bound by constitutional requirements. The basic premise is that the Constitution applies to private parties if "there is such a 'close nexus between the State and the challenged action' that seemingly private behavior 'may be fairly treated as that of the State itself'" (*Brentwood Academy v. Tennessee Secondary School Athletic Association et al.* 2001, 930). Unfortunately for those who like their constitutional law to come with bright lines, determining what constitutes state action is often "a matter of normative judgment" (*Brentwood Academy v. Tennessee Secondary School Athletic Association et al.* 2001, 295).

In general, a contractor may become a state actor when it (1) engages in a public function, such as incarceration; (2) exercises government's coercive power (e.g., to seize property); (3) acts as a government's agent for some unconstitutional purpose, such as promoting racial discrimination; (4) is nominally private but largely or wholly controlled by a government unit; or (5) is entwined with government or acts as a joint participant with it (*Brentwood Academy v. Tennessee Secondary School Athletic Association et al.* 2001).

Private parties will not be state actors merely because they are heavily regulated or funded by government. Neither will governmental subsidization of their clients or customers transform them into state actors. Private entities engaged in public-private partnerships, collaborative relationships, and contracting with government agencies should pay close attention to state action doctrine. For instance, a private physician on part-time contract with a state prison and guards employed by a private company operating a prison are state actors with Eighth Amendment obligations to prisoners and attendant potential liability for violating their rights against cruel and unusual punishments (*West v. Atkins* 1988; *Richardson v. McKnight* 1997).

Public Mental Health Patients

Since the early 1970s, patients involuntarily confined to public mental health facilities have had a constitutional right to treatment. Earlier, they were often warehoused indefinitely or otherwise inadequately treated. In *Wyatt v. Stickney* (1971), a federal district court held that confining such patients without treatment constitutes a violation of their right to liberty under the Fourteenth Amendment. Although the decision applied directly only to the Alabama mental health system, its logic was soon adopted nationwide.

The constitutional right to treatment was eventually defined in broad terms. It includes reasonable care, safety, and freedom from confinement, as well as individualized treatment (or training for the mentally disabled). Implementation requires a humane physical and psychological environment as well as adequate staffing. In practice this may require far-reaching architectural and medical reforms. The *Wyatt* litigation eventually required Alabama either to release patients or to provide the following: (1) protection of patients' right to wear their own clothes, freedom of religious worship, and opportunity for physical exercise; (2) physical building conditions in which there were no more than six patients per room, at least one toilet for each eight patients and one shower or tub for every fifteen, not less than fifty square feet per person in the dayroom, at least ten square feet per person in the dining room, and a temperature range between sixty-eight and eighty-three degrees Fahrenheit; and (3) various per patient staffing ratios for professionals, clerical workers, and other staff.

Initially, judicial involvement in public mental health care was sometimes characterized as misguided interference in professional psychiatry. However, eventually the American Psychiatric Association supported the constitutional right to treatment. Along with other factors, including better psychoactive drugs, crowding was reduced through deinstitutionalization and shorter stays, and the overall conditions in public mental health facilities improved substantially. On the downside, deinstitutionalization contributed to homelessness (Rosenbloom, O'Leary, and Chanin 2010, 256–257).

Prisoners' Constitutional Rights

Since the 1970s, the treatment of prisoners has been thoroughly constitutionalized. The Eighth Amendment prohibition of cruel and unusual punishments was reinterpreted to apply to the conditions of confinement rather than to the sentence alone. This required prison reforms in more than forty states to reduce overcrowding, provide adequate medical care and safety, and guarantee inmates at least a minimal level of nutrition, hygiene, and civilized life's other necessities. The scope of what is prohibited by the Eighth Amendment changes as society progresses and standards of decency evolve. For instance, in the 1990s prisoners gained the right to challenge exposure to secondhand tobacco smoke when it poses a risk of serious harm due to their personal respiratory or other health problems (Rosenbloom, O'Leary, and Chanin 2010, ch. 7).

In addition to Eighth Amendment protections, prisoners have a right to procedural due process when proposed discipline creates extraordinary hardships within the framework of normal prison life. Similarly, within the confines of what incarceration requires in practice, they have the right to free exercise of religion and to marry. The general test is whether restrictions on the prisoners' constitutional rights, including their impact on other inmates and guards, serve legitimate penological interests. Prison administration has become so thoroughly infused with constitutional concerns that some prison systems engage in constitutional audits to ensure their compliance with the latest judicial decisions.

Street-Level Regulatory Encounters

Street-level public employees engage in face-to-face regulatory interaction with the public. They are police, social workers, public school teachers, public health workers, health and safety inspectors, and others who (1) tend to work in the absence of close proximate supervision, (2) have a great deal of discretion in dealing with members of the public, (3) are largely self-reporting, and (4) are often in a position to have a substantial positive or negative impact on the individuals with whom they deal. It is also common for street-level employees to work with heavy caseloads and inadequate resources. Their work environment may be charged with physical and/or psychological threats (Lipsky 1980; Maynard-Moody and Musheno 2003).

The Fourth Amendment and the Equal Protection Clause are most relevant to individuals' rights in street-level encounters. However, these protections are porous and subject to circumvention.

Fourth Amendment Constraints.   Fourth Amendment law is notoriously uneven because it is fact specific in its application. It applies only when an individual has a reasonable expectation of privacy. The courts treat this expectation as a continuum. On one end, individuals who are in their own homes with the windows and doors closed and curtains drawn have a great expectation of privacy. On the other end, the same individuals would have a minimal expectation of privacy with regard to their baggage when seeking to board a scheduled commercial airplane at a US airport. In between, there are many gradations. The slope from a conventional home, to a permanently parked mobile home, to one moving on an interstate highway, to a minivan camper, to a public bus can prove slippery. Moreover, some individuals have reduced Fourth Amendment protections due to their special relationship with an administrative function and its personnel. For example, public school administrators have greater leeway to search students because the schools have special custodial and tutelary responsibilities (*Vernonia School District 47J v. Acton* 1995; *Board of Education of Independent School District No. 92 of Pottawatomie County v. Earls* 2002).

A distinction is usually drawn between law enforcement searches and administrative inspections. Whenever practicable, the Fourth Amendment requires law enforcement officers to seek a warrant from a judge, magistrate, or other judicial official. The warrant is issued upon probable cause, which essentially means there is specific evidence that a violation of law may exist or a breach of law is imminent. When time or other considerations make obtaining a warrant impractical, law enforcement agents can proceed upon probable cause alone. Administrative inspections of nonpervasively regulated businesses may also require warrants. However, it is not necessary to show probable cause, as these warrants may be issued when reasonably necessary for the enforcement of the statute involved. Administrative searches involving special relationships or needs, such as public school discipline, are generally governed by reasonableness in their inception and scope rather than probable cause. Pervasively or closely regulated entities have a reduced expectation of privacy and therefore may be inspected without a warrant under a rational regulatory scheme (see the "Enforcement" section in Chapter 4). Precisely what constitutes such an entity is sometimes a judgment call.

The constraints on street-level administration generated by this framework often appear inconsistent and sometimes close to nonexistent. On the one hand, for instance, an individual can be arrested for any traffic infraction, however minor, and consequently subjected to a legitimate personal and vehicle search. The Supreme Court has eschewed inquiry into whether such stops or arrests following them are merely pretexts used by the police to search individuals and their vehicles. Even arrest and subsequent search for a nonjailable offense, such as not wearing a seatbelt, are permitted (*Atwater v. City of Lago Vista* 2001; *Whren v. United States* 1996). On the other hand, a federal Occupational Safety and Health Administration inspector may need a warrant in order to inspect a workplace—depending in part on how open the facility is to the public or how pervasively the government regulates it (*Marshall v. Barlow's, Inc.* 1987). The constitutionality of a public hospital's drawing of bodily fluids from patients may depend on its purpose. For law enforcement, the hospital needs the patients' consent or a warrant, though apparently the same fluids can be taken for diagnostic purposes without implicating the Fourth Amendment (*Ferguson v. City of Charleston* 2001).

Equal Protection Constraints.   The main problem for individuals who challenge street-level administrators' behavior on equal protection grounds is that the burden of persuasion rests on the challenger to demonstrate that the government employees have explicitly or implicitly created a classification. Explicit invidious racial, ethnic, or gender classifications are highly unusual in contemporary street-level administration. Public personnel and governments know better than to openly categorize people by such social characteristics in order to discriminate against them. Implicit classifications, based on these characteristics, may be inferred from patterns of administrative behavior. However, establishing their existence to a court's satisfaction is difficult. This is why the Equal Protection Clause has been of limited efficacy in combating racial and ethnic profiling by law enforcement agents when there is no written or verbal evidence. Unless profiling is the only plausible explanation for the administrative behavior at issue, it may be impossible to show that an implicit classification exists. Of course, equal protection is a more effective constraint against street-level behavior that follows directly from racist, ethnically derogatory, or sexist statements (Larrabee 1997).

Public Administrators' Liability for Constitutional Torts

There is often a notable gap between formal constitutional requirements and actual administrative practice. Constitutional law may be unclear or poorly communicated to administrators. As already noted, sometimes it is highly subjective or requires an elaborate balancing of multiple factors. Specific constraints may seem counterintuitive to administrators or impractical due to scarce resources or lack of time. They may also run counter to deep-seated administrative and organizational values. Furthermore, individuals whose constitutional rights are violated may lack the incentive or resources to sue the government or its employees for redress.

In a series of decisions crystallizing in the 1980s, the Supreme Court sought to protect individuals' constitutional rights in their encounters with public administrators by invigorating the law of constitutional torts (i.e., injuries to constitutional rights). The Court made it far easier for individuals to sue most public administrators personally in federal court for money damages for violations of their constitutional rights. In terms of legal doctrine, the Court changed the presumption that public employees and officials are absolutely immune from civil suits for money damages (meaning they could not be sued for their constitutional torts) to one that affords them only a qualified immunity from such suits. The Court reasoned that making it easier to bring constitutional tort suits serves to deter violations of constitutional law as well as to compensate victims. The current standard for qualified immunity requires public administrators, at all levels of government, to have reasonable knowledge of constitutional law and to factor it into decisionmaking.

Since 1982, most public administrators in the United States have been potentially personally liable for money damages for conduct violating "clearly established [federal] statutory or constitutional rights of which a reasonable person would have known" (*Harlow v. Fitzgerald* 1982, 818). This standard expands the requirements of administrators' job competence to include constitutional law. In the Supreme Court's words, "A reasonably competent public official should know the law governing his conduct" (*Harlow v. Fitzgerald* 1982, 819). Suits may be for punitive, exemplary, and compensatory damages (*Smith v. Wade* 1983). The major exception is that public administrators cannot be sued for constitutional torts committed while engaging in adjudicatory or legislative functions. There are also some technical differences in how local, state, and federal employees may be sued. However, the vast majority of public administrators are subject to suit, and constitutional torts produce considerable litigation. Local governments and their agencies are also liable to such suits for compensatory damages when their policies directly cause violations of individuals' constitutional rights (*Pembaur v. City of Cincinnati* 1986). Under limited circumstances, cities and counties can also be sued for failure to train their employees to protect individuals' constitutional rights (*City of Canton v. Harris* 1989). Local governments cannot be sued for punitive damages in constitutional tort cases.

It should be emphasized that the "clearly established" constitutional law a reasonable administrator should know is not synonymous with the latest judicial precedent on some matter. In *Hope v. Pelzer* (2002, 741), the Supreme Court emphasized that "officials can be on notice that their conduct violates established law even in novel factual circumstances." Conduct may be obviously unconstitutional even though it has never been the subject of litigation. The broad purpose of qualified immunity is to encourage public administrators to follow the case law and be responsive to the judiciary's constitutional reasoning and values. Qualified immunity is designed to give federal judges a greater role in defining appropriate public administrative behavior. The courts labor hard to give substance to constitutional rights. They do not want their decisions to be hollow. Knowing that they face personal suits for constitutional torts gives public administrators a strong incentive to think twice before taking an action that might tread on someone's constitutionally protected rights.

Relatively speaking, qualified immunity protects the public interest in allowing public administrators to act without fear of frivolous or other unwarranted lawsuits. Depending on the circumstances, private individuals engaged in state action may either have no immunity at all, meaning they are vulnerable to suit regardless of whether the constitutional law was clearly established or likely to be known by a reasonable person;

alternatively, they may have qualified immunity or simply not be subject to such suits (*Richardson v. McKnight* 1997; *Filarsky v. Delia* 2012; *Minneci v. Pollard* 2012).

Conclusion

The US Constitution is central to the organization and practice of public administration in the United States. The separation of powers defines the scope of legislative, executive, and judicial authority for public administration. Each branch brings different—and often competing—core values to public administrative practice. Constitutional federalism allocates sovereignty and power between the federal government and the states. It also adds to the complexity of public administration. During the second half of the twentieth century, the federal courts, often led by the Supreme Court, vastly expanded individuals' constitutional rights in their encounters with public administration. Constitutional law became relevant, if not central, to administrative decisions and operations regarding clients and customers, public personnel systems, outsourcing, the treatment of patients in public mental health facilities, incarceration, and the exercise of regulatory authority in street-level encounters. The courts also greatly strengthened the opportunity for aggrieved individuals to vindicate their newfound rights through constitutional tort suits.

Constitutional law is dynamic rather than static. It affords the federal judiciary continual opportunities to exercise influence over public administrative decisionmaking and values at all levels of government. Perhaps most important, the federal judiciary expects public administrators to follow the development of constitutional law, to understand how it bears upon their official functions, and to treat it as a central element of job competence. It is no longer true—if it ever was—that US public administration "at most points stands apart even from the debatable ground of constitutional study" (Wilson [1887] 1987, 18). Rather, contemporary public administration is informed by and infused with constitutional concerns.

Additional Reading

Barron, Jerome, and C. Thomas Dienes. *Constitutional Law in a Nutshell.* 8th ed. St. Paul, MN: West Group, 2013.

Rosenbloom, David H., Rosemary O'Leary, and Joshua Chanin. *Public Administration and Law.* 3rd ed. Boca Raton, FL: CRC/Taylor and Francis, 2010.

Discussion Questions

1. The US constitutional separation of powers was designed well before federal administration became central to how the national government now operates. Some other countries have adopted new constitutions to deal with the rise of large-scale administration (i.e., "the administrative state"). By contrast, the United States has tried to "retrofit" the administrative state into the constitutional design. If you could make any three changes to the separation of powers to improve control over administration by the president, Congress, or both, what would they be? Why?

2. Do you think governmental benefits, such as welfare and civil service jobs, should be treated as "new property" and protected by constitutional procedural due process? In your view, what are the pros and cons of new property theory?

3. Do you think constitutional equal protection interpretation should apply strict scrutiny to classifications based on biological sex, as it is applied to racial classifications based on race? How about to classifications based on sexual orientation? What would be the advantages and disadvantages of doing so, if any?

4. What is the current standard for public administrators' potential liability for committing constitutional torts? If you could change it, would you? If not, why, and if so, how?

3

Administrative Rulemaking

Introduction: Smoking Whitefish

A lot of people like smoked whitefish. Some 2.75 million pounds of it were produced annually in the United States during the 1960s and 1970s. Between 1960 and 1963, a problem arose—eight cases of botulism, the only US cases involving whitefish since 1899. All eight involved a vacuum-packing process, which the industry soon abandoned. From 1964 through 1970, no botulism whatsoever was reported in the 17.25 million pounds of US-produced whitefish. Nevertheless, in 1970 the Food and Drug Administration (FDA) issued time-temperature-salinity rules requiring the heating of fish brined to 3.5 percent salinity at 180 degrees Fahrenheit for at least thirty minutes, or, alternatively, at only 150 degrees for the same period when the fish had salinity of 5 percent.

The Nova Scotia Food Products Corporation, however, maintained that the time-temperature-salinity standards would kill more than just the very remote possibility that toxic *Clostridium botulinum* type E spores would form in its smoked whitefish; the new standards would kill its business. According to Nova Scotia and the industry interest group, the Association of Smoked Fish Processors, Inc., the FDA's requirements "could not be met if a marketable whitefish was to be produced" because they would "completely destroy the product." The company sued to block FDA enforcement action against its smoked whitefish.

The legal issues were specific to whitefish but common to much rulemaking. With remarkable clarity, the reviewing court averred,

The key issues were (1) whether, in the light of the rather scant history of botulism in whitefish, that species should have been considered separately rather than included in a general regulation which failed to distinguish species from species; (2) whether the application of the proposed [time-temperature-salinity] requirements to smoked whitefish made the whitefish commercially unsaleable; and (3) whether the agency recognized that prospect, but nevertheless decided that the public health needs should prevail even if that meant commercial death for the whitefish industry. The procedural issues were whether, in light of these key questions, the agency procedure was inadequate because (i) it failed to disclose to interested parties the scientific data and methodology upon which it relied; and (ii) because it failed utterly to address itself to the pertinent question of commercial feasibility.

In the court's view, the FDA failed on two counts. First, "when the basis for a proposed rule is a scientific decision, the scientific material which is believed to support the rule should be exposed to the view of interested parties for their comment. One cannot ask for comment on a scientific paper without allowing the participants to read the paper." Here, the court was prescient—making such papers public is a major purpose of the Data Quality Act (2000) mentioned in Chapter 1. Second, the rule was not accompanied by a "concise general statement" explaining the rationale behind it, as is required by the Administrative Procedure Act (APA). Nowhere did the FDA address the issue of commercial feasibility. As the court noted, "It is not in keeping with the rational process to leave vital questions, raised by comments which are of cogent materiality, completely unanswered. The agencies certainly have a good deal of discretion in expressing the basis of a rule, but the agencies do not have quite the prerogative of obscurantism reserved to legislatures." The whitefish industry (though not the whitefish) won a reprieve (*United States v. Nova Scotia Food Products Corp.* 1977, 250, 252).

Rulemaking: Definitions and General Concerns

The scope of federal rulemaking is astounding. To a very large extent, public policy in the United States is established through administrative rulemaking. Federal rules govern the purity of the food we eat, the water we drink, and the air we breathe. They regulate the safety of our workplaces, homes, vehicles, and many of the products we use and consume. They determine much about the health care available to us as well as the practices used in banking, industry, business, agriculture, and many other areas of economic life. From 1993 through 2013, federal agencies routinely promulgated roughly 3,500 to 4,000 rules per year, totaling 81,883, which significantly exceeded the volume of congressional lawmaking (Kerwin 1999, 18, 21; Crews 2013, 2). In 2013, agency final rules took up 24,690 pages in the *Federal Register*. On average, a law or rule was passed every 2.5 hours throughout the year, but rules outnumbered statutes by a ratio of twenty-nine to one (Crews 2013, 2). In the same year, ignoring the value of benefits, the gross cost of rules for the typical American family was almost $15,000, or 23 percent of their annual income (Crews 2013, 2; Clark 2013). The number of federal employees working in agencies with regulatory authority tops 290,000 (Zajac 2012, A14). Of this mass of rules, 48 percent were issued by the Departments of the Treasury, Commerce, Interior, Agriculture, and Transportation and the Environmental Protection Agency (EPA) (Crews 2013, 3). Many rules are highly specific to particular technologies and processes used in broadcasting, generating energy, farming, extracting natural resources, fishing, manufacturing, refining, and so forth. Cumulatively, along with rules having more general effects on the overall economy and environment, they do much to determine the quality of American life.

Federal government rulemaking can be tracked through the *Unified Agenda of Federal Regulatory and Deregulatory Actions*, which "provides uniform reporting of data on regulatory and deregulatory activities under development throughout the federal government" (Office of Information and Regulatory Affairs [OIRA], n.d.). The agenda covers about sixty agencies, commissions, and departments. It includes their regulatory agendas and information about their priorities and "about the most significant regulatory activities planned" for the year ahead (OIRA, n.d.). The *Unified Agenda* is published in the *Federal Register* in the fall and is also available online (see OIRA, n.d.).

There is no single definition of administrative rules. The federal Administrative Procedure Act defines them as "the whole or part of an agency statement of general or particular applicability and future effect designed to implement, interpret, or prescribe law or policy or describing the organization, procedure, or practice requirements of an agency" (sec. 551[4]). Its definition also includes the "approval or prescription for the future of rates, wages, corporate or financial structures or reorganizations thereof, prices, facilities, appliances, services or allowances," as well as the accounting and other practices relating to them. Several general characteristics of rules are buried in this federal prose:

1. Rules are usually prospective. Their requirements will become effective and enforced at some future date, giving those directly governed by them time to comply. US administrative and constitutional law especially disfavors rulemaking as a means of assessing the legality of past behavior. Adjudication rather than rulemaking is typically used to determine the legal status of past or continuing activity. Adjudication is often called "ordermaking" to distinguish it from rulemaking. Sometimes, however, when there is good cause, rules may go into effect immediately.

2. There are three general types of rules. *Legislative rules* (or *substantive rules*) are like statutes and have the force of law. The FDA's time-temperature-salinity rule was a legislative rule. Such rules regulate conduct, impose performance standards on products and processes, and establish eligibility for licenses and benefits. For instance, the US Occupational Safety and Health Administration (OSHA) enacts a wide range of legislative rules to regulate hazards and toxic substances in the workplace; the National Highway Traffic Safety Administration similarly issues rules governing motor vehicle safety; Federal Aviation Administration rules regulate the safety of air travel; Securities and Exchange Commission rules regulate financial reporting by companies whose stock is sold publicly; the FDA issues rules regarding food purity; and Federal Trade Commission rules regulate advertising and other economic practices.

   Procedural rules govern an agency's internal organization and operations, such as how it will process requests from the public for information or benefits of various kinds, deal with its own employees' challenges to adverse actions or equal employment opportunity complaints, and prioritize its enforcement actions. *Interpretative rules* (also called *interpretive rules*) are essentially policy statements and guidelines establishing an agency's understanding of the terms of its statutory mandate. They should not, in theory, establish new legal obligations but rather should explain the basis for existing ones. Sometimes, however, the distinction is blurry. For instance, the 1964 Civil Rights Act specifically allows employers to use hiring and promotion examinations that are "professionally developed"—a term subsequently defined by the Equal Employment Opportunity Commission (EEOC) as requiring that the exams actually be job related, something that is often very difficult for employers to demonstrate (*Griggs v. Duke Power Co.* 1971, 433–434).

3. Rules can be of general or particular application. They can regulate a very wide range of industry and activity (clean air) or a single process

(use of a pesticide). As the application of a rule narrows to only a few firms or persons, constitutional due process may require the rulemaking agency to provide notice and a hearing of some sort to those directly affected (*Bi-metallic Investment Co. v. State Board of Equalization of Colorado* 1915).

As suggested by the FDA's experience with smoked whitefish, a key political and legal question is how administrative rules should be made. How should a time-temperature-salinity standard be formulated and applied? What voice in the development of such a rule should a food-processing company have? What voice, if any, should consumers and/or public health professionals have? What scientific or other information should underlie the rule? How much of that information should be disclosed? To what level of rationality should an agency be held?

If whitefish doesn't appeal to you, then try peanut butter. Any product labeled as "peanut butter" must contain peanuts. But how should an agency go about determining how much of the product can be derived from nonpeanut products? Should it take nine years and a 7,736-page transcript to determine whether the appropriate level is 87.5 percent or 90 percent? Should the allowable nonpeanut products include up to thirty insect fragments per one hundred grams, or fewer, or more (Warren 1996, 253; Rosenbloom and Kravchuk 2002, 454)?

There is a wide range of options for regulating administrative rulemaking. Agencies can be left completely to their own devices and allowed to make rules however they see fit. Alternatively, their processes and decision criteria can be so heavily regulated that they have very limited discretion in formulating and enacting rules. In between, there are many possibilities. In administrative law, these are often viewed as existing on a continuum from informal (less regulated) to formal (more regulated) processes. Each end of the continuum and every step along the way will maximize some values at the expense of others. The following are of major concern, as are the potential trade-offs among them:

1. *Flexibility:* When agencies make rules like those for smoked whitefish and peanut butter, they are exercising delegated legislative authority. Flexibility enables administrators to bring their expertise and discretion to public policy issues, such as food purity. Decisions sometimes rest on different views of the public interest, contested science, or competing assumptions about behavior. Some degree of uncertainty is generally present. (When is peanut butter no longer peanut butter?) Flexibility allows agencies to use their best judgment in determining

what kinds of information should be used, from where and from whom, and which criteria should be met in formulating rules. Flexibility would place the burden of persuasion on those opposed to an agency's rule. For example, the FDA has more flexibility if the burden is on food companies to demonstrate that a regulation is commercially infeasible than if it has to show that a rule, as applied to each product, is feasible.

2. *Policy criteria:* In contrast to having unfettered flexibility, rulemakers can be required to consider specific policy criteria, such as costs and benefits, the interests of small entities, and the impact of rules on the environment, economic competitiveness, families, and specific groups such as farmers or minorities.

3. *Faithfulness to legislative intent:* Rules can be more or less in keeping with the legislative intent behind them. Gross deviations from statutory intent or criteria are problematic in terms of the rule of law and democracy. Unelected administrators, who often have civil service protection, should not take the place of legislators. However, legislative intent and statutory standards may be vague, or it may be necessary to reinterpret them in light of new knowledge, conditions, and technologies. Judicial and legislative review of agency rules can be applied, in varying degrees, to hold rulemakers accountable to legislative intent (see Chapter 6).

4. *Rationality:* Rulemaking can be subject to a variety of standards of rationality. An agency can be required to explain the rationale for a rule, the information or science used, the likely costs and benefits and perhaps their distribution, and the level of probability that the rule will achieve its intended purpose. Rulemaking may include mandatory consideration of various alternative means of achieving the desired objective, such as safe smoked whitefish. Legislatures can use the same criteria when passing laws, but typically majority support is a surrogate for legislative rationality. Requiring high levels of rationality may undercut flexibility.

5. *Participation:* Rulemaking can be limited to one or a few agency personnel or opened up to the universe of interested or affected parties. Broad participation may yield better information and greater acceptance of the legitimacy of administrative rulemaking. Agencies can be required to include enforcement agents in their rulemaking. Participation also has costs; for example, it can reduce flexibility by encumbering and delaying rulemaking. Although it is easy to poke fun at the FDA for taking nine years to issue its peanut butter standard, not all of the snail's pace was of its own making.

6. *Efficiency:* Rulemaking can be an efficient alternative to legislative processes, which are usually cumbersome and laden with opportunities to block action. Rulemaking can be more timely and precise. Agencies can be required to produce rules within a fixed time frame. However, as policy criteria and opportunities for participation multiply, efficiency may suffer. Higher standards of rationality may also impede efficiency. Nova Scotia urged the FDA to adopt specific processing requirements for each species of fish, which would have been more rational but also would have required much more science and time. The fish could have consumed a huge amount of the agency's resources.

7. *Enforceability and the ability to conform:* Administrative law can encourage agencies to produce rules that are clear, coherent, and enforceable. The ability of regulated parties to conform, and at what cost, is always relevant to rulemaking, though rulemakers may give the issue limited attention. Nova Scotia flatly refused to comply with the FDA's regulations. Agencies can be required to assess the impact of proposed rules on the different categories of entities that will be affected by them, such as small businesses and local governments, arid versus wet regions, and those who process a particular species of fish.

A good general checklist of rulemaking criteria is contained in Executive Order 12,866 issued by President Bill Clinton in 1993. It provides that federal agencies' regulatory action should be guided by twelve principles: (1) identify the problems addressed; (2) assess the contributions, if any, of existing regulations to those problems; (3) identify alternatives to regulations; (4) consider risks; (5) assess cost-effectiveness; (6) weigh costs and benefits; (7) base decisions on the best obtainable information; (8) assess alternatives among regulatory possibilities; (9) seek the views of state, local, and tribal governments; (10) avoid inconsistency; (11) impose the least burden on society; and (12) write regulations in simple, understandable language.

President Barack Obama's Executive Order 13,563 (2011) augmented Clinton's list. It states that the federal "regulatory system must protect public health, welfare, safety, and our environment while promoting economic growth, innovation, competitiveness, and job creation" (sec. 1[a]). It urges agencies to take "equity, human dignity, fairness, and distributive impacts" into consideration in their regulatory efforts (sec. 1[c]). The order emphasizes the importance of public participation and indicates that proposed rules should generally be open for public comment for "at least 60 days," which is thirty days longer than the APA requires (sec. 2). The order also calls on agencies to "harmonize" their rules across the government and to engage in "retrospective analyses of existing rules" to determine how to "modify, streamline, expand, or repeal" "outmoded, ineffective, insufficient, or excessively burdensome" rules (sec. 6).

Both the Clinton and Obama orders operate against the backdrop of APA requirements for legislative rulemaking. These rest on an idealized model of the legislative process itself. Prior to enactment of the APA in 1946, there was no single, standardized federal rulemaking process. Many agencies had great flexibility. Within the framework of broad delegations of legislative authority, they established the specific policy criteria and trade-offs, chose the participants, and set the level of rationality. Agency procedures varied so widely that an attorney might have to be specially certified to practice before any particular one, such as the Interstate Commerce Commission. A committee of the American Bar Association summarized federal rulemaking in 1934: "Practically every agency to which legislative power has been delegated (or sub delegated [by the president]) has exercised it, and has published its enactments, sometimes in the form of official printed pamphlets, bound or looseleaf, sometimes in mimeograph form, sometimes in privately owned publications, and sometimes in press releases. Sometimes they exist only in sort of an unwritten law. Rules and regulations, upon compliance with which important privileges and freedom from heavy penalties may depend, are amended and interpreted as formally or informally as they were originally adopted" (228). In one congressman's view, the federal bureaucracy was "becoming greater as a lawmaking institution than the Congress of the United States itself" (US Congress 1940, 4672). The bigger problem, as another said, was that the agencies "not only pay too little attention to the viewpoint of the public, but pay less attention to the clearly expressed intention of Congress" (US Congress 1939, 46).

Congress's solution was to require the agencies, "when acting in a quasi-legislative capacity," to "follow the legislative practice of Congress, which from the beginning has held open public hearings on proposed legislation of general public interest" (US Congress 1940, 4591). In this model, administrative rulemaking is a search for the broad public interest. It draws on the insights, information, knowledge, and perspectives of the community at large, especially those who have the greatest stake or concern in the substance of a rule. Just as congressional committees hold hearings on proposed legislation or policy issues, administrators should approach rulemaking with open minds, listen to the public, and be responsive to it. In short, administrative rulemaking is a legislative process; therefore, it should be informed by legislative values.

A major difficulty with the idealized model is precisely that—it is idealized. Politics in the United States tends to flow to the point of policy decision (Lowi 1969). When administrative rules make important policy choices, political influence—rather than a neutral search for the public interest—will be exerted (Stewart 1975). Political parties and groups will seek to protect and promote their interests. They will attempt to ensure that rulemakers pay attention to particular values, such as vibrant federalism, preventing environmental degradation, and protecting small businesses. Groups with enough political clout may convince Congress, the president, or an agency such as the Office of Management and Budget to require impact statements or impose other procedures that will slow or block the adoption of rules that contravene their interests or values. They may also try to achieve their favored substantive policy outcomes or generate delay by influencing an agency's choice among available administrative procedures for rulemaking. Additionally, they may litigate and, over time, essentially compel agencies to use expansive procedures in order to establish comprehensive and defensible rulemaking records that reviewing courts will find convincing. After *Nova Scotia*, presumably the FDA was less likely to withhold the scientific basis for its rules or fail to issue a more comprehensive "concise general statement" of their purpose. Eventually, organized groups seeking to promote their own interests will tend to make rulemaking more elaborate.

It is highly unlikely that in enacting the APA in 1946 Congress could have foreseen what federal rulemaking would look like more than six decades later. The APA is based on an idealized model. It established three rulemaking processes and, for better or worse, left ample flexibility to build upon them. To varying degrees, the same general approaches are available at the state level.

Rulemaking Processes

The APA's rulemaking processes range from unregulated to highly formalized, trial-like procedures.

Limited or No Procedural Requirements

Rules relating to military and foreign affairs, agency management, personnel, public property, loans, grants, benefits, and contracts are exempt from APA requirements. Rulemaking on these matters may nevertheless be regulated by other statutes and/or internal agency procedures. The only APA requirement for procedural and interpretive rules is publication in the *Federal Register* (sec. 552[a][1][C][D]). The constitutionality or legality of specific exempt, procedural, and interpretive rules can be challenged in federal court, but how they are made is up to the agencies. Of course, an agency may want to consult with outside interests or even hold hearings on such rules, but it is not required to do so.

Agencies can also make legislative rules in unrestricted fashion (other than required publication in the *Federal Register*) when they have "good cause," meaning more elaborate procedure is "impracticable, unnecessary, or contrary to the public interest" (sec. 553[b][3][b]). This is a large loophole. The US General Accounting Office found that in 1997 the good-cause provision was used in about half of all potentially covered rulemakings. Most instances involved administrative or technical matters of limited applicability. However, eleven substantial rules were published with no prior public notice or participation. In some cases, the agencies use one of two variants for obtaining public input after a rule is made. In *direct final rulemaking*, a rule is published in the *Federal Register* and goes into effect at a specified future date, unless adverse comments are filed. *Interim final rules* are immediately effective but subject to postpublication comments and potential withdrawal or revision (US General Accounting Office 1998, 2–3, 6–8; the General Accounting Office's name was changed to the Government Accountability Office in 2004).

Informal Rulemaking

Informal rulemaking requirements are modest but subject to considerable amplification. Also known as *notice and comment rulemaking*, informal rulemaking imposes five requirements on the agencies. First, they must either specifically notify affected persons or publish a notice of the proposed rulemaking (NPRM) in the *Federal Register*. The notice must contain "(1) a statement of the time, place, and nature of public rule making proceedings; (2) reference to the legal authority under which the rule is proposed; and (3) either the terms or substance of the proposed rule or a description of the subjects and issues involved" (sec. 553[b]). Second, "the agency shall give interested persons an opportunity to participate in the rule making through submission of written data, views, or arguments with or without opportunity for oral presentation" (sec. 553[c]). Third, "after consideration of the relevant matter presented, the agency shall incorporate in the rules adopted a concise general statement of their basis and purpose" (sec. 553[c]). Fourth, after publication of a final rule in the *Federal Register* at least thirty days must elapse before it can take effect, unless there is good cause, explained with the published rule, for it to apply sooner. Fifth, the agencies have to "give an interested person the right to petition for the issuance, amendment, or repeal of a rule" (sec.

553[e]). If the agency significantly revises a proposed rule after receiving initial comments, it may publish a new version in the *Federal Register* to obtain additional feedback. On their face, these requirements do not appear particularly burdensome. However, the potential for litigation and unfavorable judicial review of rules has prompted the agencies to treat the APA's requirements copiously.

Agency notices regarding the substance of proposed rules have sometimes been found inadequate. Reviewing courts may want "to see what major issues of policy were ventilated by the informal proceedings and why the agency reacted to them as it did" (*Automotive Parts & Accessories Association v. Boyd* 1968, 338). A final rule may be invalidated if a significant issue addressed by it was not identified in the NPRM or if it is not a logical outgrowth of the proposed rule. After receiving comments, an agency can write a substantially different rule. However, the original notice must always enable the parties potentially affected by a final rule to know that their interests are involved. An agency's notice cannot be so cryptic that interested parties are unable to comment upon it meaningfully. This was the problem with the FDA's failure to disclose the scientific basis for its proposed rule in *Nova Scotia*. Additionally, as *Nova Scotia* illustrates, an agency's concise statement of purpose may be defective. Finally, although the APA does not require rulemakers to respond to individual comments, agencies routinely docket them with some kind of assessment in order to build a record that will convince a court that a final rule is reasonable. Rules can have huge effects on the economy, environment, and public. Courts often take a hard look at their logic and rationality (see Chapter 6 on judicial review of agency actions).

Assessments of informal rulemaking vary. Notice and comment was intended to be straightforward, not straitjacketing. In practice, however, agencies tend to use more elaborate procedures than those outlined in the APA itself. As noted above, this is partly because they need to build a satisfactory record for judicial review. But as discussed later in this chapter, it is also due to additional requirements imposed by statutes and executive orders. Rulemaking has become laborious enough for agencies to use a variety of techniques to obtain input from interested publics before writing, or deciding to write, proposed rules. They may chose or be required by statutes other than the APA to issue an advance notice of proposed rulemaking (ANPRM) to help frame their notice of proposed rulemaking. In fact, as a means of exercising influence, response to an ANPRM or informal contacts with the agency both before and after publication of an NPRM may be equally or more effective than submitting written comments or attending hearings, if any are held (Kerwin 1999, 195).

Formal Rulemaking

Also known as *rulemaking on the record*, formal rulemaking is very elaborate—so much so that it can be counterproductive in terms of timeliness and efficiency. This is why the 1981 Model State Administrative Procedure Act avoids it (Bonfield 1986, 186). Federal agencies are also apt to dispense with it whenever possible, which is often. The APA sets forth the structure for formal rulemaking but does not require agencies to engage in it. Formal rulemaking is mandated by separate statutes when Congress considers it appropriate, as in some sections of the FDA's Federal Food, Drug, and Cosmetic Act.

Formal rulemaking is a quasi-judicial, trial-like process. Hearings, which are central to congressional lawmaking, are mandatory for formal rulemaking. A panel or specific officer, who can be an administrative law judge or similar hearing examiner, presides. The presiding officer or panel regulates the course of the hearing, administers oaths, decides on the information that may be offered as evidence, tries to arrange for agreement among the parties, and, failing that, issues a decision. The parties to the hearing submit evidence and may engage in cross-examination (sec. 556). The APA places the burden of persuasion on the proponent of the rule, which may be the agency or an outside interest. Ex parte (one-sided) contacts between the decisionmaker and a participant in the hearing in the absence of any other are improper. The agency maintains a complete transcript, and its decision must be supported by substantial evidence on the record as a whole.

The presiding officer or panel can issue an initial or recommended decision. Initial decisions become final unless they are appealed; recommended decisions are automatically subject to review by the agency head or governing board or commission. The final rule, if any, is published in the *Federal Register* and takes effect, as specified, after at least thirty days have elapsed to enable those affected to comply. In unusual cases, the agency, board, or commission may issue a tentative decision for comment by the parties and possible revision. These provisions may be modified by whatever statute requires the agency to use formal rulemaking.

The weight of opinion among administrative law scholars, legislators, and judges is that "the formal rulemaking procedure normally 'does not work,'" or at least works so badly that it ought to be avoided (Warren 1996, 253). The courts, including the US Supreme Court, seem to agree. They are unlikely to force agencies to use it unless "(1) a specific statute clearly requires formal rule-making; (2) an oral, evidentiary hearing is mandated by a statute; and (3) adjudicative facts specific to an individual involving 'property' or 'liberty' interests must be resolved through a [constitutional] due process, formal rule-making agency hearing" (Warren 1996, 254; *United States v. Florida East Coast Railway Co.* 1973).

Hybrid and Negotiated Rulemaking Processes

Two additional general rulemaking approaches have gained currency since enactment of the APA in 1946.

Hybrid Rulemaking

Hybrid rulemaking was developed by some federal agencies, promoted by Congress, and, until 1978, sometimes imposed on administrators by the courts. Hybrid rulemaking follows a Goldilocks-type principle. As a means of making public policy, formal rulemaking is informational and procedural overkill, whereas informal rulemaking is potentially inadequate in providing agencies with the comprehensive data and perspectives they need to formulate sound rules. The APA allows the agencies to search for a middle ground that is just right. Most notably, they can hold public hearings in conjunction with notice and comment rulemaking and invite interested parties to participate or solicit their views in some other fashion. With wider information, the agency can build a more complete record and, presumably, a stronger rationale for its final rule.

Hybrid rulemaking is related to a shift toward greater public and public interest group participation in administrative policymaking (Stewart 1975). Prior to the 1960s or 1970s, individual agencies were often considered "captives" of specific, narrow-based economic interest groups (Bernstein 1955). In a classic case, the Interstate Commerce Commission was once considered a ward of the railroad industry. The same interest group capturing the agency would have considerable influence with the congressional (sub) committees that formulated legislation in the particular policy area and exercised oversight of the agencies involved. Relations among the group, committee, and agency tended to be harmonious—and nearly impervious to influence from outsiders. The terms "iron triangle" and "cozy triangle" (or "subsystems," as some political scientists call them) were used to describe these policymaking arrangements.

In the 1960s and 1970s, political demands for wider group representation and greater attention to the public's interest in administrative policymaking reached a crescendo. The period witnessed the enactment of the Freedom of Information Act (1966) and the Government in the Sunshine Act (1976) (see Chapter 5 on transparency), as well as the Federal Advisory Committee Act (1972), which is discussed later in this chapter. As the agencies responded to both the new statutes and the political mood, the iron triangle image gave way to one portraying far more open, participatory *issue networks* or *policy networks* (Heclo 1978). These are made up of groups and individuals who share technical knowledge and interest in policy areas but not necessarily the same political perspectives. For instance, whereas energy policy may once have been dominated by economic interests, such as oil and electric power companies, issue networks bring environmental and conservation groups into the policymaking (rulemaking) process.

The growth of hybrid rulemaking was instrumental in the shift from iron triangles to issue networks. By expanding participation in rulemaking, "agency personnel give shape to the heretofore formless issue networks" and, importantly, may serve as "arbiters" of their perspectives (Golden 1998, 12). This frees the agencies from captivity, or at least inordinate influence, by a single interest and brings rulemaking closer to the idealized legislative model. Airing competing perspectives in the rulemaking process should enhance rationality and enable agencies to compile better explanations of the basis for their final rules. It should also lend more political legitimacy to rulemaking.

The federal courts boosted hybrid rulemaking in the late 1960s and early 1970s. As litigation became a staple of the administrative process, judges were looking for better agency records upon which to review the legality of final rules. In particular, they might require the agencies to grant greater participation to environmental or other public interest groups. Judicially imposed hybrid rulemaking came to a dead end with the Supreme Court's unanimous decision in *Vermont Yankee Nuclear Power Corp. v. Natural Resources Defense Council, Inc.* (1978). In no uncertain terms, the Court held that the judiciary should not graft additional procedural requirements onto informal rulemaking. The agencies need only meet the minimal APA requirements. Otherwise, rulemaking requirements would be unpredictable, and from a practical perspective, the agencies would have to make the informal procedure much more like the laborious formal one. However, nothing in *Vermont Yankee* prohibited the agencies from using hybrid rulemaking on their own or Congress and the president from augmenting APA informal rulemaking requirements by statutes and executive orders.

Negotiated Rulemaking

Negotiated rulemaking was developed in the 1980s, also as a means of bringing rulemaking closer to the idealized legislative model. It relies on face-to-face negotiation among interested parties, including agencies, to formulate rules. Also known as *regulatory negotiation* (Reg-Neg), it gained full legitimacy via the federal Negotiated Rulemaking Act of 1990, which amends the APA's rulemaking procedures. Reg-Neg is considered appropriate when only a limited number of identifiable interests will be affected by a rule. The general procedure is for agencies to establish rulemaking committees after notice and comment in the *Federal Register*. Committees will typically comprise up to twenty-five members drawn from the agency, regulated entities, trade associations, unions, citizen groups, and other relevant interests. The committee should adequately represent all the affected interests. Its meetings are open to the public. A facilitator or mediator can be used to steer the proceedings in search of a consensus. Unanimity is required for a rule to be successfully negotiated, though members who oppose the majority can withdraw from the committee rather than block its efforts. If consensus is reached, the agency publishes the negotiated rule in the *Federal Register* for notice and comment (and possible revision). Although the agencies are treated as any other participant in the negotiations, they retain ultimate control of whether a final rule will be issued and, if so, what its text will be.

The premise behind Reg-Neg is that it can improve on "the poor quality of rules produced, the burdensome nature of the rulemaking process, the length of time it takes to promulgate rules, and the frequency of litigation that follows" (US Senate 1989, 2). Compared with informal rulemaking, Reg-Neg is thought to be less adversarial, more problem solving and creative, supported by better information and perspective, and more educational for the parties (Strauss et al. 1995, 405). The Negotiated Rulemaking Act was permanently reauthorized in the 1996 Administrative Dispute Resolution Act.

Critics of Reg-Neg contend that it fails to deliver on its promise and "has the tendency to obscure, if not pervert, the public interest to the benefit of private interests" (Funk 1987, 57; quoted in Strauss et al. 1995, 405). Timeliness and litigation rates do not seem to have been dramatically affected by Reg-Neg, though the data are not conclusive (Coglianese 1997; Kerwin and Furlong 1992). By one count, the EPA's Farmworker Protection Standards rule took 2,528 days, or nearly seven years, to complete, whereas the US Coast Guard took only 179 days to negotiate a rule regarding drawbridges on the Chicago River (Coglianese 1997, 1279). Negotiated rules, both before and after the 1990 act, include such matters as residential woodstoves, nondiscrimination in air travel, asbestos in public schools, handicapped parking, clean fuels, wood furniture coatings, direct student loans, disadvantaged students, and Indian self-determination.

Additional Features of the
Idealized Legislative Model for Rulemaking

Several other elements of the legislative rulemaking model are noteworthy.

Representation: Advisory Committees

Federal agencies have long used quasi-governmental advisory committees to guide them in setting rulemaking agendas, writing proposed rules, and performing other policymaking activities. Many of these committees have a relatively narrow focus, dealing, for instance, with a single geographic region, crop, animal, food, disease, chemical, or technology. The advisory committee system is fluid—committees come and go—but the following titles indicate their nature: Pediatric Advisory Committee, Allergenic Products Advisory Committee, Medical Devices Advisory Committee, Cascade Head Scenic Research Area Advisory Council, National Advisory Council on Safety in Agriculture, National Cotton Marketing Study Committee, Cattle Industry Advisory Committee, National Advisory Council on Child Nutrition, Advisory Committee on Hog Cholera Eradication, Expert Panel on Nitrates and Nitrosamines, National Peanut Advisory Committee, and Raisin Advisory Board (Leahy 1976). Both Congress and the president establish such committees, which are a valued resource in bringing greater expertise, perspective, and legitimacy to administrative policymaking. They also promote the democratic-constitutional values of participation and representation in agency decisionmaking (Steck 1984). The system is quite active. There are about 1,000 advisory committees. In fiscal year 2006, they had 67,346 members, held over 7,000 meetings, and produced almost 1,000 reports (Center for Effective Government 2014).

Advisory committees have sometimes been considered a powerful "fifth branch" of the government, the agencies being the fourth (US Senate 1978, 48, 217, 293, 299–300). Despite their acknowledged value, there is always concern that they will be skewed in favor of some interests at the expense of others, generate conflicts of interest, or exercise untoward influence over the agencies.

The Federal Advisory Committee Act of 1972 seeks to reduce the potential for abuse. It requires that the membership of advisory committees be "fairly balanced in terms of the points of view represented and the functions to be performed" (sec. 5). It also specifies that the committees "will not be inappropriately influenced by the appointing authority or by any special interest" (sec. 5). The act promotes transparency through a number of public notice, open meeting, and reporting requirements (see Chapter 5 in this book). It does not apply to committees composed entirely of federal employees.

The Federal Advisory Committee Act contemplates joint congressional and executive management of the advisory committee system. Congressional committees are charged with reviewing the activities of those advisory committees under their jurisdictions and determining whether they should be merged with others, abolished altogether, or have their responsibilities revised. The Office of Management and Budget (OMB) also has a role in reviewing the status of advisory committees and issuing guidelines to improve their effectiveness. Cost is also a concern. In fiscal 2006 the committees "cost the federal government more than $383 million in personnel, travel and support expenses" (Center for Effective Government 2014).

Protecting Specific Interests and Values

The use of advisory committees is premised on the belief that many interests are well defined and coherent enough to be represented through direct participation in agency policymaking, including establishing rulemaking agendas. But what about interests and values that are so diffuse in the economy and society that they are not readily amenable to such direct representation? The federal government's answer has been to protect them through impact assessments or analyses in notice and comment rulemaking. The Regulatory Flexibility Act of 1980 is a good example.

That statute requires agencies to analyze the effects of their rulemaking on small entities, which include small governmental jurisdictions, not-for-profits, and, most notably, businesses. Such entities often face a problem in that they are exceptionally burdened by the compliance costs associated with across-the-board regulations for clean air and water, worker safety, and other matters. Overall, small business has very strong support in Congress. But specific small enterprises, such as mom-and-pop outfits, are likely to be less effective than large firms in using their own resources and/or relying on trade associations to protect their interests through daily monitoring of the *Federal Register* for ANPRMs and NPRMs and subsequent submission of comments to the agencies.

The Regulatory Flexibility Act seeks to reduce small entities' vulnerability to unduly burdensome, prohibitively expensive, and impractical regulations by requiring the agencies to provide *regulatory flexibility* (Reg-Flex) analyses, when relevant, in notice and comment rulemaking, along with their proposed and final rules. Reg-Flex analyses focus on the impact the rules will have on small entities and potential alternatives, if any, that would be less burdensome. Enforcement is through the Small Business

Administration, with limited opportunity for judicial review (Sargentich 1997, 124–126).

The Small Business Regulatory Enforcement Fairness Act of 1996 amended the 1980 act and strengthened the Reg-Flex process in a number of ways. It broadens the scope of judicial review for aggrieved small entities. It also contains provisions requiring EPA and OSHA actively to seek input from representatives of small entities. The act continues to apply primarily to informal legislative rulemaking but also covers some Internal Revenue Service interpretive rules.

The precedent set by the Regulatory Flexibility Act gained a foothold in executive orders as well. President Ronald Reagan issued two such orders in 1987: No. 12,606 required agencies to engage in assessments of the impact of their proposed rules on "family values," and No. 12,612 required "federalism impact assessments." Clinton followed suit in 1994 with a similar order for environmental justice (No. 12,898). President George W. Bush's Executive Order 13,422 mandated that when agency rulemaking is intended to correct a "market failure (such as externalities, market power, lack of information)," that failure must be identified in writing (sec. 1[a][1]). President Obama's Executive Order 13,514 requires agencies to identify and analyze the "impacts from energy usage and alternative energy sources in all Environmental Impact Statements and Environmental Assessments" pursuant to the National Environmental Policy Act of 1969 (sec. 2[f][iv]). In 1998, Congress strengthened the family values emphasis through the Assessment of Federal Regulations and Policies on Families Act, noted in Chapter 1, which requires the agencies to engage in "family policymaking assessments." The executive orders on rulemaking are not binding on the independent regulatory commissions, such as the Federal Communications Commission and the Federal Trade Commission, which nevertheless may comply voluntarily. Although not without controversy as a matter of constitutional law, "the President . . . lacks distinct constitutional power to manage these organizations [i.e., independent regulatory commissions]" (Moreno 1994, 512). However, the orders do apply to EPA, OSHA, and similar executive branch units.

The Paperwork Reduction Acts of 1980 and 1995 also bear mention. They seek to control and reduce the enormous paperwork burden that federal rules and requirements thrust on society. In 1980, the OMB estimated the overall burden at 1.5 billion hours (Skrzycki 1998, G2). By 1994, it had apparently reached 6.5 billion hours and may have cost as much as 9 percent of gross domestic product (Strauss et al. 1995, 872). The Paperwork Reduction Acts require agencies to publish in the *Federal Register* for public comment notices of their intent to collect information. They must also estimate the burden their forms and related instruments impose. After completing these steps, if the agencies decide to proceed, they must submit their proposals for collecting information to OMB's Office of Information and Regulatory Affairs. Their submissions must include considerations of whether the information sought is duplicative or burdensome, creates special hardships for small entities, and is clearly identified or defined. The Office of Information and Regulatory Affairs (OIRA) works to prevent the collection of unnecessary information by monitoring and coordinating the agencies' use of forms and other devices. It has sixty days to clear requests, which are approved for one year by default if it fails to meet this deadline. OIRA's disapproval is binding with two exceptions: it is subject to judicial review if challenged as arbitrary and capricious, and independent regulatory commissions can override OIRA's rejection by a majority vote of their commission or board members (Lubbers 1997, 116). A public-protection provision prohibits penalizing anyone for failing to respond to a federal information-collection instrument that was not properly subjected to the required clearance process.

The paperwork reduction process seems straightforward enough, if not wholly adequate, in limiting the agencies' appetite for information. Despite the acts, the paperwork burden rose to 8.2 billion hours by 2002, in part due to population growth (Ziegler 2003, 6). Like many administrative law procedures, paperwork reduction can be used (or abused) politically to achieve public policy objectives. In 2001, a Republican congressional aide, working in concert with the head of OIRA, convened key business lobbyists in an effort to "use obscure paperwork guidelines as a back-door mechanism to gut long-established regulations" for air and water quality, lead paint, truck safety, reporting the release of toxic substances, and family and medical leaves. In short, "paperwork technicalities [are] an excuse to review otherwise untouchable rules" (Grunwald 2001).

This experience with paperwork reduction makes the idealized legislative model look less ideal. As suggested earlier, there are apt to be important value trade-offs in rulemaking processes. The Federal Advisory Committee Act's reporting and transparency provisions encumber the use of such committees, albeit in an effort to promote democratic-constitutional values. Efforts to protect particular interests and values through impact assessments and paperwork review consume time and effort. Some scholars wonder whether, in the aggregate, the addition of so many administrative law requirements to the APA's basic process for informal rulemaking has such an inhibiting effect that a "'regulatory impact analysis' impact analysis would be useful in deciding whether to undertake any further such requirements" (Strauss et al. 1995, 217)! Yet rulemaking has been further complicated by presidents.

Executive Efforts to Influence Federal Agency Rulemaking

Legislative rulemaking by administrators occupies a somewhat uncomfortable place in the constitutional structure. When Congress exercises its legislative powers by enacting laws, the president has a veto. This gives the chief executive considerable bargaining power with Congress, which needs a two-thirds majority in both chambers to override vetoes. When Congress delegates its legislative authority to the agencies, the president has no formal veto power over their rules. The 1981 Model State Administrative Procedure Act provides that a governor may "rescind or suspend all or a severable portion of a rule of an agency," and some states authorize their attorney general to review rules (sec. 3-202; Bonfield 1993, 180). However, the federal APA has no equivalent provisions. Presidents need other means of promoting their policy agendas and coordinating executive branch activity. To a large extent, they rely on their political appointees for these purposes. President George W. Bush strengthened control over rulemaking by requiring that executive branch agencies' regulatory policy offices be managed by political appointees with responsibility for supervising rules and guidance statements (Executive Order 13,422 2007; Pear 2007). Beginning in earnest during President Richard Nixon's administration, presidents have also turned to administrative law devices.

Nixon established a lasting precedent by authorizing the Office of Management and Budget to undertake quality-of-life reviews of proposed administrative regulations. The reviews focused on the regulatory objectives, costs and benefits, and plausible alternatives to proposed measures. President Gerald Ford followed Nixon's precedent by requiring the agencies to send *inflation impact statements* to OMB along with their proposed regulations. But it was President Jimmy Carter who ratcheted up presidential control of agency rulemaking toward contemporary standards.

Carter established the Regulatory Analysis Review Group to review agency rulemaking proposals likely to cost industries at least $100 million per year. Among its purposes were improving the analysis supporting proposed regulations and assuring consideration of the least costly alternatives (Kerwin 1999, 123). Carter's Executive Order 12,044 (1978) established the Regulatory Council, composed of the heads of the agencies most active in regulation, to coordinate administrative rulemaking and assess the cumulative effect of regulations. The order also called on the agencies to publish a regulatory agenda twice a year, write regulations in plain and simple language, increase outside participation in the development of regulations, prepare economic impact analyses for all significant regulations, and periodically review the efficacy of existing regulations. OMB was responsible for agency compliance, though actual review was typically conducted by the review group.

President Reagan followed Carter's lead and put OMB at the center of much federal rulemaking. Executive Orders 12,291 (1981) and 12,498 (1985) centralized executive control of covered rulemaking in OIRA. Under the orders' combined provisions, agencies had to submit draft and final regulatory analyses, regulatory agendas, and major proposed and final rules to OIRA for review. Unless prohibited by a specific statute affecting a policy area, rulemaking had to incorporate cost-benefit analysis. Agency heads retained final authority to proceed with rulemaking but were required to explain any noncompliance with OIRA's recommendations (Warren 1996, 279). Although compliance was the norm, this arrangement stuck to the letter of constitutional precedent, which allows Congress to vest legal authority specifically and directly in the agencies rather than in the president for subdelegation to them (*Kendall v. United States* 1838).

Observers agree that Reagan's approach had a permanent impact on presidential direction and control of federal rulemaking (Warren 1996, 279; Kerwin 1999, 126). President George H. W. Bush (Bush I) (1989–1993) retained Reagan's initiatives and also appointed a Council on Competitiveness to review selected major rules. President Clinton revoked the Reagan orders but adhered to their general direction regarding OMB review, though with more transparency in OIRA's operations (Executive Order 12,866 1993).

President George W. Bush (Bush II) subscribed to "unitary executive branch theory," which contends that the president has constitutional power to personally exercise legislative authority congressionally delegated to executive branch agencies. In other words, although Congress may delegate its lawmaking power to agencies with the expectation that they will use their scientific, economic, and public policy expertise to fashion rules for environmental protection and sustainability, occupational health and safety, safe pesticides, economic performance, and so forth, such rulemaking authority can be used by the president, personally or through political appointees, to write the rules (Rosenbloom 2010). Bush II's efforts to control rulemaking began in controversy on the very day of his first inauguration (January 20, 2001), when his White House chief of staff, Andrew Card Jr., issued a memorandum asking the agencies to postpone the effective date of final rules for sixty days. The new administration wanted to review what many viewed as last-minute efforts to write final rules before the presidential transition. Bush II was building on a precedent set by Reagan in Executive Order 12,291, which imposed a sixty-day moratorium on new rules. Upon taking office, Bill Clinton also slowed "regulations that were underway, including those on the verge of becoming final, without touching any completed rules about to take effect" (Goldstein 2001, A6).

The Bush II administration also sought to strengthen OMB review in five main ways. First, it favored more openness through use of the Internet to enable "the public to scrutinize how [OMB] use[s] science and economics to stop bad rules and help agencies craft better ones" (Graham 2002). Second, OIRA intended to hire more scientists and engineers to join its statisticians, economists, and information technologists in analyzing agency rulemaking proposals. Third, OIRA planned to cajole the agencies into doing higher-quality regulatory analyses. Fourth, OMB took a proactive role in rulemaking by issuing "prompt letters" "to identify publicly areas where agencies might improve regulatory policies" (Graham 2002). For example, one such letter speeded up the FDA's work on a food-labeling rule for trans fatty acids. Finally, OMB initiated a broad effort to require that the data on which rulemaking is based are "reproducible, or at least highly transparent, about research design, data sources and analytical methods" (Graham 2002).

These presidential efforts to supervise or control rulemaking are largely prospective. President Obama added a role for OIRA in overseeing agency plans to review "existing significant regulations" as part of his administration's overall effort to improve rulemaking and regulation (Executive Order 13,563 2011, sec. 6[b]). Generally, however, what is known as the "regulatory ratchet" dictates that rules are aggregative or accretive and "rarely recede" because deleting or modifying older rules is a low priority, cost-ineffective use of agency resources, potentially subject to unnecessary political controversy, and just plain "boring work" (Bardach and Kagan 1982, ch. 7). Under considerable pressure from President Clinton and Vice President Al Gore's National Performance Review in the 1990s, the ratchet was partly reversed with the elimination of 16,000 pages of outdated regulations in the *Federal Register* and revision of 40 percent of the remaining rules (National Performance Review 1995). Consequently, Obama's effort to institutionalize rule deletion and revision bears watching.

The logic behind presidential efforts to coordinate agency rulemaking and improve the quality of rules is clear. Nevertheless, presidents continue to face significant hurdles in gaining full mastery over agency rulemaking. As administrative law scholar Kenneth Warren (1996, 279–281) reminds us, with specific reference to Reagan, there are several limits to presidential authority over legislative rulemaking:

1. The independent regulatory commissions "promulgate thousands of major rules profoundly affecting public policy areas," but their rulemaking is largely unaffected by executive orders (see also Moreno 1994). Requests that they voluntarily comply tend to be ignored.
2. Reagan's executive orders did not apply to formal rulemaking, and, more generally, executive orders cannot override statutory or constitutional requirements affecting such rulemaking.
3. Bureaucratic inertia along with legal obstacles (and, one might add, agency support in Congress) make centralized control of the rulemaking process very difficult.
4. Reagan's deregulatory agenda faced a substantial number of setbacks in court. Essentially, it takes informal rulemaking, or at least a cogently reasoned analysis, to rescind final rules. A new administration cannot simply terminate rules promulgated by its predecessors (*Motor Vehicle Manufacturers Association of the United States, Inc. v. State Farm Mutual Automobile Insurance Co.* 1983; see Chapter 6).

With reference to Warren's third point above, it should also be noted that executive orders, as in No. 13,514, may contain a provision making them legally and therefore judicially unenforceable by explicitly stating that they do not "create any right or benefit, substantive or procedural, enforceable at law or in equity by any party against the United States, its departments, agencies, or entities, its officers, employees, or agents, or any other person" (sec. 20[d]). Consequently, the penalties, if any, that agencies and their personnel face for not adhering to the orders' requirements are political. Yet it may be politically infeasible for presidents and their top aides to try to compel enforcement by taking action against career employees with civil service protection against dismissals and demotions and political executives (appointees) who may enjoy congressional, interest group, or stakeholder support.

Despite such obstacles, the decades-old presidential effort to gain greater control over administrative rulemaking is likely to continue—often contentiously—through the current administration and beyond.

Conclusion: The Philosopher's Stone Versus the Bubble Effect

During congressional debate on the APA in 1946, Senator Homer Ferguson, a Michigan Republican, predicted that "there will be fewer complaints because of the activities of governmental agencies if they will attempt to live within the rules and regulations laid down by Congress" (US Congress 1946, 2205). Maybe, but complaints about federal rulemaking still abound. Finding the "best" process is like searching for the philosopher's stone. Rulemaking procedures are not neutral. They inevitably involve important value trade-offs. They also advantage some interests and participants while disadvantaging others. Members of Congress, presidents, administrators, and interest groups will tend to support procedures that favor their policy preferences and contest those that hinder them. Pressure will be brought to bear wherever key policy decisions can be made, blocked, or reversed. Interests that are able to influence rulemaking agendas and criteria, such as through the use of cost-benefit or Reg-Flex analysis, will do so; others, lacking the same avenues of influence, may turn to the courts to achieve their objectives. As a former OIRA official candidly summed up misuse of the Paperwork Reduction Acts for political gain, "The paperwork is a way in, you know?"—a way in to gut rules opposed by favored lobbyists (Grunwald 2001). Both before and after 1946, changing federal rulemaking has been like trying to squeeze an air bubble in a clear plastic tube. Putting pressure on it in one place moves the point at which it can be squeezed to another.

Additional Reading

Kerwin, Cornelius, and Scott Furlong. *Rulemaking: How Government Agencies Write Law and Make Policy.* 4th ed. Washington, DC: CQ Press, 2010.

Lubbers, Jeffrey. *A Guide to Federal Agency Rulemaking.* 4th ed. Chicago: ABA Press, 2006.

Discussion Questions

1. Almost all observers agree that federal legislative rulemaking has become highly complex and even convoluted. If you could change one or two aspects of the current processes to simplify rulemaking, what would you do? Why?

2. Presidents have used executive orders to add protection of specific interests and values, such as environmental justice, to legislative rulemaking. Do you think presidents should have the authority to do so in view of the fact that legislative rulemaking is based on congressional delegations of legislative authority, and if Congress wants to protect these values, it can do so in the delegations or by separate statutes? Why?

3. The Paperwork Reduction Acts notwithstanding, the amount of paperwork that federal agencies thrust on the American public keeps growing. Federal income tax forms are one of the most time-consuming and intrusive paperwork requirements that most Americans fill out. Can you recommend ways of simplifying the form you use? If so, what are they? Do they involve rewriting tax law?

4

Evidentiary Adjudication and Enforcement

Adjudicating *Cinderella*:
A Case of Deceit, Abuse, and Due Process

The Federal Trade Commission (FTC) has legal authority to initiate and decide cases against firms it believes are engaging in unfair and deceptive business practices. In the late 1960s, the FTC charged Cinderella Career College and Finishing Schools, Inc. (Cinderella) with thirteen counts of false advertising and deception. These included Cinderella's questionable claims that

- Miss USA 1965 owed her success to Cinderella's program
- Cinderella's courses qualified students to become retail buyers and airline hostesses and to assume executive positions
- Cinderella was the official Washington, DC, headquarters for the Miss Universe beauty pageant
- Cinderella was a college
- Cinderella's placement services rarely failed

The FTC also accused Cinderella of using high-pressure and misleading sales tactics on prospective students. In short, the FTC deemed Cinderella a cheat that should be exposed and forced to stop preying on naive teenage girls.

The FTC prosecuted Cinderella at a hearing within the FTC itself, presided over by an independent hearing examiner. The hearing took sixteen days, during which 247 exhibits were introduced, 52 witnesses appeared, and 1,810 pages of testimony were taken. The hearing examiner's 93-page initial decision absolved Cinderella of all charges. The FTC had "failed to prove by a preponderance of reliable, probative and substantial evidence" that Cinderella deceived.

The FTC's prosecutor (the complaint counsel) appealed the initial decision to the full commission, that is, to the five FTC commissioners. In this type of proceeding, the commissioners may substitute their own decision for that of the hearing examiner. The commission was chaired by Paul Rand Dixon, who had no love for Cinderella. In a well-reported speech to members of the National Newspaper Association, he cited Cinderella's ads as exemplars of deception and urged his audience to stop printing such material: "Granted that newspapers are not in the advertising policing business, their advertising managers are savvy enough to smell deception when the odor is strong enough." He specifically mentioned "carrying ads that offer college educations in five weeks, fortunes by raising mushrooms in the basement, getting rid of pimples with a magic lotion, or becoming an airline's hostess by attending a charm school." Dixon's remarks were made after FTC staff had given notice that the hearing examiner's initial decision would be appealed to Dixon and the other commissioners.

With Dixon in charge, Cinderella fared poorly at the commission level. The commissioners sustained six of the FTC's original charges and ordered Cinderella to cease and desist from engaging in the illegal practices covered. They reached this decision with scant attention to the transcript and outcome of the earlier proceeding. Instead of wading through the voluminous record before them, the commissioners decided "to independently analyze—and without assistance from consumer or other witnesses—the challenged advertisements and their impact." Consequently, it became "unnecessary" for the commissioners "to review the testimony of . . . expert and consumer witnesses." Believing that the commissioners knew deception when they saw it, "the Commission [relied] on its own reading and study of the advertisements to determine whether the questioned representation [had] the capacity to deceive."

Cinderella took the case to court on the grounds that the FTC had egregiously violated constitutional due process by (1) making its decision without reference to the record produced by the hearing, and (2) allowing Dixon to participate in deciding the appeal. The Court of Appeals for the District of Columbia Circuit agreed that it was "preposterous for the Commission to claim a right to ignore that evidence [relied upon by the hearing examiner] and, with more daring than prudence, to decide a case de novo [anew]" as it did with *Cinderella*. In plain English, "the Commissioners are not free to boil over in aggression and completely dismiss [the hearing] proceedings either because they are dissatisfied with the outcome, or for any other reason."

The court also had some choice words for Chairman Dixon, who, in its view, was no Prince Charming. He had failed to recuse (disqualify) himself in other cases, and with obvious frustration the court found "it hard to believe that . . . Chairman Dixon is so indifferent to the dictates of the Courts of Appeals that he has chosen once again to put his personal determination of what the law requires ahead of what the courts have time and again told him the law requires." It rebuked him for exercising "questionable discretion and very poor judgment indeed," being "sensitive to theory but insensitive to reality," and distorting the law "beyond all reasonable interpretation" or just ignoring it altogether.

In reiterating the fundamental legal principle requiring recusal, the court noted that "it requires no superior olfactory powers to recognize that the danger of unfairness through prejudgment is not diminished by a cloak of self-righteousness." Disqualification is necessary when "a disinterested observer may conclude that [the agency] has in some measure adjudged the facts as well as the law of a particular case in advance of hearing it." Moreover, agency adjudications "must be attended not only with every element of fairness but with the very appearance of complete fairness."

The court held that the FTC had violated Cinderella's constitutional due process. The commissioners should have taken the whole record into account and also excluded Dixon from the appeal. Some seventeen months after the commission issued its final order, Cinderella won a reprieve (*Cinderella Career and Finishing Schools, Inc. v. Federal Trade Commission* 1970, 584–586, 588, 591–592).

What Is Evidentiary Administrative Adjudication?

The violations of due process in *Cinderella* are atypical, but otherwise the case provides a good illustration of *evidentiary administrative adjudication*. An evidentiary adjudication is a proceeding—typically a hearing of some kind—in which evidence is adduced and law applied in determining the rights and obligations of individuals, corporations, and other entities. Evidentiary adjudication is used in a very wide variety of administrative decision making, including

- Determining individuals' eligibility for benefits
- Resolving charges of unfair or illegal economic, personnel, and labor relations practices
- Granting or denying licenses

- Challenging the award of a government contract
- Enforcing laws and agency regulations to protect the public, the environment, businesses, and other entities against harmful practices, threats, and dangers

The product of an evidentiary hearing is an *order*.

The structure and process of agency evidentiary adjudication is broadly controlled by procedural due process under the US Constitution's Fifth and Fourteenth amendments, as well as by administrative law provisions. Adjudications controlled by sections 554, 556, and 557 of the Administrative Procedure Act (APA) of 1946 are called "formal." As in *Cinderella*, adjudication may involve an elaborate hearing, with personal appearances and live testimony, as well as an appeals process. However, it may also be confined to written submissions and very limited opportunity for review. Unlike notice and comment rulemaking, where the model seeks to replicate an idealized version of how legislatures in the United States make law, administrative evidentiary adjudication is not intended to match courtroom procedure. Rather, the objectives are fourfold: (1) to achieve fundamental fairness, (2) to adjudicate cases competently, (3) to resolve conflicts and cases efficiently, and (4) to accomplish all of the foregoing while enhancing, or at least not impeding, organizational performance.

Fairness is usually gauged in terms of how the parties to an adjudication believe they were treated. *Competence* is measured by the extent to which hearing examiners and agencies' decisions are upheld on appeal. *Efficiency* is essentially timeliness. *Organizational performance* can involve any number of factors, including the impact of adjudication on resources, coherent decisionmaking, and personnel systems. In practice, it is difficult for adjudicatory systems to excel in all four dimensions simultaneously.

Discussions of adjudication are often confusing. First, under the APA, there is overlap in the provisions for formal rulemaking and evidentiary adjudication. Formal rulemaking is an adjudicatory procedure. However, it is apt to focus on *legislative facts* or general policy concerns, such as whether a proposed rule is necessary or cost-beneficial. Legislative facts may involve empirical or scientific matters, such as how to eliminate botulism in smoked whitefish. However, they do not pertain to the conduct of specific individuals or entities like Cinderella. Evidentiary adjudication, by contrast, focuses on *adjudicative facts*, which are concerned with individual motive, intent, and behavior. Whether individuals should have a right to cancel a contract with a school like Cinderella within a day or two of signing it is a legislative fact; whether Cinderella engaged in deceptive advertising is an adjudicative fact.

Evidentiary adjudication also differs from formal rulemaking in that it is retrospective rather than prospective. It deals with past and/or continuing conduct. By contrast, rulemaking—both formal and informal—addresses matters in the future. Another distinction is that evidentiary adjudication deals with specific parties, whereas rulemaking has general applicability. A rule prohibiting false advertising applies broadly throughout the economy; an evidentiary adjudication to determine whether a firm has violated the rule is specific, as in *Cinderella*.

A second source of confusion is that although evidentiary adjudication and rulemaking are analytically distinct, as just described, in practice sometimes they may be used interchangeably to achieve identical policy outcomes. The main problem is that although evidentiary adjudication applies directly only to the parties to a case and is retrospective, the decision reached will presumably apply to others in the future. For example, the National Labor Relations Board (NLRB) adjudicates charges of unfair labor practices by unions and businesses. Many cases are repetitive, dealing with the same basic fair labor practice principles, and the evidentiary adjudication merely determines the facts (e.g., Did the union organize an employee "sick-out," or did a large number of bargaining unit employees catch the flu at once?). Some cases, however, known as *cases of first impression*, will raise altogether new issues. When this occurs, the evidentiary adjudication will necessarily deal with legislative facts: Is the practice unfair under the governing statute? It will also address adjudicative facts: Did the union or business engage in it? When adjudication of a case of first impression by the NLRB determines that the labor practice at issue is unfair, the immediate and direct effect is on the parties to the dispute (i.e., the union and the company). Nevertheless, if the board is consistent, then the unfair practice in question will be prohibited in the future just as surely as if it had been outlawed through rulemaking. And the prohibition will apply to all other firms and unions under the NLRB's jurisdiction. Many believe that in such circumstances adjudication should be avoided because it is inferior to rulemaking as a vehicle for administrative policymaking.

Criticisms of Adjudication

Administrative adjudication is frequently criticized from two perspectives: legal and administrative.

Legal Perspectives

Administrative law scholars generally disfavor policymaking through agency adjudication in cases of first impression. First, it is a kind of "dog law" because notice is inadequate. Like a dog being trained, parties to an adjudication find out after the fact that they have done something wrong. The retroactive quality of such decisions fits uncomfortably with due process and other principles of US law. Unless specifically constrained by law, agencies usually have the choice of proceeding by adjudication or rulemaking. However, when adjudication results in a new regulation of general applicability, a court may sometimes direct an agency to engage in rulemaking instead (*Ford Motor Company v. FTC* 1981; see Warren 1996, 304).

Second, regulations and legal principles established through adjudication may be buried in hundreds or thousands of adjudicatory decisions. These form a kind of agency-specific case law that is difficult to master and far less accessible than agency rules. One may have to analyze a large number of agency adjudicatory decisions to know what is prohibited and why. Even then, it will sometimes be unclear whether a more recent decision has effectively overruled or modified an earlier one.

Third, evidentiary adjudication is not a participatory problem-solving exercise. The APA provides that in adjudication and other matters, "so far as the orderly conduct of public business permits, an interested person may appear before an agency" (sec. 555[b]). In terms of adjudication, the word "interested" may be interpreted broadly. It may also be restricted to those potentially so adversely affected by an agency's adjudicatory decision as to have standing to challenge it in court (see Chapter 6). The appearance may be in the form of a written statement or legal brief, as well as live testimony and other direct participation in the hearing. However, in many instances participation will be limited to the parties directly involved and the experts and witnesses who testify. When controversial policy choices are involved, greater participation is apt to be generated through rulemaking than by adjudication. Less participation can limit the amount of information and range of perspectives available to the agency decisionmakers. This problem is compounded by adversary procedure, which inhibits the parties from volunteering anything that may weaken their cases. The agency decision must be supported by the record, but what goes into the record may be less than sufficient for making complex policy decisions.

Fourth, agency adjudicatory decisions may be inconsistent with one another because different hearing examiners, administrative law judges

(ALJs), and other decisionmakers come to disparate conclusions in similar cases. Federal agencies hold millions of hearings annually (Warren 2011, 257). The odds of deciding them with complete consistency are extremely low. This can be frustrating not only for the parties involved but also for reviewing courts. For instance, in a case involving the Federal Labor Relations Authority (FLRA), a court complained, "In the two cases at hand, the effects of the FLRA's failure adequately to set forth its governing rule are clear. With respect to the identical violation, one ALJ awarded back pay; the other did not. . . . The confusion and inconsistency within the Authority itself is abundantly evident" (*Professional Airways Systems Specialists, MEBA, AFL-CIO v. FLRA* 1987, 860).

Finally, oversight of agency adjudication is difficult, especially compared to rulemaking. Congressional committees cannot engage in direct discussion with agency adjudicators about pending cases or those being heard. If Congress is dissatisfied with the policy direction of an agency's adjudicatory ordermaking, its primary recourse is to rewrite the pertinent statutes. Neither can an executive unit like the federal Office of Management and Budget (OMB) do much to steer or coordinate agency adjudicatory decisionmaking. Political executives—hence the governors and presidents who appoint them—have limited controls over ALJs and other hearing examiners. The ability of elected chief executives to affect the direction of agency adjudication is also weakened by the fixed and staggered terms and bipartisan composition of many boards and commissions.

Administrative Perspectives

A second set of criticisms of evidentiary adjudication focuses more on the administrative difficulties in achieving high levels of the values mentioned earlier: fairness, efficiency, competence, and neutral or positive effect on organizational performance. The federal personnel system, which uses evidentiary adjudication in its equal employment opportunity (EEO), labor relations, and merit systems protection programs, is illustrative.

Federal EEO adjudication has been particularly problematic. Historically, only a very small percentage of the thousands of cases filed annually have resulted in clear findings of discrimination. For instance, in fiscal year 2011, of the 17,436 complaints of prohibited discrimination closed, only 1.2 percent (212) resulted in findings of discrimination. In part this is because the US Equal Employment Opportunity Commission (EEOC), which has adjudicatory and oversight responsibility for federal EEO, emphasizes alternative dispute resolution (ADR) such as mediation and conciliation.

However, among the 36,642 employees who completed the first step in the EEO complaint processing system—counseling—20,846 (57 percent) did not go on to file formal complaints. Agencies offered 78 percent of those who completed counseling an opportunity for ADR, which was accepted by 48.6 percent (17,822) (EEOC, n.d.). Therefore, of the total number who received counseling, more than half neither filed formal complaints nor engaged in ADR. Precisely why these employees did not continue with the complaint process is unknown. The issues may have been resolved, or counselors or others may have dissuaded the complainants from continuing, for both good and bad reasons. According to the American Federation of Government Employees, agency EEO investigations, which could provide evidence of discrimination, are a sham—"almost a complete waste of time" (Shafritz et al. 2001, 537–541).

Other data suggest that there is a broad perception among federal employees that the personnel system is less than a model of fairness, and, importantly for adjudication, employees who say they have been personally subject to prohibited discrimination do not necessarily file complaints. In 1996, only a minority of all federal employees agreed that their agencies had "no problem, or a minor one, in providing fair and equitable treatment" (US Merit Systems Protection Board [MSPB] 1997, 8–9). Only 21 percent of African Americans could say that about their agencies, as could about 30 percent of Hispanics, Asian Pacific Americans, and Native Americans. Among non-Hispanic whites, less than half—43 percent—shared this perspective (US MSPB 1997, 8–9). In 2000, 54 percent of African American civilian federal employees thought their group was extensively or moderately subject to "flagrant or obviously discriminatory practices"; 31 percent of Hispanic employees, 27 percent of Native American employees, and 23 percent of Asian Pacific American employees thought the same with regard to their groups (US MSPB 2002a, 3). In 2013, the Merit Systems Protection Board (MSPB) reported that "about one in four Federal employees believe their supervisor practices favoritism" (2013, ii).

When these generalized perceptions are translated into concrete knowledge and experience, the extent of prohibited discrimination appears to be much more limited. For example, in 2011, the MSPB reported that 9.1 percent of respondents indicated that within the past two years an agency supervisor had "discriminated in favor or against someone in a personnel action based on race"; 3.4 and 7.8 percent said the same with regard to discrimination based on national origin and gender, respectively. Even smaller percentages of the respondents claimed to have personally experienced discrimination: 4.6 percent based on race, 2.1 percent based on national origin, and 3.9 percent based on gender (Naff, Riccucci, and Fox

Freyss 2014, 355). However, each of these percentages is greater than the 1.33 percent of all executive branch employees who initiated EEO counseling in fiscal year 2011. In other words, although prohibited discrimination based on these factors in the federal service is far from pervasive, more federal employees say they have personally experienced it than use the EEO complaint system.

Studies of sexual harassment in the 1980s and 1990s revealed some reasons why a significant number of federal employees fail to file complaints. Employee surveys indicated that more than 40 percent of all female and about 19 percent of all male civilian employees were likely to be sexually harassed during any given two-year period. Of these, only 6 percent took formal action. Why? Many gave one or more of the following reasons for not filing formal charges: the harassment was not serious enough (50 percent); it would make the work situation unpleasant (29 percent); nothing would be done about it (20 percent); confidentiality would be breached (19 percent); and it would have adverse career ramifications (17 percent). Eight percent thought the victim would be blamed (US MSPB 1995, figure 1, tables 7, 10, 11).

The EEO complaint processing system also scores low on efficiency. It generally takes agencies a year or longer to close complaints. In the 1990s, it took the EEOC an average of 707 days to close complaints from its own workforce (Shafritz et al. 2001, 537; Rivenbark 1998, 3)! In fiscal 2011, the agency took an average of 378 days to complete appeals, and the average age of pending appeals in its backlog was 284 days (EEOC, n.d., 2[b][i]). Long processing times mean that employees may be at work for extended periods with the supervisors they have accused of discrimination while their cases slowly wend their way through the complaint system. This also bears on employees' reluctance to file complaints and the overall fairness of the EEO adjudicatory system.

The handling of EEO complaints weakens the federal personnel system's adjudicatory performance on the dimensions of fairness and efficiency. The difficulty of establishing competence was best illustrated by the FLRA. Although its record has since improved, between 1979 (when it was created) and 1987, the FLRA was overruled in slightly more than half the reported cases in which the federal courts reviewed its decisions on substantive legal issues (as opposed to procedural matters). In one case, the court sent the case back to FLRA with instructions to "address and resolve the conflict [in its decisions] candidly and in a manner that persons affected by the Authority's decisions can comprehend" (*American Federation of Government Employees, Local 32 v. FLRA* 1985, 506). In another, the court would not say FLRA's interpretation was wrong, only that "it was assuredly not right for the reasons stated" (*National Association of Government Employees v. FLRA* 1985, 1227). FLRA's problem was not bias against unions or management but an inability to adjudicate coherently (Rosenbloom 1992).

The federal government's adverse action system exemplifies how adjudication that works well in terms of fairness, efficiency, and competence may have a substantial detrimental impact on organizational performance. The adverse action system is designed to ensure that disciplinary measures against employees, including dismissals, comport with merit system requirements. Agency decisions may be appealed to the MSPB, whose adjudicatory decisions form a major component of federal personnel policy. The MSPB generally has received high marks for fairness, efficiency, and competence (Vaughn 1992). For instance, in 1997, a remarkable 96 percent of the 444 MSPB decisions appealed to federal court were upheld without modification (US MSPB 1998, 4). However, it is widely believed that merit system adjudication dampens agency performance. In 1996, 28 percent of federal supervisors were unwilling to take adverse actions against employees, even though they considered them warranted. Among the multiple reasons cited were the time required to go through the adverse action process (67 percent), lack of support by upper management (62 percent), impact on the work group (48 percent), the prospect of facing an EEO complaint (40 percent), lack of familiarity with procedures (25 percent), and the cost to the agency if the employee appealed (18 percent) (US MSPB 1998, 4). At the same time, a majority of supervisors (59 percent) and employees (51 percent) agreed that "their agencies have a major problem . . . separating employees who cannot or will not improve their performance to meet required standards" (US MSPB 1997, 7). In 2008, the US Office of Personnel Management found that 37 percent of federal employees disagreed with the statement "In my work unit, steps are taken to deal with a poor performer who cannot or will not improve." Only 30 percent agreed, while 27 percent neither agreed nor disagreed, and 7 percent answered that they did not know (US Office of Personnel Management 2008, table 3; percentages exceed 100 percent due to rounding). As recently as April 2013, the poor-performer issue was still in the news (T. Fox 2013).

The legal and administrative problems with adjudication reviewed above are inherent and substantial. As a policymaking format in cases of first impression, adjudication has intrinsic shortcomings. The difficulties illustrated by evidentiary adjudication in the federal personnel system are also endemic. They cannot be attributed to the newness of systems, inexperience, or the federal government's inability to provide adequate human and financial resources. Where underfunding exists, it may be due as much to inadequate agency performance as to a lack of congressional support for a particular adjudicatory program. If adjudication is so problematic, then why use it?

Why Adjudicate?

Adjudication is used primarily for five overlapping reasons: (1) agency convenience, (2) advantages presented by incrementalism, (3) suitability for resolving conduct and application cases, (4) equity and compassion, and (5) satisfaction of constitutional procedural due process.

Agency Convenience

Despite its costs and difficulties, adjudication has several advantages for agencies. It generally affords them considerable flexibility in enforcing policy. This is especially true when agencies have the discretion to initiate cases and invest their enforcement resources wherever they deem most appropriate. In *Cinderella*, the court chided Chairman Dixon for "pouncing on the most convenient victim" (*Cinderella Career and Finishing Schools, Inc. v. FTC* 1970, 591). Such an enforcement strategy may or may not be less efficacious than tackling a more substantial and visible firm. Picking easy cases that can be adjudicated relatively quickly may help an agency recruit high-quality, newly minted lawyers who want to gain experience and build winning records before moving to the private sector. Cases against large, prominent firms may have a great impact, but they can also consume an inordinate share of agency resources. The key point is that whatever the court thought about the appropriateness of the FTC's move on Cinderella as a legal matter, the choice of where to invest enforcement resources ordinarily lies with the agency unless its actions violate statutory or constitutional restrictions.

When agencies have broad discretion because there is no clear law to apply, they may find it easier to change policy by adjudicating than by rulemaking. Rulemaking and rule rescission are publicized through the *Federal Register*. They can prompt comments from any person, group, or entity that cares to offer them. Broad participation, coupled with requirements for cost-benefit or various impact analyses, can make establishing a satisfactory rulemaking record arduous. Adjudication generally attracts less public attention. As noted earlier, participation can be restricted, and adjudication is subject to weaker legislative and executive oversight than rulemaking. Agency adjudicators are not required to consider the impact of their decisions on sets of specific policy concerns that are extraneous to their agencies' core missions, such as environmental justice, families, protecting small business, and federalism.

Adjudication also affords agencies flexibility in that it is difficult to win legal challenges against incremental—or even abrupt—policy changes introduced in individual adjudicatory decisions. An agency can usually distinguish the basis of a new adjudicatory order from an earlier precedent in terms of the specific facts, changes in public policy or economic concerns, technological developments, and other considerations that a rational decisionmaker should take into account. As Supreme Court Justice Felix Frankfurter once said, adherence to precedent "is not, to be sure, an imprisonment of reason" (*United States v. International Boxing Club of New York, Inc.* 1955, 249). Moreover, the parties to whom a policy is first applied through adjudication may assume that it will bind others in the future. They may therefore decline to challenge the agency for being inconsistent or discriminatory. It may take years to see if the assumption is correct. Using adjudication, in 1969 the Federal Communications Commission (FCC) required the Boston *Herald-Traveler* newspaper to divest itself of Boston TV station 5 on the basis that "it is important in a free society to prevent a concentration of control of the sources of news and opinion" (Woll 1977, 81). The reviewing court held that the decision was within the FCC's discretion. However, the FCC's decision turned out to be anomalous: "In case after case, the FCC has permitted media concentration that directly contradicts its Boston *Herald-Traveler* decision, and the Court of Appeals has upheld the Commission in every case" (Woll 1977, 83). By the time it was clear that the *Herald-Traveler* had been singled out, it was too late for the newspaper to take effective legal action against the FCC.

Multiheaded boards and commissions may especially prefer adjudication to rulemaking when they have highly fragmented policy preferences or are uncertain about the direction in which their agency should move. Adjudication provides board members and commissioners with a forum to resolve their policy differences and arrive at compromises, often in an incremental fashion. Each can explain why he or she would decide the case in a certain way and what the policy and other advantages would be. A board or commission that would become deadlocked in a rulemaking might nevertheless be able to carry out its functions through case-by-case adjudication.

Advantages Presented by Incrementalism

When an agency is charged with regulating and implementing law in a new or uncertain field of public policy, incrementalism may be advantageous. This is especially true when a legislative delegation is particularly vague or a technology is new and in flux. For instance, an agency might

find the task of defining the "public interest" or "unfair" practices daunt-
ing, especially when it is just beginning to deal with a policy area. The
meaning of such terms is not self-evident. If it were easy, the legislature
probably would have defined key terms in the relevant statute. It is often
precisely because terms like "public interest," "convenience," "necessity,"
"just cause," "reasonable," and "adequate" gain meaning only in specific
contexts that the task of interpreting them is delegated to administrative
agencies. Adjudication allows for incremental definition on a case-by-case
basis. When the NLRB started out in 1935, how could it write a rule iden-
tifying the full range of possible unfair labor practices or even a relatively
complete set of principles distinguishing "fair" from "unfair"? In time,
through sufficient adjudication, what is in the public interest, reasonable,
unfair, and so forth might be comprehensively established in an agency's
adjudicatory decisions. At that point, an agency could (many would say
should) write a rule essentially codifying the principles in its adjudicatory
case law.

Adjudication is also helpful in regulating new and rapidly changing
technologies where there are significant hazards and unknowns. This is
especially true if the number of cases is sufficient to promote substantial
agency learning. Adjudication in the face of uncertainty may reduce the
scope and cost of mistakes. As the Supreme Court noted in *City of Ontario, California v. Quon*, it is prudent to "proceed with care when considering the whole concept of privacy expectations in communications made
on electronic equipment owned by a government employer. The judiciary
risks error by elaborating too fully on the Fourth Amendment implications
of emerging technology before its role in society has become clear" (2010,
2629). If a new and potentially dangerous technology is not well under-
stood, rulemaking may be more prone to error and resistant to correction
than adjudication. For example, according to Kenneth Warren, the Nuclear
Regulatory Commission should have regulated by ordermaking rather
than rulemaking: it "has been severely criticized for failing to prevent unnecessary and dangerous accidents in nuclear power plants because the
commission irresponsibly promulgated rules not based on a thorough collection and evaluation of crucial scientific facts and questions concerning
the safety of nuclear power plant operations, including the disposal of nuclear waste" (Warren 1996, 305).

Conduct and Application Cases

Broadly construed, conduct and application cases encompass a very wide
range of administrative decisions. They include matters such as sanctioning

firms like Cinderella, retention of benefits, governmental licensing, and dealing with unfair or illegal labor and other personnel practices. Adjudication is desirable in conduct and application cases because they turn on specific facts or individual motives. By allowing affected parties to present their claims and challenge those raised against them, adjudication guards against arbitrary governmental action. This is true whether the matter involves an individual's retention of welfare benefits or a multimillion-dollar false advertising action. Adjudication is so preferred as a means of making such decisions that it is often required by constitutional procedural due process (as discussed below).

Unless there is no factual or legal dispute at all, adjudication is usually the safest approach in significant conduct cases. For example, the *Cinderella* court explained,

> While it may be true that some advertisements are so glaringly misleading that anyone can recognize that fact, we think it could only benefit the ultimate determination if the Commissioners had before them the testimony both of experts on youth and of teenage girls themselves, in addition to their own reading of the statements alleged to be misleading. While they might initially decide that a given statement had the capacity to mislead, perhaps testimony of experts and consumers would reveal that the group at which the statements were directed was in fact more knowledgeable and sophisticated than the Commissioners had originally anticipated. In any event, we think it can only help, and certainly it will not hurt, to have the testimony before the reviewing Commissioners. (*Cinderella Career and Finishing Schools, Inc. v. FTC* 1970, 586)

In other words, things are not always as they may appear to administrators. Adjudication helps to ensure that agency decisions are based on correct factual premises. Congress fashioned the APA's adjudicatory requirements against a background in which it was widely believed that "[t]he rights of individual citizens have been arrogantly disregarded" in administrative decisionmaking (US Congress 1940, 4649).

Equity and Compassion

Adjudication may be particularly favored in cases involving individuals' eligibility for welfare and other safety net–type governmental benefits because it has the capacity to promote equity and compassion. Welfare and safety net decisions are a subset of conduct and application cases that are set apart by involving individuals only, rather than firms or other entities, and by being nonadversarial and nonrival. The governments administering welfare and safety net programs and the claimants seeking benefits share a common interest. Both want the benefits to be available to those in need. These programs sometimes contain regulatory aspects, such as requiring individuals seeking unemployment compensation payments to be actively job hunting. However, deserving claimants are not in an adversarial relationship with government or in rivalry with one another, as the parties to licensing decisions for TV stations and other types of mutually exclusive public benefits might be.

Equity and compassion may be important factors in promoting the policy objective of helping people who need welfare and safety net programs to deal effectively with their economic and other problems. In this context, equity entails the ability to make principled exceptions to general regulations when they serve the interests of both the government and the individual. The phrase "I feel your pain" has become a cliché. But compassion may sometimes be a necessary component of successful rehabilitation or sociotherapy, as in some aspects of public health administration and social work. Compassion may also encourage equitable waiver or modification of clearly counterproductive legal requirements.

The advantages of adjudication over rulemaking in providing equity and compassion are illustrated in *Heckler v. Campbell* (1983), a case dealing with Social Security disability benefits. Eligibility is established in a two-stage process. First, a medical assessment is made to determine the level of work, if any, a physically or mentally impaired applicant can perform. Second, applicants who are capable of some level of work are eligible for benefits only when there are few or no jobs in the national economy that they could handle. Until 1978, ALJs from the Social Security Administration (SSA) relied on the testimony of vocational experts to gauge whether jobs might exist for individual claimants. The vocational experts' testimony was often inconsistent, perhaps being swayed by equity and compassion but leading to contradictory outcomes. In 1978, the SSA decided to replace the vocational experts, who were personally familiar with the claimants' impairments, with rules known as *grid regulations* (grid-regs or grids).

Grid-regs are individual rules that use age, education, and work experience to specify whether jobs exist for claimants who can perform certain levels of work. Individuals can receive benefits only if they are considered disabled under the grids. The following are examples:

1. For individuals whose impairment permits them to perform light work:

Rule	Age	Education	Previous Work Experience	Decision
202.02	55 & over	Limited or less	Skilled/semi-skilled, not transferrable	Disabled
202.03	55 & over	Limited or less	Skilled/semi-skilled, transferrable	Not disabled

2. For individuals whose impairment permits them to perform medium work:

Rule	Age	Education	Previous Work Experience	Decision
203.10	55 & over	Limited or less	None	Disabled
203.11	55 & over	Limited or less	Unskilled	Not disabled

Overall, there were more than thirty such sequentially numbered individual rules for light and medium work (US Department of Health and Human Services 1978). They acted to severely constrain the ALJs' discretion and ability to bring considerations of equity and compassion into their decisionmaking.

Carmen Campbell applied for disability benefits when a back condition and hypertension forced her to stop working as a hotel maid. She was fifty-two years old, had limited education, and was classified as unskilled. She was also from Panama, and although she could read and understand English fairly well, she had difficulty speaking and writing it. Her initial application was denied. She then requested a hearing, which was held before an ALJ who determined that she was capable of light work. Based on the grid-regs, the ALJ also found that she was not disabled (i.e., jobs that she could perform existed). After the Social Security Appeals Council upheld the ALJ's decision, Campbell sued the SSA.

The district court ruled against Campbell, who then pressed on to the court of appeals. That court found the grid-regs defective. It reasoned that the SSA was required to "identify specific alternative occupations available in the national economy that would be suitable for the claimant," to provide descriptions of such jobs, and to demonstrate that they do "'not require' exertion or skills not possessed by the claimant." The court reasoned that without this information, "the claimant is deprived of any real chance to present evidence showing that she cannot in fact perform the types of jobs that are administratively noticed by the guidelines [i.e., the grid-regs]." In short, the determination based on the grids was defective; therefore the ALJ's decision was not supported by substantial evidence.

The Supreme Court reversed the court of appeals. It noted that the Social Security Act "contemplates that disability hearings will be individualized determinations based on evidence adduced at a hearing." However, this did not preclude the SSA from using rules (i.e., the grid-regs) to provide ALJs and other decisionmakers with a factual determination regarding the existence of jobs in the national economy. Two justices raised a cautionary note regarding the desirability of building equity and compassion into disability determinations.

Justice William Brennan concurred with the majority but admonished that ALJs should exercise a "duty of inquiry" "in these nonadversarial proceedings to develop a full and fair record" and "scrupulously and conscientiously explore for all the relevant facts." "In a case decided under the grids," this includes inquiry "into possible nonexertional impairments and into exertional limitations that prevent a full range of work." In plain English, the ALJ ought "to inquire whether factors besides strength, age, or education, combined with her other impairments, rendered [Campbell] disabled." What was her mental state, energy level, threshold for pain?

Justice Thurgood Marshall concurred and dissented in part. In his view, the hearing was defective because Campbell never had the opportunity to show that she was unable to perform light work, which under the grid-regs was the "central issue." Additionally, the ALJ was ill prepared to exercise equity or compassion because "he conducted little inquiry into the effect of her medical problems on her capacity to perform work. Yet reasonably complete questioning concerning the claimant's ability to function in her daily activity was essential to resolving this question in a fair manner."

Although the grid-regs were valid and Campbell lost the case, the different perspectives raised by the court of appeals and Justices Brennan and Marshall illuminate some of the concerns for equity and compassion in welfare and safety net adjudication. Campbell and other claimants would clearly be better off with more elaborate and probing hearings in which their status was determined by individualized factors rather than boxes on the grid-regs. The Supreme Court's majority was unwilling to require a different hearing process because compelling the SSA "to relitigate the existence of jobs in the national economy at each hearing would hinder needlessly an already overburdened agency" (*Heckler v. Campbell*, 1983, 464, 467, 468, 471, 474–475). Its opinion speaks to the immediate needs of efficiency rather than the desirability of individualized and compassionate treatment in the abstract.

Procedural Due Process

The Fifth and Fourteenth amendments prohibit the federal, state, and local governments from depriving individuals of "life, liberty, or property, without due process of law." *Procedural due process* does not have a fixed meaning. It requires fundamental fairness when a government decision dealing with one or a few individuals creates a deprivation of life, liberty, or property. It does not apply to legislation or decisionmaking that affects the population generally, such as raising taxes. Neither does it apply when the deprivation is unintentional, being caused by governmental negligence. Its overall structure and application were explained in Chapter 2. For the most part, its requirements are incorporated into the adjudicatory provisions of the APA and state administrative law statutes. When these statutes apply and are properly followed, a violation of due process is unlikely. The greater problem is determining what procedural due process requires in an adjudication that is not regulated by administrative law.

In some administrative contexts, it will be uncertain whether a property or liberty interest protected by procedural due process exists. This is because the Due Process Clause does not create property or liberty interests; it only protects those that are established independently by other constitutional provisions, statutes, administrative rules, or governmental practices. Procedural due process is implicated in the termination and/or revocation of welfare benefits, parole, driver's and occupational licenses, and civil service and tenured public university employment, as well as in public school expulsions and suspensions, some forms of prison discipline, and deportations. But this list by no means exhausts the range of interests to which procedural due process might apply (W. Fox 2000, 133–137; Gellhorn and Levin 2006, ch. 6). The levying of significant governmental sanctions, as in *Cinderella*, also engages procedural due process, as does termination of service by a municipal electric, gas, or water utility (*Memphis Light, Gas & Water Division v. Craft* 1978). As a general rule, the more harm the governmental deprivation of liberty or property interest causes an individual, the greater the likelihood that procedural due process will apply. If welfare, other benefits, or licenses terminate automatically at a fixed date or according to a legislative scheme, there is no right to procedural due process. For example, civil service employees have no due process protection when their jobs are eliminated by reductions in force. Neither will procedural due process be required when there is no factual dispute, unless the deprivation of liberty or property is punitively excessive.

When procedural due process applies, what it requires is also an issue. *Goldberg v. Kelly* (1970) outlined comprehensive protection for individuals being deprived of a benefit by administrative action. The case involved the termination of a means-tested welfare benefit, which John Kelly presumably needed in order to survive. The Supreme Court held that he was entitled to a pretermination hearing with the following safeguards: (1) notice of the government's intent and reasons for terminating the benefit, (2) an oral hearing before an impartial decisionmaker, (3) confrontation and cross-examination, (4) representation by counsel (though not to counsel provided by the government), (5) the maintenance of a record of the proceedings, (6) a decision based exclusively on the record, and (7) a statement of reasons for the decision (*Goldberg v. Kelly* 1970). In *Gagnon v. Scarpelli*, the Supreme Court expanded these requirements in reasoning that "though the State is not constitutionally obliged to provide counsel in all cases, it should do so where the indigent probationer or parolee may have difficulty in presenting his version of disputed facts without the examination or cross-examination of witnesses or the presentation of complicated documentary evidence" (1973, Syllabus 788). An odd feature of the right to counsel is that agencies can nevertheless set "absurdly low" limits—such as $10—on lawyers' fees for representing clients in adjudicatory matters (Warren 2011, 286).

By contrast, *Goss v. Lopez* (1975) set forth the apparent minimal requirements when procedural due process applies at all. There, the Supreme Court held that procedural due process is satisfied in a one-day suspension from public school by "at least an informal give-and-take between the student and the disciplinarian, preferably prior to the suspension" (*Goss v. Lopez* 1975, 584). Many cases lie in between these extremes. Sometimes notice and opportunity to respond prior to the administrative action are coupled with more elaborate due process afterward. In other cases, a post-termination or deprivation process with varying due process elements is sufficient. By following the case law or consulting an attorney or someone else who does, one can determine what, if anything, procedural due process requires in circumstances that have been previously litigated. In other situations, precedents can serve only as an uncertain guide.

Caveat Estoppel

As it applies to governmental benefits, the law of estoppel negates the application of procedural due process when individuals receive misinformation from the government that causes them to forego something to which they are actually entitled. To "estop" means to stop, prevent, preclude, or impede. The problem of estoppel is well illustrated in *Schweiker v. Hansen* (1981). Ann Hansen met for about fifteen minutes with an SSA field representative who incorrectly told her she was ineligible for "mother's insurance benefits." The SSA rep violated the SSA's thirteen-volume *Claims Manual* by failing to tell her to file a written application anyway. About a year later, Hansen learned she was eligible for the benefits and received them after filing a written application. Under the relevant statute, Hansen was also entitled to twelve months' retroactive benefits, which she received. However, she wanted retroactive benefits for the twelve months prior to her initial meeting with the field representative, whose mistakes cost her about a year's worth of benefits in the first place. The question for the Supreme Court was whether the SSA was estopped (i.e., prevented) from withholding those retroactive payments. Put positively, did the field representative's errors compel the SSA to give Hansen the retroactive benefits she sought? The Court's answer was that the SSA was not estopped; legally it could withhold the benefits.

The law of estoppel is far from crystal clear. Justices Marshall and Brennan charged that it amounts to the Court saying, "We will know an estoppel when we see one." However, to win an estoppel, Hansen had to satisfy two requirements. First, she had to have been harmed by the agency's misinformation. Hansen was clearly harmed, though the Court questioned whether the injury was sufficient for an estoppel. Second, there must be no other way in which the individual can obtain the correct information. The two requirements are related. Because correct information was available, Hansen could have undone the harm at any time.

The general principle of the law of estoppel is that agency heads should not be bound by the mistakes of subordinate employees. Making estoppel easy in cases like Hansen's would undercut hierarchical control and could drain the agency's budget. Marshall was joined by Brennan in a dissent that emphasized the unfairness of estoppel doctrine: "It is quite clear that [Hansen] provided [the field representative] with sufficient information on which to make a correct judgment, had he been so inclined. . . . Such preliminary advice is inevitably accorded great weight by applicants who—like [Hansen]—are totally uneducated in the intricacies of the Social Security laws. . . . The fault for [Hansen's] failure to file a timely application for benefits that she was entitled to must rest squarely with the Government" (*Schweiker v. Hansen* 1981, 789, 792, 794–95). The bottom line: their fault, her loss, no remedy unless the SSA would voluntarily pay the retroactive benefits.

Adjudicatory Hearings

The APA provides for elaborate adjudicatory hearings, which are triggered by separate statutes or constitutional due process. Coverage does not extend to decisions based entirely on inspections, tests, or elections, military and foreign affairs, and some additional matters (sec. 554[a]). When adjudication is required, "persons entitled to notice of an agency hearing shall be timely informed of: (1) the time, place, and nature of the hearing; (2) the legal authority and jurisdiction under which the hearing is to be held; and (3) the matters of fact and law asserted" (sec. 554[b]). Hearings are to be scheduled with regard to the "convenience and necessity of the parties or their representatives." The agency must provide the parties the opportunity for the "submission and consideration of facts, arguments, offers of settlement, or proposals of adjustment when time, the nature of the proceeding, and the public interest permit" (sec. 554[c]). Additional provisions include the following:

1. The right to be represented by retained (not agency-provided) counsel
2. The conclusion of hearings within "a reasonable time"
3. Prompt notification of the outcome of the hearing, as well as a brief explanatory statement of the grounds for the denial of an application or other request
4. A decision based on substantial evidence in the record
5. The appointment of impartial ALJs (originally, "hearing examiners") or other employees to preside over hearings when the agency itself does not do so
6. An opportunity for parties to present their "case or defense by oral or documentary evidence, . . . submit rebuttal evidence, and . . . conduct such cross-examination as may be required for a full and true disclosure of the facts"
7. Maintenance of a complete and exclusive record, including a transcript of testimony
8. A statement of the "findings and conclusions, and the reasons or basis therefor, on all the material issues of fact, law, or discretion presented on the record"
9. Judicial review of final agency action (secs. 555, 556, and 557; ch. 7)

The APA also contemplates the potential to appeal initial ALJ decisions within the agencies, but the opportunities and procedures available depend on agency rules. As substantial as the APA's adjudicatory requirements are, they differ in significant ways from judicial trials, primarily in the interests of more flexibility and less formality.

Presiding Officers

The federal employees who preside over adjudications have several different titles and levels of skill and independence. For the sake of convenience, they can be considered under two headings: ALJs and all others.

Administrative Law Judges. The title "administrative law judge" replaced that of "hearing examiner" in 1972. Whatever the name, the main concerns with ALJs have always been impartiality, competence, and efficiency. Prior to enactment of the APA in 1946, hearing examiners were subject to discipline by the agencies in which they worked. They might combine investigatory, prosecutorial, and judicial functions. The APA requires a separation of functions and insulates ALJs from supervision by agency investigators and prosecutors. It also prohibits communication outside the hearing on matters "relevant to the merits of the proceeding" with individuals who are not employed by the agency (sec. 557[d]). More generally, such one-sided communications (called "ex parte"), whether with outsiders or agency personnel, are disparaged because they give an appearance of unfairness. Although discipline is adjudicated by the MSPB, the ALJs are still employed by the individual agencies. The vast majority of the federal government's 1,400 or so ALJs are in the SSA, though significant numbers also work for the Department of Labor and NLRB. Federal ALJs perform the following functions:

1. "Administer oaths and affirmations"
2. "Issue subpoenas"
3. "Rule on offers of proof and receive relevant evidence"
4. Handle depositions
5. Manage the hearings
6. Hold conferences, which the parties are required to attend, for consideration of the settlement or simplification of cases
7. Encourage the parties to engage in alternative means of resolving the case (discussed below)
8. "Dispose of procedural requests"
9. Make initial or recommended decisions
10. Take other actions consistent with APA procedures (APA sec. 556[c]; see Lubbers 1994, 293–294)

This list makes it clear that ALJ performance is a major component of administrative adjudicatory systems.

The problem of ALJ impartiality is complicated. Despite their independence from agency hierarchies, ALJs are part of the organizations in which they work. They are likely to share many organizational goals and values. Their responses to political and media criticisms of their agencies may be identical to those of other employees. Association with an agency, especially over a long period, is likely to have an impact on their worldviews and judgments. Even if this were not the case, the whole arrangement of allowing an agency to employ a judge who rules on its own enforcement efforts creates an appearance of bias. The FCC has openly recognized this by physically separating its ALJs from other agency personnel (W. Fox 2000, 246). Another approach to maintaining impartiality is to place ALJs in a special corps to be assigned on a rotational basis to the various agencies by a central agency, such as the Office of Personnel Management or the MSPB. Several states, including Florida and New Jersey, have used such a system, with apparent success (W. Fox 2000, 245). The idea has been discussed at the federal level for years but never adopted. The flip side concern is that federal adjudication is too specialized and complex to make rotation practicable (Lubbers 1994).

Administrative law is tolerant of the appearance of bias in another context as well. Prehearing bias does not automatically disqualify agency adjudicators, including ALJs, from participating in adjudicatory decision-making. If the bias involves legislative facts (i.e., general information relevant to policy matters), adjudicators are excluded only if they have an "unalterably" or "irrevocably closed" mind on the matter under consideration (*Housing Study Group v. Kemp* 1990, 332; *FTC v. Cement Institute* 1948, 701; Warren 2011, 266–269). The rationale for this standard is that FTC, FCC, and other commissioners advocate and promote policies as part of their jobs, often indicating a preference for enforcement in one area or another. If such statements precluded them from participating in adjudication, they would essentially have to give up one function or the other. Either way, they would be less effective in implementing their agencies' missions. Moreover, in drafting the APA, Congress clearly gave broad adjudicatory authority to boards, commissions, and agency heads.

By contrast, if the prehearing bias involves adjudicative facts (matters pertaining to the parties to the case), it is highly likely that the adjudication will be unfair, and the ALJ or other decisionmaker should be disqualified. The *Cinderella* court emphasized that chairman Dixon's conclusive public statement of adjudicative facts was particularly offensive. Essentially he had prejudged Cinderella's lack of virtue. Any adjudication with his participation would be poisoned. Even though Dixon's vote was not necessary for a majority of the commissioners to find Cinderella shady, "Litigants are entitled to an impartial tribunal whether it consists of one man or twenty and there is no way which we know of whereby the influence of one upon the others can be quantitatively measured" (*Cinderella Career and Finishing Schools, Inc. v. FTC* 1970, 592).

Personal bias, which sometimes manifests itself during hearings, can also lead to disqualification. ALJs and other adjudicators are, after all, human beings with a variety of personal preferences and prejudices. Personal bias may be displayed in open derogatory statements about a participant in the adjudication. At other times, it is derived from an adjudicator's overall record of favoring one set of interests over another (e.g., management over labor).

An exception to disqualification for any of these biases may be made under the *rule of necessity*. This occurs when enforcement would be impossible because there are no impartial adjudicators who can hear the case. The point is that from a public policy perspective, biased enforcement is better than none at all, and it can be subsequently checked by judicial review.

ALJs' competence and efficiency are also of concern, though perhaps more so to the agencies than to private parties. Federal ALJs are not subject to performance appraisals, but they can be disciplined or fired for *good cause*. Consequently, their performance can be evaluated, but only within limits that do not unduly compromise their impartiality. This was illustrated during the 1980s when the SSA embarked on controversial initiatives to encourage better and quicker ALJ decisionmaking. One effort dealt with competence by tracking the rate at which individual ALJs ruled in favor of disability claimants (so-called allowance rates). Those with the highest rates had all their decisions reviewed by the SSA Appeals Counsel, presumably on the assumption that many were incorrect. The SSA also developed, but did not implement, a comprehensive plan to counsel ALJs with the highest allowance rates. Additionally, it set allowance-rate goals for the ALJs in an attempt to rein in the disability budget. These practices were challenged in court but changed before a definitive decision was handed down (Lubbers 1994, 295–296).

The SSA also created monthly production goals for the ALJs in order to increase their efficiency. The goals established the minimum number of dispositions expected. The ALJs charged that the goals infringed on their independent decisionmaking. However, the courts disagreed and found no violation of the APA (Lubbers 1994, 296). Further, the SSA tried to fire several ALJs for low productivity. It was successful in getting the MSPB to agree that this constituted good cause, though it was unable to carry the heavy burden of persuasion required. In the MSPB's view, the productivity rate by itself was an inadequate indicator of poor performance because cases are not "fungible." Some are more difficult than others and take more time to resolve. Perhaps the SSA's greatest victory was promoting agreement that guidelines could feasibly be used to maintain or improve the quality and efficiency of ALJ decisionmaking (Lubbers 1994, 296–297).

Other Presiding Officers.   Neither the APA nor procedural due process requires that ALJs preside over all types of adjudications and hearings. For instance, the adjudication of veteran benefit claims and many federal personnel matters takes place before non-ALJ presiding officers. Overall, there are more non-ALJ presiding officers than ALJs. Many of these are not insulated from the agencies' hierarchical authority. They may be hired and fired like other federal employees. Most do not work solely as adjudicators. Their performance has not been systematically tracked, and they may be considered "the real 'invisible' judiciary" (Lubbers 1994, 306). On occasion, an agency commission or board may preside over the hearing stage of a case, though usually its role is to hear appeals or review recommended decisions.

Decisions and Appeals

Under the APA, ALJs and other hearing officers make initial and recommended decisions at their agency's direction. Initial decisions are generally issued in ordinary cases and become final unless they are appealed within the agency or reviewed by it. Recommended decisions are more likely to involve unsettled policy questions. They have no legal effect until reviewed by the agency's reviewing authority, be it the head, commission, board, or a designated unit. In licensing and formal rulemaking, the reviewing authority sometimes issues a tentative decision after receiving a record (without a decision or recommendation) from an ALJ. Tentative decisions are submitted to the parties for comment and may subsequently be revised by the reviewing authority (Gellhorn and Levin 1997, 264).

Evidentiary adjudicatory decisions must be based on acceptable evidence and include findings and conclusions with regard to facts and law. Agencies are not required to use the same rules of evidence that would apply in judicial trials. The evidence should be relevant, reliable, probative (tending to prove), and substantial. However, such terms lack precision, and the extent to which presiding officers rely on evidence that would be inadmissible in court varies. It was once settled doctrine that decisions had to be supported by a "residuum" of evidence that could be used in a judicial trial, but since the Supreme Court's decision in *Richardson v. Perales* (1971), the federal courts and most states no longer adhere strictly or at all to the "residuum rule" (see Warren 1996, 327–334; Funk and Seamon 2012, 87).

The APA does not include a standard of proof for adjudicatory decisions. Its requirement that decisions be supported by "substantial evidence" is taken as referring to the quantity of evidence in the record. This is somewhat confusing, because when the term is used in the context of judicial review of an agency action, substantial evidence essentially means "reasonable" (see Chapter 6). The Supreme Court has ruled that "preponderance of evidence" is the minimum standard for APA evidentiary adjudications (*Steadman v. Securities and Exchange Commission* 1981). This means that the evidence in the record as a whole must make the presiding officer's decision more likely correct than incorrect. In some types of cases, a higher standard, "clear and convincing evidence," is imposed by statute, court decisions, or perhaps agency policy. This requires a substantially higher level of likelihood that the decision is correct (roughly, a 75 to 80 percent or greater probability). These standards are, of course, significantly lower than "beyond a reasonable doubt," which applies in criminal trials (almost 100 percent probability).

Before the presiding officer issues the initial or recommended decision, the parties may submit proposed findings and conclusions, with explanations, to guide his or her judgment. Agencies use a variety of approaches for internal appellate review. In multiheaded agencies, commissioners or board members may perform this function or delegate it to subordinate boards. Single-headed agencies are likely to use review boards. However, appeals and reviews may also be decided by agency heads, who are not required to go through the entire record and need only be briefed on it by subordinates who have. The Occupational Safety and Health Administration has followed a "split-enforcement" process in which ALJ hearings and review are conducted within a separate body, the Occupational Safety and Health Review Commission (Funk, Shapiro, and Weaver 1997, 206).

The APA specifies that when dealing with appeals, the "agency has all the powers which it would have in making the initial decision." In theory, this protects hierarchical authority and allows great flexibility. However, the Supreme Court has cautioned appellate decisionmakers to give great weight to the presiding officer's decision when it is largely based on his or her assessment of witnesses' credibility (*Universal Camera Corp. v. NLRB* 1951). As held in *Cinderella*, the appellate decisionmakers must also take the hearing record into account (*Morgan v. United States* 1936; *Morgan v. United States* 1938). Presumably an agency will have good reasons for overturning a presiding officer's decision, as the matter may be appealed to the courts.

Alternative Dispute Resolution

The APA was intended to make administrative evidentiary adjudication fair, competent, efficient, and workable. It envisioned adjudicatory hearings that were far less formal than judicial trials. Over the years, the initial level of informality has given way to greater formality in response to judicial decisions, the establishment and evolution of the ALJ position, and the accretion of precedent. Hearings and appeals have become less timely and more cumbersome, arduous, and expensive. In 1990, Congress enacted the Administrative Dispute Resolution Act (ADRA) to counter this trend. The act was strengthened by the 1996 Administrative Dispute Resolution Act.

The ADRA is premised on the belief that "administrative proceedings have become increasingly formal, costly and lengthy resulting in unnecessary expenditures of time and in a decreased likelihood of achieving consensual resolution of disputes" (sec. 2[2]). Congress also noted that alternative dispute resolution "can lead to more creative, efficient, and sensible outcomes" (sec. 2[4]). The APA specifically calls on agencies to try to settle disputes without adjudicatory hearings, and several federal agencies used ADR prior to 1990. The main purpose of the ADRA was to provide comprehensive regulations for ADR and to resolve some of the legal questions associated with it.

ADR is a mutually acceptable way of resolving a dispute by means other than a formal hearing or trial (Hawes and Rieke 1998). The following are the most common approaches:

1. The use of ombudsmen and ombudswomen (ombuds) in the agencies. Ombuds can be contacted by aggrieved parties or otherwise called upon to resolve administrative errors or disputes.
2. Mediation by a third party who helps the parties resolve the dispute by suggesting "win-win" or otherwise acceptable solutions. Mediators often meet independently with each of the parties in an effort to determine what would be acceptable to them.
3. Facilitation by a third party who coordinates meetings and discussions to aid the parties in finding a resolution. Facilitators are less involved than mediators in the actual effort to resolve or settle the dispute.
4. Fact-finding to resolve a dispute over some factual issue through empirical investigation or, possibly, expert opinion. For example, fact-finding could determine whether Cinderella's ads had a significant propensity to deceive.

5. Arbitration by a third party who offers a resolution of the dispute. Arbitration, which is frequently used in public-sector labor relations, can take several forms. First, entrance into it can be voluntary or compulsory. Voluntary arbitration allows the parties to leave a dispute unresolved; compulsory arbitration requires that an unresolved dispute be settled. Second, arbitration can be binding or advisory. A binding arbitration award has the same effect as a final adjudicatory order. It decides the dispute, though under limited circumstances it may be challenged in court. Advisory arbitration (nonbinding arbitration) offers the parties a resolution and can create pressure for one or both to end the dispute. However, it has no legal force.

Third, arbitration can be conventional, or "final offer" (also called "last best offer"). In the conventional format, the arbitrator hears the dispute and questions the parties. He or she then writes up an award based on the proceedings. Final-offer arbitration requires each party to make a final offer for settling the dispute and limits the arbitrator's decision to accepting one or the other. There are two variants: "whole package," and "issue by issue." In whole-package arbitration, the arbitrator cannot modify the favored final offer. In issue-by-issue arbitration, he or she can choose, without modification, the final offer of one side on a particular issue and that of the other side on a different issue. The rationale behind final-offer arbitration is that it prods the parties to make reasonable offers lest the arbitrator choose the other side's. Logically, it must be binding to function as anticipated, as well as to bring finality to the dispute.

Fourth, arbitration can be combined with mediation (so-called med-arb). Here, the third party first mediates the dispute to reduce the issues on which there is disagreement; then he or she arbitrates any remaining ones.

The ADRA provides for voluntary arbitration only; the parties cannot be compelled to submit to it. (However, federal agencies and unions do negotiate labor-grievance resolution procedures that rely on compulsory binding arbitration.) Agency decisions to use arbitration are not subject to judicial review, except when an arbitral award adversely affects a third party. The 1996 ADRA requires the agencies to specify the maximum amount of money that can be included in an arbitral award in each case. Panels of arbitrators may be used in some jurisdictions.

6. Minitrials structured to enable the parties to present the core of their cases to one another before personnel from each side who are authorized to reach a settlement. A neutral third party may be present to orchestrate the proceeding and/or to offer an advisory resolution.

7. Mock trials with advisory resolution by mock juries to avoid formal hearings and trials (Funk, Lubbers, and Pou 2000, 299–300).

The 1990 ADRA instructs agencies to consider ADR in a very wide range of activities, including anything for which adjudication might be used. However, it also cautions them to consider avoiding ADR when (1) it would be better to resolve the matter in a fashion that establishes an authoritative precedent, (2) policy issues are involved, (3) consistency is important, (4) outside parties would be significantly affected, (5) a comprehensive record of the proceedings is important, or (6) "the agency must maintain continuing jurisdiction over the matter with authority to alter the disposition . . . in light of changed circumstances" (sec. 572[b]). The act also instructs each agency to designate a high-level dispute resolution specialist. The 1996 act protects the confidentiality of ADR proceedings.

Satisfaction with ADR is bound to vary among agencies, programs, and parties. It should always be measured against the alternative, which is adjudication. The MSPB listed ADR's major virtues as improving timeliness, reducing costs, fashioning win-win outcomes, giving the parties "ownership for the solution," revealing the underlying causes of conflicts, and increasing managers' willingness to take necessary disciplinary action (US MSPB 2002b, 3). A comprehensive study of ADR in the Environmental Protection Agency (EPA) also found highly favorable views in general but pointed to the need for better education of managers about ADR, higher-quality mediators, continuing evaluation by the agency, and greater integration of ADR into the dominant administrative culture. It also called for independent evaluation of ADR by the EPA's ALJs (O'Leary and Raines 2001).

Enforcement

Agencies can impose a wide variety of civil sanctions on individuals, firms, and other entities that violate laws or administrative rules. Ordinarily, sanctions are levied after notice and the opportunity to adjudicate the matter. Exceptions may occur in emergency situations—that is, where there is an imminent specific danger to the public's health or welfare. Civil sanctions include cease-and-desist orders, financial penalties, forfeitures, product seizures and recalls, and the revocation and/or suspension of licenses. At the federal level, the authority to take such actions must be delegated to an agency by Congress. Frequently, these penalties are negotiated rather than imposed in a strict sense. Without admitting guilt, violators agree to stop or remedy a practice and perhaps pay a financial penalty. In return, the agency takes no further action. Agencies do not have the power to impose criminal penalties, though U.S. Immigration and Customs Enforcement can physically confine individuals. Criminal wrongdoing may be brought to the attention of the Department of Justice for prosecution. In some cases, financial penalties require civil lawsuits. Although not technically a sanction, adverse publicity can have a harsh impact on a violator, and the threat of it may be sufficient to change behavior.

Agencies use several common means to detect violators and pursue sanctions. First, there are *informational requirements*. As the discussion of paperwork reduction in Chapter 3 suggests, agencies require regulated entities to provide them with a great deal of information. They also impose record-keeping requirements on the regulated, including taxpayers. Additionally, many agencies have the power to subpoena individuals and records. The APA regulates, but does not convey, the subpoena power, which must be "authorized by law" (sec. 555[c]). Aside from the possibility that an agency will be acting ultra vires (outside the scope of its authority), limits on the subpoena power require that the information sought be relevant and specific, not unduly burdensome, and not subject to attorney-client or other privilege. The Fifth Amendment's protection against self-incrimination can sometimes be invoked to defeat the subpoena's utility. However, the amendment does not apply to civil matters and is available only to individuals, not firms and other entities. Even in criminal matters, individuals can be compelled to testify under a grant of immunity from prosecution (Gellhorn and Levin 1997, 127–138).

Second, there are *inspections*. Physical inspections of businesses and other entities are a staple of regulatory enforcement. Inspectors play a variety of roles. They deter violations, help educate the regulated about what compliance requires, and try to persuade them that cooperation with the agency is the best approach for the long term (Scholz 1994, 425–426). Insofar as agencies have statutory authority to undertake inspections, legal issues are likely to arise only with respect to the Fourth Amendment.

The Fourth Amendment applies directly to the federal government and to the states through incorporation into the Fourteenth Amendment. It affords individuals, other entities, and some physical facilities protection against unreasonable governmental searches and seizures. It applies to administrative as well as criminal searches. Inspectors sometimes need to obtain warrants in order to do their jobs. These are generally easier to obtain in the administrative context than in criminal investigations. They are likely to be issued by judges or other judicial officers when the inspection is part of a reasonable, systematic administrative enforcement strategy or is based on specific information regarding violations. In several circumstances, warrants are not required at all.

As noted in Chapter 2, the Fourth Amendment applies to searches only when one has a reasonable expectation of privacy. If someone voluntarily consents to a search, then that person no longer has such an expectation. Similarly, there is no reasonable expectation of privacy when something is in plain view. An open field or smokestack that can be seen from the air is fair game for an airborne EPA or other inspector. If a facility is open to the public, an inspector can enter it and look for violations. Searches in emergency situations, such as firefighting or dealing with hazardous materials, are likely to be considered reasonable (*Michigan v. Tyler* 1978). Customs agents have broad authority to search individuals, containers, and vehicles at ports of entry. Under relatively narrow circumstances, the homes of welfare recipients may be subject to inspections by social workers (*Wyman v. James* 1971; W. Fox 2000, 106–108).

Pervasively or closely regulated entities may also be subject to an administrative search without a warrant. They are considered to have reduced expectations of privacy. But what constitutes such an entity? In *New York v. Burger* (1987), which involved a junkyard believed to be engaged in "chop shop" automobile theft, the Supreme Court identified three factors that permit warrantless searches: (1) there is a substantial governmental interest in the regulatory scheme, (2) the warrantless inspections are necessary under that scheme, and (3) the certainty and regularity of the inspections "provides a constitutionally adequate substitute for a warrant" by (a) notifying the business that inspections will occur, and (b) placing "appropriate restraints upon the inspecting officers' discretion" (*New York v. Burger* 1987, 691–692; Schwartz 1994, 209).

Third, there are *tests*. Agencies rely on tests to ensure that products meet regulatory standards. Testing may take place before a product can be marketed or afterward. Premarket testing is common for drugs, food additives, and other substances for human consumption. The Food and Drug Administration relies heavily on testing, but primarily by evaluating the tests done by the drug companies and others. New drug applications have contained as many as two hundred volumes of information (Quirk 1980, 207). Postmarket tests may be initiated in response to consumer complaints, accidents, illnesses, and other indicators that a product or service is not performing properly. Safety testing is common, but tests can also be used to ensure that products live up to required performance standards and/or satisfy advertising and labeling claims. The Fourth Amendment is relevant when tests occur within the producer's facility and when product seizures are required. The APA specifically provides that hearings are unnecessary in "proceedings in which decisions rest solely on inspections, tests, or elections" (sec. 554[a][3]).

Contemporary administrative thinking associated with the "reinventing government" and new public management movements of the late twentieth century favors alternatives to traditional "ruthless and efficient investigation and enforcement capability" as a means of deterring violations (Sparrow 1994, ix; Osborne and Gaebler 1992; Hood 1991). In a movement that parallels substituting ADR for formal adjudication, regulators may now seek cooperation and partnership as alternatives to the standard enforcement tools of the past. Although agencies retain the capacity to deal forcefully with the worst offenders, they also try to conserve resources and reduce hassles by treating regulatees as customers and by focusing on genuine problems and serious violations rather than on writing up countless minor infractions (Sparrow 1994, ix, xxiii–xxiv). Today, a great deal of administrative enforcement is consensual, albeit with legal sanctions available as a backup. If the partnership approach proves successful, it will reduce agency adjudication, both internally and in court.

Conclusion: Should Adjudication Be Reformed?

Improving federal agencies' evidentiary adjudication was one of the APA's core objectives. Prior to 1946, adjudicatory processes varied among the agencies, and Congress and others viewed many practices as patently unfair. If 1946 is used as a baseline, there is no doubt that federal evidentiary adjudication has advanced vastly in terms of fairness. Presumably, it is more competent today as well. In addition to the APA's specific provisions, the establishment and professionalization of the ALJ position have been major contributors to improvement. However, the ALJs have also promoted greater formality and the growth of court-like procedure in hearings. Some ALJs wear judicial robes. The ALJs have their own professional advocacy associations, which weigh in on proposed reforms and agency practices affecting adjudication. The SSA's ALJ Association took the SSA to court to prevent the imposition of allowance-rate goals (Lubbers 1994, 296). Several agencies now have chief ALJs with administrative and managerial responsibilities for the operation of adjudicatory systems.

The increasing formalization of administrative evidentiary adjudication is often referred to as "judicialization." It promotes fairness and competence but, as enactment of the ADRA indicates, also inefficiency and adverse effects on organizational performance. The act's section on congressional findings concludes that "the availability of a wide range of dispute res-olution procedures, and an increased understanding of the most effective use of such procedures, will enhance the operation of the Government and better serve the public" (sec. 2[8]). Congress's expectation was that in time ADR would supplant adjudication as a means of resolving many disputes.

But some adjudication will always remain, as will the challenge of en-suring that it is fair, competent, efficient, and workable in terms of other major administrative values. As the MSPB maintained with respect to ALJ productivity, adjudications are not fungible. Their subject matter, proce-dural due process requirements, and roles in agency policymaking and enforcement vary widely. Some are "formal" and presided over by ALJs; others are not. Consequently, it is highly likely that within broad parame-ters, tailoring reforms, if desirable, to the particular needs and missions of individual agencies will be more successful than one-size-fits-all, across-the-board approaches. Federal agencies and many at the state and local levels are required to engage in periodic strategic planning and to develop performance measures. Many benchmark their current operations against past performance and "best practices" developed by other agencies. In-cluding evidentiary adjudication in these plans, measures, and assess-ments, along with other facets of their operations, may lead to continuing incremental improvements in agencies' adjudicatory processes and even better integration of them with their overall missions.

Additional Reading

Mashaw, Jerry. *Due Process in the Administrative State.* New Haven, CT: Yale University Press, 1985.

Warren, Kenneth. "Agency Hearings: How Fair Are They?" *Adminis-trative Law in the Political System,* 278–339. 5th ed. Boulder, CO: Westview Press, 2011.

Discussion Questions

1. Fairness is an obvious concern with respect to administrative adjudi-cation. Do you think some aspects of adjudication mentioned in the chap-ter are unfair? What about the "grid-regs" or the law of estoppel?

2. The idea of rotating federal administrative law judges across various agencies, perhaps employing them as a corps rather than as agency em-ployees, has been around for decades but never adopted. What would be the advantages and disadvantages of forming such a corps?

3. The commissioners and board members of multiheaded federal agencies are political appointees. In your view, should they be authorized to overrule administrative law judges when cases are appealed? Why or why not?

4. Agencies sometimes enforce their regulations through product testing. Identify several products that you have used in the past few days and try to develop principles for determining whether they should be subject to premarket, postmarket, or no testing at all. What are the main considerations underlying the principles you develop?

5

Transparency

Introduction: The Central Intelligence Agency's Budget? What Budget?

The US Constitution seemingly requires that "a regular Statement and Account of the Receipts and Expenditures of *all* public Money shall be published from time to time" (Art. I, sec. 9, cl. 7 [emphasis added]). Now, suppose you want to know how much the Central Intelligence Agency (CIA) spends and on what. Suppose further that you suspect the CIA is spending your hard-earned tax and deficit dollars wastefully or on illegal domestic surveillance. A logical first step would be to take a look at the CIA's budget—the account of receipts and expenditures mentioned in the Constitution. However, one would search in vain. The CIA's budget is secret, and under the Central Intelligence Act of 1949, it accounts to the Treasury for its expenditures by a nonpublic "certificate."

In the 1970s, William Richardson, a member of the electorate, loyal citizen, and taxpayer, sued to have the CIA Act declared unconstitutional. A lawyer with a background in military intelligence, he was apparently incensed by the CIA's secretive domestic spending (Wharton 1995). He had a dual constitutional complaint. On the one hand, he could not obtain the CIA's budget; on the other, without the CIA's budget numbers, the Treasury's published "Combined Statements of Receipts, Expenditures, and Balances of the United States" was "a fraudulent document" (*United States v. Richardson* 1974, 169). How could Richardson be an informed citizen and voter if the government was withholding some budget information from him and putting out disinformation in its constitutionally mandated account of receipts and expenditures?

Richardson never received an answer. When the case reached the Supreme Court, a slim majority of five justices decided not to give him one. Instead they found that he lacked standing to bring the suit in the first place. He had no concrete personal injury, only a generalized grievance, perhaps shared with millions of others (see Chapter 6 on standing). The four dissenting justices would have granted standing for a variety of reasons. One justice, William O. Douglas, had a good deal of sympathy for Richardson's cause:

> The sovereign of this Nation is the people, not the bureaucracy. The statement of accounts of public expenditures goes to the heart of the problem of sovereignty. If taxpayers may not ask that rudimentary question, their sovereignty becomes an empty symbol and a secret bureaucracy is allowed to run our affairs. . . .
>
> The public cannot intelligently know how to exercise the franchise unless it has a basic knowledge concerning at least the generality of the accounts under every head of government. No greater crisis in confidence can be generated than today's decision. Its consequences are grave because it relegates to secrecy vast operations of government and keeps the public from knowing what secret plans concerning this Nation or other nations are afoot. (*United States v. Richardson* 1974, 201–202)

Douglas was in the minority, but his views succinctly capture one of the chief concerns that frame administrative law's requirements for open government.

In 2013, by contrast, Edward Snowden's "leaks" raised a countervailing concern for public consideration of transparency in national security policy. According to his information, some of which the *Washington Post* published, the CIA requested $14.7 billion for fiscal year 2013. Of this total, $2.3 billion was for human intelligence; $2.5 billion for security, logistics, and missions; $2.6 billion for paramilitary and covert operations, probably including drone strikes; $1.7 billion for "technical collection" efforts such as intercepting radio and telephone communications; and $68.6 million for providing cover for its operatives (Ehrenfreund 2013; Gellman and Miller 2013).

As Richardson contended, knowledge of the CIA's budget could shed a great deal of light on what it does and where. As one observer explained,

> The CIA's dominant position [in national intelligence] will likely stun outside experts. It represents a remarkable recovery for an agency that

seemed poised to lose power and prestige after acknowledging intelligence failures leading up to the Sept. 11, 2001, attacks and the 2003 U.S.-led invasion of Iraq.

The surge in resources for the agency funded secret prisons, a controversial interrogation program, the deployment of lethal drones and a huge expansion of its counterterrorism center. The agency was transformed from a spy service struggling to emerge from the Cold War into a paramilitary force. (Ehrenfreund 2013)

This conclusion speaks to Douglas's point. The shift in an agency that spends billions of dollars annually from gathering intelligence to paramilitary activity in Afghanistan, Pakistan, and elsewhere is presumably something of which citizens—the "sovereign of this Nation"—ought to be aware. But as Director of National Intelligence James R. Clapper Jr. maintained, it is presumably also something that should be secret: "Our budgets are classified as they could provide insight for foreign intelligence services to discern our top national priorities, capabilities and sources and methods that allow us to obtain information to counter threats" (Gellman and Miller 2013). Therein lies the core of the problem of government transparency: What information should be public, what should be secret, why, and if the "sovereign people" do not decide, who should and how?

The Administrative Law Framework for Transparent Government

(As Douglas argues, open government is a prerequisite for government by the people.) The Constitution's framers were acutely aware that without a good measure of transparency, the system they designed would fail. James Madison, author of the Bill of Rights and chief architect of the separation of powers, ranked openness alongside other fundamental constitutional values: "A popular Government, without popular information, or the means of acquiring it, is but a Prologue to a Farce or a Tragedy; or, perhaps both. (Knowledge will forever govern ignorance.) And a people who mean to be their own Governors, must arm themselves with the power which knowledge gives" (1999, 790; see also US House of Representatives 2001, 1; US Senate 1974, 37–38). In addition to the Receipts and Expenditure Clause, the Constitution requires that "each House [of Congress] shall keep a Journal of its Proceedings, and from time to time publish the same" (Art. I, sec. 5, cl. 3). It also requires a record of presidential vetoes and publication of the names of those members of Congress voting to override or sustain them (Art. I, sec. 7, cl. 2).

Nevertheless, the framers recognized that some matters would have to be secret. Constitutionally, whatever material Congress wants to keep secret it may omit from its journals (Art. I, sec. 5, cl. 3). The Constitution itself was framed under a veil of strict secrecy.

(American constitutional democracy relies heavily on administrative law to determine what should be open, what should be secret, and how decisions regarding governmental transparency should be made, challenged, and reviewed.)Since adoption of the Administrative Procedure Act (APA) of 1946, five main approaches to regulating openness have become widely used: public reporting, freedom of information, protection against invasions of privacy, open meetings, and whistle-blowing.

Public Reporting

As amended, section 552 of the APA requires all covered agencies to publish the following in the *Federal Register*: (1) descriptions of their organization and location, along with whom to contact for information, to make submittals or requests, or to obtain decisions; (2) explanations of their operations and procedural requirements; (3) procedural rules, descriptions of forms and where to obtain them, and information regarding the content of papers, reports, and examinations; (4) substantive and interpretive rules and policy statements; and (5) amendments, revisions, and repeals of any of the above.(A public protection clause provides that no person may be held responsible for noncompliance with an agency requirement in any of these categories that was not properly published.)

The agencies are also required to make some documents available for public inspection and copying, unless they are published. These include final adjudicatory opinions, concurrences, and dissents; adopted policies and interpretations that are not available in the *Federal Register*; and staff manuals and instructions that affect the public. These materials must be indexed for public inspection or sale. They may be posted on the Internet in what are often referred to as "electronic reading rooms." Anything in a document that creates a "clearly unwarranted invasion of personal privacy" should be deleted.

These requirements are important. They go a long way toward overcoming what Congress perceived as excessive administrative secrecy in the 1930s and 1940s. However, they are really just the tip of the iceberg. Agencies face myriad reporting requirements. Along with special reports mandated by Congress, they routinely publish annual reports on their performance and finances. The Government Accountability Office publishes reports on virtually every significant aspect of administration, including personnel practices, organizational design, budgets and financial management, performance, and the implementation of specific statutes.

Agencies also issue news releases and public relations material. As electronic government continues to develop in the digital age, more and more agencies at all levels are maintaining websites. The federal government puts a massive amount of information online—sometimes, perhaps, too much. After the terrorist attacks of September 11, 2001, many agencies removed information about water resources, chemicals, nuclear energy, and other potentially dangerous topics (OMBwatch 2001).

Today, the emphasis is on performance reporting. For instance, the Government Performance and Results Act Modernization Act of 2010 requires the US Office of Management and Budget (OMB) to maintain a website that includes descriptions of the federal government's priority and performance goals with "an identification of the agencies, organizations, program activities, regulations, tax expenditures, policies, and other activities that contribute to each Federal Government priority goal" (sec. 7[c6]). Executive Order 13,514 (2009), titled "Federal Leadership in Environmental, Energy, and Economic Performance," requires OMB to prepare scorecards (available at sustainability.performance.gov) related to agencies' promotion of environmental sustainability. The scorecards rate agencies on reduction of greenhouse gases and energy, use of renewable energy, potable water intensity, fleet petroleum usage, and green buildings. In total, all the reports, scorecards, and other information made public by the federal government would probably overwhelm any citizen diligently trying to understand and evaluate federal administration.

However, not all information is equal. Government reports are sometimes criticized for blurring the distinction between factual reporting and spinning information for favorable public relations. Reading *The United States Government Manual*, one might assume that the federal government houses the most benevolent, caring, rights-protecting, and efficient agencies imaginable. Never mind that federal agencies are routinely denounced by politicians and the media, largely distrusted by the public, and frequently sued.

Agencies may change their mission statements as they update their strategic plans. In the recent past, two particularly sweet-sounding mission statements belonged to the Department of Health and Human Services and the US Botanic Garden. The former portrayed itself as "the Cabinet-level department of the Federal executive branch most involved in the Nation's human concerns. In one way or another, it touches the lives of more Americans than any other Federal agency. It is literally a department of people serving people, from newborn infants to persons requiring health services to our most elderly citizens." The Botanic Garden has informed "visitors about the aesthetic, cultural, economic, therapeutic, and ecological importance of plants to the well-being of humankind." Not to be outdone, the Department of Justice, usually a no-nonsense law enforcement agency that includes the Federal Bureau of Investigation and the Bureau of Prisons, has presented itself as "the largest law firm in the Nation [serving] as counsel for its citizens" (Office of the Federal Register 1999, 271, 45, 323).

Freedom of Information

Freedom of information is aptly defined as regulations and laws "that provide members of the community with a legally enforceable right of access to information in the possession of government" (Zifcak 1998, 941–942). The first freedom of information law was apparently introduced in Sweden in 1766, but contemporary US federal freedom of information did not begin to develop until enactment of the APA in 1946. The APA's provisions were rudimentary, perhaps naive, and they largely failed. The act provided, "Save as otherwise required by statute, matters of official record shall in accordance with published rule be made available to persons properly and directly concerned except information held confidential for good cause found" (sec. 3[c]). Between a citizen's need to show that he or she was "properly and directly concerned" and an agency's ability to withhold information for undefined "good cause," the APA became "a basis for withholding information" despite "the clear intent of the Congress to promote disclosure" (US Senate 1974, 6–7). The Freedom of Information Act (FOIA) of 1966 amended the APA in an effort to fix these problems. The Presidential Records Act of 1978 later applied the basic principle of open government to presidential materials.

The Freedom of Information Act

After its initial enactment in 1966, FOIA was significantly amended in 1974, 1986, and 1996 and again in 2007 by the Openness Promotes Effectiveness in Our National Government Act (OPEN Government Act). From its inception, FOIA sought to balance four concerns: open access, privacy, necessary secrecy, and the government's ability to obtain information. FOIA promotes access by giving all individuals a right to information. There is no requirement that they be properly and directly concerned with the information sought. With one exception explained below, anyone can ask for anything, although the fees agencies charge to supply information may vary with the purpose for which it is sought.

By itself, FOIA is primarily a disclosure statute. However, it instructs and permits agencies to withhold substantial categories of information at their discretion. These categories are called "exemptions," of which there are nine. (They guard individuals' privacy, trade secrets, and commercial, geological, and geophysical information, as well as protect governmental secrecy in the interests of national security, law enforcement, effective decisionmaking and management, and administrative efficiency.)Personal privacy is also protected by the Privacy Act of 1974, as reviewed later in the chapter. The ability to collect information is crucial to contemporary governmental policymaking and regulatory enforcement. FOIA works in conjunction with other statutes, such as the Federal Trade Secrets Act (1948), to protect some types of commercial information, whether submitted voluntarily or under compulsion.

Basically, FOIA operates as follows. Activity is triggered by the submission of a FOIA request to an agency. Requests may be submitted by corporations and associations as well as by individuals. Foreigners may also request information. Federal agencies cannot make FOIA requests of one another. There is no standard form, though the US Department of Justice publishes the *FOIA Reference Guide* (2010), which provides advice on how to request information. Individual agencies also provide online forms for FOIA requests. The requester is obligated to "reasonably describe" the agency records he or she is seeking—that is, to provide enough specificity to enable a professional employee, familiar with the material, to locate it without undue effort. Only information in the form of records is covered. One could ask an agency for a record on John Lennon but should not request all the information it might have on him scattered throughout its documents or organized as records on other subjects (Weinberg 2000). If the information is electronic, the agency may create the requested record, depending on the circumstances. Requesters should indicate whether they want a record in electronic form. Under the OPEN Government Act, agencies are also required to "make the raw statistical data used in [their] reports available electronically to the public upon request" unless it falls under one of the exemptions or is protected by another statute (sec. 8[c]). Until the OPEN Government Act made records maintained and managed for agencies by contractors subject to FOIA requests, agencies were responsible only for records under their control, generated within the agency or placed in its files, and used by the agency for some work purpose (*Bureau of National Affairs, Inc. v. U.S. Department of Justice* 1984). The agency bears the burden of persuasion in demonstrating that the requested information is not an agency record. Requests should be in accordance with the agency's published rules regarding time, place, fees, and procedures.

FOIA's coverage is very broad, applying to the CIA, Federal Bureau of Investigation, military, executive departments and agencies, independent regulatory commissions, and government corporations. As noted above, today it can extend to records held by contractors. FOIA also covers those units in the Executive Office of the President that have statutory responsibilities, such as the Office of Management and Budget, but not those that are purely advisory (e.g., the Council of Economic Advisers) (Funk, Shapiro, and Weaver 1997, 595). It does not apply to Congress, the judiciary, or the president.

Timeliness has been a long-standing FOIA problem. There has been far more FOIA activity than Congress foresaw in 1966, and efforts have been made to prod the agencies to process requests more promptly. Today, agencies have twenty days (up from the original ten) to tell a requester whether the information sought will be released. This can be extended by ten days to channel the request to the proper agency unit. The agency may "toll" the twenty-day period (that is, stop the clock) when it "reasonably" asks the requester for additional information or clarifies fee assessments with him or her. The clock starts running again when the requester responds (OPEN Government Act 2007, sec. 6[a][1][I, II]). If the agency's response is positive, it still may take years to supply the information itself to the requester. Agencies are required to explain their denials of requests. These may be appealed within the agency, in which case the agency has another twenty days to decide whether to release the information.

Along with timeliness, fees have been an issue. When FOIA went into effect, some agencies levied exorbitant charges for reviewing, searching, and copying. Amendments adopted in 1974 limited these but had the effect of subsidizing searches initiated for commercial gain, as when a business seeks information on its competitors. Additional amendments passed in 1986 regulate fees according to how the information will be used. These are highly detailed, but their gist is that requests for information of value to scholarship, research, news reporting, and the public's understanding of government are billed for less than those seeking information for commercial purposes. The OPEN Government Act defines "representative of the news media" to include any entity, be it a person or organization, that "gathers information of potential interest to a segment of the public, uses its editorial skills to turn the raw materials into a distinct work, and distributes that work to an audience." "News" means information dealing with "current events" or of "current interest" (OPEN Government Act 2007, sec. 3).

Although FOIA applies broadly across the federal executive branch, as amended the nine exemptions exclude a considerable amount of information from mandatory release:

1. National defense or foreign policy information that is properly classified for secrecy.
2. Information "related solely to the internal personnel rules and practices of an agency."
3. Information that is specifically prohibited from disclosure or regulated by another statute.
4. "Trade secrets and commercial or financial information obtained from a person and privileged or confidential."
5. Inter- or intra-agency memos or letters that would not be available by law to a party in litigation with the agency.
6. "Personnel and medical files and similar files the disclosure of which would constitute a clearly unwarranted invasion of personal privacy."
7. "Records or information compiled for law enforcement purposes, but only to the extent that the production of such law enforcement records or information (A) could reasonably be expected to interfere with enforcement proceedings, (B) would deprive a person of a right to a fair trial or an impartial adjudication, (C) could reasonably be expected to constitute an unwarranted invasion of personal privacy, (D) could reasonably be expected to disclose the identity of a confidential source, including a State, local, or foreign agency or authority or any private institution which furnished information on a confidential basis, and, in the case of a record or information compiled by a criminal law enforcement authority in the course of a criminal investigation or by an agency conducting a lawful national security intelligence investigation, information furnished by a confidential source, (E) would disclose techniques and procedures for law enforcement investigations or prosecutions, or would disclose guidelines for law enforcement investigations or prosecutions if such disclosure could reasonably be expected to risk circumvention of the law, or (F) could reasonably be expected to endanger the life or physical safety of any individual." Exemption 7(C) was the focus of litigation creating an important exception to FOIA's usual operation and is detailed below.
8. Information pertaining to the regulation of financial institutions.
9. "Geological and geophysical information and data, including maps, concerning wells." (sec. 552[b][1–9])

Two points about the exemptions should be borne in mind. First, information in these categories may be released at an agency's discretion unless it would violate some other law. In other words, the fact that requested information falls into one of the exemptions does not necessarily determine whether it will be released. Over the years, federal attorneys general have provided different guidance. Some, such as Janet Reno (1993–2001), have promoted disclosure; others, including John Ashcroft (2001–2005), have sought to dampen it. Reno authorized the Department of Justice to defend the agencies in FOIA suits only when release of the information sought would create "foreseeable harm." Under Ashcroft, the department defended agencies whenever they had a "sound legal basis" for withholding information (Office of Information and Privacy 2001). President Barack Obama's attorney general, Eric Holder (2009–), replaced this standard with a "presumption of openness" by asserting that "the Department [of Justice] will defend a denial only if the agency reasonably foresees that disclosure would harm an interest protected by one of the statutory exemptions, or disclosure is prohibited by law" (Office of Public Affairs 2009). Nevertheless, the Obama administration has demonstrated a penchant for secrecy (J. Ball 2012). For instance, Obama's Executive Order 13,526 (2009) authorizes agencies to classify information after they receive FOIA requests (sec. 1.7[d]).

Second, FOIA specifically provides that "any reasonably segregable portion of a record shall be provided to any person requesting such record after deletion of the portions which are exempt" from release (sec. 552[b]). To the extent technically feasible, the agencies should identify the places where deletions were made.

FOIA has engendered far more litigation than can be reviewed here. A great deal of it is incredibly detailed and fact specific. This seems particularly true in suits over what constitutes a record. One example should be of particular interest to public managers. In *Bureau of National Affairs, Inc. v. U.S. Department of Justice* (1984), a US court of appeals had to decide whether government officials' telephone message slips, daily agendas, and appointment calendars were agency records. It reached the following conclusions:

1. The telephone message slips "are not 'agency records' within the meaning of FOIA. No substantive information is contained in them. No one but the official for whom the messages were taken used the telephone slips in any way. And, in many cases, there might be no way for the official to segregate personal from business calls."
2. "The daily agendas are 'agency records' within the meaning of FOIA. They were created for the express purpose of facilitating the daily activities of the Antitrust Division. Even though the agendas reflected personal appointments, they were circulated to the staff for a business purpose." They were created "for the convenience of [the] staff in their conduct of official business."

3. "The appointment calendars are the most difficult to categorize. . . . We conclude, however, that *these particular* appointment calendars are not 'agency records.' They are distinguishable from the daily agendas in two important respects. First, they were not distributed to other employees, but were retained solely for the convenience of the individual officials. Second, . . . the appointment calendars were created for the personal convenience of individual officials so that they could organize both their personal and business appointments." (*Bureau of National Affairs, Inc. v. U.S. Department of Justice* 1984, 1495–1496 [emphasis added]).

Public managers sometimes assume that anything work related may be obtained under FOIA for all the world to see. *Bureau of National Affairs* suggests FOIA's operation is more complex and less governed by categorical rules. This also tends to be the case with regard to the specific exemptions. Although it is not possible to treat each of these in detail here, the following general points are important:

- Exemption 1, for national security, does not affect the government's ability to classify documents. Where an agency's very admission that it does or does not have a record could compromise national security or foreign policy, it may respond that it can neither confirm nor deny the existence of the record. For historical reasons, this is called a "Glomar denial" or "Glomarization"[1] (Funk, Shapiro, and Weaver 1997, 607).
- Exemption 2, for personnel rules and practices, covers less than its language suggests. The Supreme Court interpreted it to exempt only internal information that would be of no interest to the public. For example, records pertaining to the Air Force Academy's internal disciplinary system are not exempt (*Department of the Air Force v. Rose* 1976).
- Exemption 3, for information protected by another law, occasionally gives rise to an issue of statutory interpretation. However, the principle is clear enough: agencies may withhold information when disclosure is prohibited or regulated by other statutes. As explained immediately below, releasing such information may violate the APA.
- Exemption 4, for confidential commercial information and trade secrets, has had a difficult history. FOIA by itself would allow the

---

1. The term comes from a FOIA request for information about the CIA's connection to Howard Hughes's effort, using the Glomar Explorer, to retrieve a sunken Soviet submarine. See *Phillippi v. CIA* (1976).

release of such secrets, however defined. To defend against this possibility, firms developed "reverse FOIA" suits. A business can file suit in a district court to block an agency from disclosing information requested on it. The firm's challenge takes the form of contending that release would be arbitrary, capricious, an abuse of discretion, or otherwise not in accordance with law as defined by section 706 of the APA (see Chapter 6). For example, all things being equal, releasing information covered by an act protecting trade secrets would violate section 706. Under Executive Order 12,600 (1987), agencies are required to inform businesses that their commercial information is being sought.

- Exemption 5, dealing with inter- and intra-agency memos, is interpreted to privilege (i.e., shield from disclosure) two types of information. One is information generated by an attorney-client relationship that would not be available in litigation. The other is information covered by executive privilege. This is a somewhat more amorphous concept derived from judicial interpretation of the separation of powers that permits the president to withhold some executive branch information from Congress and the judiciary (*Nixon v. Administrator of General Services* 1977; *United States v. Nixon* 1974). The general principle underlying exemption 5 is that predecisional information is privileged to protect the free flow of ideas within and among agencies. In other words, before a decision is made, participants should be able to engage in uninhibited brainstorming and feel free to bounce half-baked ideas off one another. Who would start a thought with, "This may sound crazy, but . . . " if the rest might be on the front page of a newspaper someday? The predecisional exemption applies to private parties who participate in a decision as well as to agency employees. Predecisional material is not privileged if it becomes specifically incorporated into the final decision. Executive privilege is more central to the Presidential Records Act, as explained in the next section.
- Exemption 6 protects only against "unwarranted" invasions of personal privacy. It should be considered in conjunction with the Privacy Act, which is discussed below. It applies only to human beings, not to corporations or associations. Under some circumstances, its coverage is broad enough to allow withholding information to protect the privacy of the relatives of an individual on whom information is being sought.
- Exemption 7(C), which allows withholding law enforcement information that "could reasonably be expected to constitute an unwarranted invasion of personal privacy," was the subject of *National Archives and*

Records Administration v. Favish (2004), a major Supreme Court decision, which is discussed below.

- Exemptions 8 and 9, dealing with financial institutions and geology, are of less importance to public managers generally. Nine was included to assuage oil industry concerns that information about potential oil and natural gas fields, developed at great expense through exploration, would be released to competitors or speculators.

Returning to exemption 7(C), Allan Favish sought photographs taken at the scene of Vincent Foster's suicide. Foster was President Bill Clinton's deputy White House counsel, and the photos were held by the National Archives and Records Administration (NARA). The issue was whether NARA could withhold them under section 7(C). Foster was dead and, of course, could not assert a right to privacy. However, his family did so, and this led the Court to establish two important principles. First, it is appropriate "to conclude from Congress' use of the term 'personal privacy' that it intended to permit family members to assert their own privacy rights against public intrusions long deemed impermissible under the common law and in our cultural traditions." Second, the usual FOIA rule holding that it is irrelevant why a requester seeks information does not apply to section 7(C). Here, the Court spoke to the essence of government transparency:

FOIA is often explained as a means for citizens to know "what the Government is up to." . . . This phrase should not be dismissed as a convenient formalism. It defines a structural necessity in a real democracy. The statement confirms that, as a general rule, when documents are within FOIA's disclosure provisions, citizens should not be required to explain why they seek the information. . . . The information belongs to citizens to do with as they choose. . . . The disclosure does not depend on the identity of the requester. As a general rule, if the information is subject to disclosure, it belongs to all.

When disclosure touches upon certain areas defined in the exemptions, however, the statute recognizes limitations that compete with the general interest in disclosure, and that, in appropriate cases, can overcome it. In the case of Exemption 7(C), the statute requires us to protect, in the proper degree, the personal privacy of citizens against the uncontrolled release of information compiled through the power of the state. . . .

Where the privacy concerns addressed by Exemption 7(C) are present, the exemption requires the person requesting the information to establish a sufficient reason for the disclosure. First, the citizen must show that the public interest sought to be advanced is a significant one, an interest more specific than having the information for its own sake. Second, the citizen must show the information is likely to advance that interest. Otherwise, the invasion of privacy is unwarranted. (*NARA v. Favish* 2004, 167, 171–172)

In reaching its decision, the Court was careful to distinguish between the narrow wording of exemption 6, which speaks to creating "a clearly unwarranted invasion of personal privacy," and the broader language of 7(C), which requires only a reasonable expectation that the release of information would be an "unwarranted invasion of personal privacy." "Personal" in 7(C) does not protect nonhuman "legal persons," including corporations and other "artificial entities" (*Federal Communications Commission v. AT&T* 2011).

Enforcement of FOIA depends heavily on the federal district courts. The act places the burden of persuasion on the agency to show that nondisclosure is legal. The district court makes its determination de novo (afresh) rather than being bound by the agency record. It may review the records at issue in camera (i.e., privately in chambers). When requesters substantially prevail, agencies may have to pay their attorneys' fees and related costs. The OPEN Government Act makes these fees available when the requester has a substantial claim and the agency changes its position prior to trial. This is intended to potentially compensate requesters for their legal fees when agencies agree to release information just before going to trial, as well as to deter agencies from dissuading requesters from suing with the prospect of incurring heavy, nonreimbursable pretrial costs. The act also specifies that attorneys' fees will be paid from the agencies' own budgets rather than the Treasury Department's Claims and Judgment Fund (sec. 4[b]).

Theoretically, a court's finding that an agency acted arbitrarily and capriciously can result in a Merit Systems Protection Board (MSPB) disciplinary action against an official, though apparently by 1997 there was only one such finding and no actual discipline (Funk, Shapiro, and Weaver 1997, 593). When a suit involves discovering what information actually exists, the agency is required to provide an index of its relevant records to both the court and the requester (known as a "Vaughn index"; see Funk, Shapiro, and Weaver 1997, 607).

Evaluations of freedom of information radically differ. In principle, it is broadly accepted as necessary for representative government. Voters like Richardson need information to fulfill their roles as citizens. The OPEN Government Act is premised on the belief that "the effective functioning of a free government like ours depends largely on the force of an informed public opinion" (sec. 2[1][c]). Access to public information, as Madison maintained, is a key to governmental accountability. Every US state has a statutory-based freedom of information policy, as do most, if not all, democracies abroad. As early as 1946, the United Nations General Assembly resolved that "freedom of information is a fundamental human right and is the touchstone for all the freedoms to which the United Nations is consecrated" (Zifcak 1998, 942). Nevertheless, there may still be some holdouts. In 1982, when he was still merely a law professor, Supreme Court Justice Antonin Scalia denounced the premise "that the first line of defense against an arbitrary executive is do-it-yourself oversight by the public and its surrogate, the press" (quoted in Strauss et al. 1995, 909).

There is broad agreement that implementation of FOIA is costly, litigious, and time-consuming. Explanations vary with respect to why the act has not worked better. Clearly, the volume and expense were unanticipated. In fiscal year 2012, there were 651,254 requests government-wide and a backlog of 71,790 requests (FOIA.gov, n.d.). The government spends an estimated $300 million to $400 million annually on FOIA requests (National Security Archive 2006). No doubt many requests are frivolous, and most may be for commercial information that has no immediate value to the public. However, requesters' ardor for information is not the sole problem. The federal government's administrative culture has been slow to change from valuing secrecy to embracing openness (Warren 1996, 187). As of 2000, the vast majority of agencies paid no attention to FOIA activities in their annual performance plans (Piotrowski and Rosenbloom 2002). The OPEN Government Act seeks to change this culture by requiring agencies to report on their timeliness in processing requests and to appoint chief FOIA officers with responsibility for compliance, monitoring and improving implementation, and designating FOIA public liaisons to help resolve disputes with requesters (sec. 10[k]).

The OPEN Government Act will promote better agency reporting and processing of requests. However, at least for the near future it is likely to remain true, as Professor Robert Vaughn, for whom the Vaughn index is named, maintains, that "the Founding Fathers would be proud of the act—unless they could see how the people['s] government often frustrates its purpose" (Mashaw, Merrill, and Shane 1992, 697). Federal judge Patricia Wald's summary may be best: "Something like [FOIA] had to be invented to prevent a 'curtain of fog and iron' from falling between the American public and its government," but "FOIA, like all basic freedoms, sometimes hurts the worthy and sometimes helps the unworthy" (Strauss et al. 1995, 909).

The Presidential Records Act

The Presidential Records Act was adopted to resolve an issue simmering in the demise of Richard M. Nixon's presidency. Who has control over the release of presidential papers, tapes, and related materials—a former president, claiming executive privilege, or the federal government? The act placed presidential and vice presidential materials in the custody of the archivist of the United States, with the "affirmative duty" to make them public "as rapidly and completely as possible" (sec. 2203[f][1]). It allows former presidents and vice presidents to prevent access to some records for twelve years after they leave office. Most of the FOIA exemptions apply to disclosure by the archivist. However, papers and so forth that might be covered by FOIA exemption 5 should not be withheld simply because they reveal internal White House deliberations or staff advice. The act allows a former president or vice president to sue the archivist to prevent access to specific documents by asserting constitutional executive privilege, the full scope of which is uncertain and depends on case-by-case judicial interpretation. The act is considered of great value to historians, public interest groups, the media, and, ultimately, the American people.

Its first application was to President Ronald Reagan (1981–1989), whose papers became eligible in 2001. However, implementation was frustrated by President George W. Bush (Bush II), whose father, President George H. W. Bush, was Reagan's vice president and could figure prominently in the released documents. Bush II issued Executive Order 13,233 (2001), blocking the archivist from permitting access to any papers that either a former or incumbent president wanted withheld. In some cases the order would have allowed the family members of incapacitated or deceased former presidents to prevent access. It also increased vice presidents' control over their papers. Bush II's order was broadly based on claims of constitutional executive privilege. It flipped the legal process regarding access. Under its terms, the burden was on those seeking access, not former presidents seeking to prevent it. Individuals and associations suing for access to blocked material would have to demonstrate a specific need for the records involved (US House of Representatives 2001; Allen and Lardner 2001).

Bush's order provoked criticism in Congress, legislative attempts to nullify it, and at least one lawsuit, brought by the American Historical Association, the National Security Archive, the Reporters Committee for Freedom of the Press, Public Citizen, the American Political Science Association, and independent scholars (*American Historical Association v. NARA* 2007; see Miller 2001; Lardner 2001). In the lawsuit, the US District Court for the District of Columbia narrowly ruled that a section (3[b]) of the Bush

II order that would have extended a president's or vice president's ability to prevent the archivist's release of records indefinitely was "arbitrary, capricious, and contrary to law in violation of the Administrative Procedure Act" (*American Historical Association v. NARA* 2007, 3, 33).

On the second day of his presidency, Obama replaced Bush II's order with Executive Order 13,489 (January 21, 2009). It specifies that in the absence of a claim of executive privilege, presidents and vice presidents can only prevent the release of records for "a time certain" rather than indefinitely (sec. 2[b]). However, like Bush II's order, it apparently limits the release of records that might fall under FOIA exemption 5 by stating, "A 'substantial question of executive privilege' exists if NARA's disclosure of Presidential records might impair national security (including the conduct of foreign relations), law enforcement, or the deliberative processes of the executive branch" (sec. 1[g]). The order also requires NARA to "abide by any instructions given . . . by the incumbent President [regarding a claim of executive privilege] . . . unless otherwise directed by a final court order" (sec. 4[b]). Eventually, the federal courts are likely to determine when assertions of presidential executive privilege can override the presumption that records covered by FOIA exemption 5 are subject to disclosure under the Presidential Records Act.

Privacy

The federal Privacy Act of 1974 reflects the APA's broad interest in protecting individual rights against administrative encroachment. Its coverage within the executive branch is similar to FOIA, though somewhat broader because it extends to advisory units in the Executive Office of the President. The act was a congressional response to a variety of issues that crystallized in the Watergate years (1972–1974), especially concern over the abuse of agency information about private individuals. There was also a sense that the federal government was collecting too much personal information and safeguarding it poorly. For example, during the 1960s some federal agencies used personality tests and privacy-invading questionnaires that contained items such as the following true-false questions: "My sex life is satisfactory" and "There is little love and companionship in my family as compared to other homes" (Westin 1967, 256–268). A congressional investigation concluded that there was a high potential for misuse of such information because "confidentiality of government files is a myth. Such files float from agency to agency. Federal investigators in some instances are given access to information far removed from the subject of their inquiry" (US Congress 1966, 398). At one point, some nondefense agencies were routinely requiring their employees to fill out a questionnaire that was originally designed for use by patients in government hospitals. The form asked numerous detailed questions about physical and mental health symptoms, including bed-wetting and nightmares (see Rosenbloom 1971, 213).

The Privacy Act is primarily concerned with regulating the collection, management, and release of information regarding individual citizens and permanent residents. It does not apply to corporations, associations, or other organizations. The following are its main features:

1. Access to records: Individuals have a right to review agency records on them. If they find errors, they may request that the records be amended. If the agency refuses, the individual involved may file a statement of disagreement, which essentially becomes part of the record. A person may also request information about the purpose, nature, and date of agencies' disclosure of records on him or her. A general exemption prevents individual access to CIA and law enforcement agency records.

2. Management of records: Agencies are required to publish notices in the *Federal Register* explaining the nature of their record systems and policies regarding access, disposal, storage, and related matters. They must also develop safeguards against inaccuracies and misuse of information, including through computer matching. The information contained in an agency's records should be relevant to its mission.

3. Restrictions on disclosure: In principle, the act prohibits the disclosure of any record on an individual without his or her prior consent. However, there are twelve specific exceptions in which such consent is not required. The most important among these are that records may be disclosed to Congress, to law enforcement agencies at all levels of government, in response to a FOIA request, and in "compelling circumstances" regarding an individual's health or safety. Records may also be released for "routine use," which is rather circularly defined as use "for a purpose which is compatible with the purpose for which it was collected." (sec. 552a[b][1–12], [a][7])

In a case with odd protagonists, *U.S. Department of Defense v. Federal Labor Relations Authority* (FLRA) (1994), the Supreme Court noted that the relationship between FOIA and the Privacy Act is "convoluted." Information protected by the Privacy Act may nevertheless be disclosed under FOIA's sixth exemption unless it would "constitute a clearly unwarranted invasion of personal privacy." How does one determine what is "unwarranted"?

In *U.S. Department of Defense v. FLRA,* two local unions were seeking the names and home addresses of the employees in the bargaining units they represented, some of whom were not union members. The Department of Defense (DoD) supplied the employees' names and workstations but, citing the Privacy Act, not their home addresses. The unions filed unfair labor practice charges with the FLRA, which ultimately ordered the DoD to supply the home addresses. The DoD refused, and the conflict went to court.

The Supreme Court applied the following framework for analyzing the relationship between the Privacy Act and FOIA exemption 6. First, "in evaluating whether a request for information lies within the scope of an exemption that bars disclosure when it would amount to an unwarranted invasion of privacy, a court must balance the public interest in the disclosure against the interest Congress intended the exemption to protect." Second, and the key point, "the only relevant public interest to be weighed in this balance is the extent to which disclosure would serve FOIA's core purpose of contributing significantly to public understanding of the Government's operations or activities." Third, "whether an invasion of privacy is warranted cannot turn on the purposes for which the information request is made." (*NARA v. Flavish,* discussed above, was decided under exemption 7(C) but may have implications for this third point in the *DoD v. FLRA* framework for interpreting exemption 6. See also *U.S. Department of Justice v. Reporters Committee for Freedom of Press* 1989).

In applying this three-step analysis to the facts, the Court had no trouble finding that the home addresses were protected by the Privacy Act. The public interest in disclosure was "negligible, at best"—"virtually nonexistent." This interest must be defined in terms of what the public might learn from disclosure, not whether releasing the home addresses would improve collective bargaining in the federal government. Consequently, "a very slight privacy interest would suffice to outweigh the relevant public interest." The Court reasoned that even though home addresses are often available through phonebooks and other published sources, "the employees' interest in nondisclosure is not insubstantial" because "many people simply do not want to be disturbed at home by work-related matters." It also noted that if the unions could obtain the addresses, they would likewise be available to commercial advertisers and solicitors (*U.S. Department of Defense v. FLRA* 1994, 487–489 [Syllabus], 497–501).

The Privacy Act is enforced through civil lawsuits and criminal prosecutions, though instances of the latter are very rare (Funk, Lubbers, and Pou 2000, 819). There have been a few highly publicized allegations of violations of the act. During the 1992 election campaign, one Elizabeth Tamposi allegedly went rummaging through the State Department's passport files on candidate Bill Clinton and his mother, Virginia Dell. Toward the end of Clinton's presidency, agency information on Linda Tripp, a key figure in the Monica Lewinsky episode, was improperly released. However, enforcement for anything other than an agency's failure to provide access or correct its records is difficult. Suits for money damages require a showing of actual damages and that the violation at issue was intentional. Damages for mental and emotional distress are not available (*Federal Aviation Administration v. Cooper* 2012). The Privacy Act has not produced a great deal of litigation, perhaps because its exceptions are broad and winning damages is so difficult (Bonfield and Asimow 1989, 560). Every state has a counterpart of the federal act. Privacy may be further protected by regulations requiring agencies to develop "privacy impact assessments" dealing with personal information held in electronic form and shared among agencies and levels of government such as contained in the Implementing Recommendations of the 9/11 Commission Act of 2007.

Open Meetings

The federal government and all fifty states promote transparency through open meetings laws. Their purpose is to place agencies' oral policymaking in full public view in order to obtain better decisions, promote greater understanding of government, and generate more trust and confidence in it. Open meetings laws complement freedom of information by creating public access to verbal decisionmaking, where there may be a relatively thin paper trail for subsequent retrieval. Such laws are based on two major premises. First, when agencies exercise delegated legislative authority orally in formulating and adopting binding public policy decisions, they ought to emulate legislatures by doing so in the open rather than behind closed doors. Second, openness combats political favoritism, corruption, and opportunities for special interests to wield undue influence.

Open meetings laws are often called "sunshine laws," presumably in the spirit of Supreme Court Justice Louis Brandeis's well-known statement that "sunlight is said to be the best of disinfectants; electric light the most efficient policeman" (quoted in *Buckley v. American Constitutional Law Foundation* 1999, 223). However, despite their popularity, these laws are often criticized for being cumbersome, having a chilling effect on informal collegial discussions, and driving agency decisionmaking backstage, which leads to "scripted," "perfunctory" open meetings (May 1997, 421; Coyle 1995, A12). At the federal level, the major open meetings laws are the Government in the Sunshine Act of 1976 and the Federal Advisory Committee Act of 1972.

The Sunshine Act applies to multiheaded federal boards and commissions to which a majority of the members are appointed by the president with the advice and consent of the Senate. There are about fifty such units, including the Securities and Exchange Commission, Federal Trade Commission, Federal Communications Commission, and Consumer Product Safety Commission. Covered agencies are required to give at least one week's advance notice of their meetings. In principle, all meetings of a quorum of the agency members necessary for official business should be open to the public. By majority vote, meetings or portions of them may be closed in the public interest for reasons that parallel the FOIA exemptions. However, a major difference is that a meeting cannot be closed simply to protect predecisional discussions from public scrutiny. The act's purpose is to force as much of the decisionmaking process into the open as possible. Meetings may also be closed when public decisionmaking would frustrate implementation of the proposed policy. A vote to close meetings must be made public. Depending on the reason for closure, the agency must keep either a transcript, recording, or set of minutes of the meeting. This record is available to the public, except for discussion that may be withheld under an exemption. The act contains a number of requirements for reporting to Congress.

Enforcement is by civil lawsuit, though the Sunshine Act has not produced much significant litigation. The remedy for improper closure of a meeting is likely to be access to the agency's transcript. Under the federal act, an agency action cannot be invalidated on the basis that a meeting should have been open. Some state laws do provide such a remedy (Bonfield and Asimow 1989, 554). Litigation by Common Cause and Public Citizen established that meetings cannot be closed to shield budget decisions or simply to promote more candid discussions (Funk, Lubbers, and Pou 2000, 542).

Several features of the Federal Advisory Committee Act (FACA) were discussed in Chapter 3 on rulemaking. The whole thrust of the act was to bring the advisory committee system aboveboard. It seeks to make openness in advisory committee meetings the general rule (sec. 10). Notices of meetings must be published in the *Federal Register*, and "interested persons shall be permitted to attend, appear before, or file statements with any advisory committee" (sec. 10[a][3]). FACA requires that detailed minutes of meetings be kept and provides public access to these as well as to written materials supplied to advisory committees, including reports, working papers, and studies. These documents may be withheld under a FOIA exemption. Open meetings are the norm; exceptions may be made based on the same criteria as apply to agencies under the Sunshine Act. FACA does not apply to committees composed solely of federal employees, the CIA, the Federal Reserve System, and local civic groups.

FACA has produced considerable litigation, mostly over what constitutes an "advisory committee." Remedies for improper secrecy may include a court injunction against the use of an advisory committee report, but in some cases there may be no remedy even for clear violations—except to prevent their repetition (Strauss et al. 1995, 957). Enforcement against presidential advisory committees raises constitutional questions involving the separation of powers and executive privilege. Perhaps the most publicized case to date is *Association of American Physicians and Surgeons, Inc. v. Hillary Rodham Clinton* (1993). Is the First Lady a federal employee for FACA purposes? If she is not, then the President's Task Force on National Health Care Reform was an advisory committee, and its closed meetings violated FACA. Applying dexterous statutory interpretation "to the point of disingenuous evasion," as one judge put it, the court concluded that First Lady Clinton was a federal employee, at least in the FACA context. The court articulated some general principles that provide useful guidance:

1. A "group is a FACA advisory committee when it is asked to render advice or recommendations, as a group, and not as a collection of individuals."
2. "In order to implicate FACA, the President, or his subordinates, must create an advisory group that has, in large measure, an organized structure, a fixed membership, and a specific purpose."
3. "When an advisory committee of wholly government officials brings in a 'consultant' for a one-time meeting, FACA is not triggered because the consultant is not really a member of the advisory committee."
4. "When we examine a particular group or committee to determine whether FACA applies, we must bear in mind that a range of variations exist in terms of the purpose, structure, and personnel of the group." Formal groups of private citizens "brought together to give publicized advice as a group" are clearly covered; "an unstructured arrangement in which the government seeks advice from what is only a collection of individuals who do not significantly interact with each other" is not regulated by the act. (*Association of American Physicians and Surgeons, Inc. v. Hillary Rodham Clinton* 1993, 913–915)

FACA was back in the news in 2001–2002 in conjunction with Vice President Richard Cheney's refusal to release the records of the National Energy Policy Development Group, which he chaired. The Bush II administration claimed that the task force was not a government unit subject to FOIA.

But it may have been an advisory group subject to FACA. The Natural Resources Defense Council sued for records on its membership and meetings, and in an unprecedented step, the US General Accounting Office took similar legal action (Nakashima 2001; Milbank 2002). Eventually, after reaching the Supreme Court, which sent it back to the district court for further action, the case was dismissed in *In re Cheney* (2005) (see also *Cheney v. District Court* 2004).

It is difficult to predict the future of FACA. On the one hand, the law has significant implications for reinvented government, in which it is common to form public-private partnerships and collaborative governance arrangements with private organizations and multilevel governmental units. Some public-private partnership meetings may fall under the act. Hillary Clinton's case also drew attention to the potential for using the act to delay, if not upend, federal policymaking. On the other hand, remedies for violations have been tepid thus far.

Whistle-Blower Protection

Providing legal protection to whistle-blowers is another way to promote transparency. Public-sector whistle-blower protection regulations are intended to prevent reprisals against public employees, contractors, and others who expose wrongdoing observed in their relationships with government agencies. Exposure of maladministration can be internal to an inspector general or other agency official. It may also be external to some outside agency, a legislature, media outlets, or some other party. More broadly, whistle-blower protections seek to transform organizational cultures to view whistle-blowing as a civic obligation and public virtue rather than as insubordination, snitching, or tattling. The premise is that insiders are in an excellent position to reveal maladministration and protect the public from it. At the federal level, whistle-blowing is defined as disclosing violations of laws, rules, or regulations, mismanagement, "gross waste of funds," abuses of authority, and substantial and specific dangers to public safety or health (Civil Service Reform Act 1978, sec. 1206[b]). This covers a very broad array of activity encompassing everything from illegal handling of radioactive materials to run-of-the-mill violations of federal personnel law.

As noted in Chapter 2, all civilian public employees in the United States enjoy a measure of constitutionally protected free speech on matters of public concern. This includes whistle-blowing but excludes "work-product" speech as explained earlier with reference to the Supreme Court's decision in *Garcetti v. Ceballos* (2006). However, even public employees' speech on matters of public concern may legitimately provide cause for discipline when it significantly harms the employer's interests in confidentiality, efficiency, performing ongoing operations, and similar matters. Although whistle-blowing is a form of protecting the public's interests, it can also create unnecessary public anxiety and disdain for government or hinder administrative agencies in implementing their missions effectively. The free speech rights of government contractors parallel those of public employees, as may those of individuals who are engaged in preexisting commercial relationships with public agencies (*Board of County Commissioners, Wabaunsee County v. Umbehr* 1996; *O'Hare Truck Service, Inc. v. City of Northlake* 1996).

A problem for whistle-blowers is that vindicating these rights may involve a tortuous path of litigation. Under constitutional law, the public employee, contractor, or supplier of goods or services to a government has the initial burden of persuasion in showing that his or her protected speech triggered a reprisal. The burden then shifts to the agency involved to show that its action served a substantial governmental purpose or that it would have taken the action based on other factors even if the speech had not occurred. An agency may also prevail if it can show that the action is justified based on information it gained after disciplining an employee or terminating an economic relationship with a contractor or other party. Statutory whistle-blower protection regulations are intended to afford an easier—though sometimes still difficult—route for combating reprisals.

The 1978 federal Civil Service Reform Act prohibited taking any personnel action as a reprisal against a federal employee's whistle-blowing. The Merit Systems Protection Board and the Office of Special Counsel were charged with enforcement. These provisions were strengthened by the Whistleblower Protection Act of 1989, (which (1) extends protection to cover threats of retaliation; (2) provides protection if an employee can show that retaliation was a factor, rather than the dominant factor, in an adverse action; (3) raises the government's burden of persuasion in showing that the action was taken for reasons other than retaliation; and (4) permits employees to initiate action for redress before the MSPB when the Special Counsel does not act on the matter (Warren 1996, 401).)

Interpretation of federal whistle-blower protection law by the US Court of Appeals for the Federal Circuit and the MSPB is highly detailed, often turning on the precise meaning of a single word. In general, a federal employee is not protected if he or she (1) reports the wrongdoing to the wrongdoer, even if that person is his or her supervisor, because the wrongdoer is probably aware of the wrongdoing and, consequently, the employee is not "disclosing" it to him or her; (2) discloses wrongdoing to a wrongdoing supervisor who is aware of his or her conduct because in that situation the disclosure is about the nature of the conduct rather than the conduct itself; (3) discloses wrongdoing through normal channels as part of his or her regular job responsibilities; (4) lacks a reasonable belief that wrongdoing occurred; or (5) discloses information in contravention of a law or regulation. By contrast, disclosure is likely to be protected if it is part of one's normal responsibilities but reported "outside normal channels" or disclosed outside assigned responsibilities to a proper party (see US MSPB 2010, esp. 17–18).

Thirty-four states provide some degree of whistle-blower protection. Some protect state employees; others, public and private employees; and North Dakota's law applies to private employees only. Most regulations cover violations of law, though they may pertain to breaches of state, but not federal or local, law. Louisiana's coverage extends only to federal, state, and local environmental protection laws. Alaska "prohibits public employers from discharging, threatening, or otherwise discriminating against a public employee who reports to a public body or participates in a court action or inquiry on a matter of public concern." Colorado protects disclosures about state agency actions that are not in the public interest. Nebraska provides employees with a right to disobey illegal orders: "It is unlawful for an employer with 15 or more employees, or a union or employment agency to discriminate against a person who has opposed any practice or refused to carry out an action that is a violation of state or federal law." Pennsylvania appears to be the only state that covers violations of ethical codes (National Conference of State Legislatures 2010).

A whistle-blower's charges will not be protected if he or she makes them knowing them to be false or, depending on the specifics of the law, with disregard for their truth or falsity. Claims that turn out to be false may be protected if they were made in good faith—that is, the whistle-blower reasonably believed them to be true. Under some laws, individuals seeking personal gain by whistle-blowing may be afforded less protection.

Whistle-blower protection statutes vary in their procedural requirements. Some require that the first effort to expose wrongdoing be made internally within the organization in which it is occurring. Others allow disclosure directly to an external state agency, such as the federal Office of Special Counsel, a personnel board, an auditor's office, or a law enforcement authority.

Remedies for retaliation against protected whistle-blowing also vary. Public employees are generally made whole through reinstatement and back pay, benefits, and seniority. They may also recoup attorney's fees. Punitive damages are sometimes available. However, fines for violating whistle-blower protection laws may be light, such as $500 in Pennsylvania. The MSPB notes that at the federal level "perceptions of retaliation against those who blow the whistle remain a serious concern. In both 1992 and 2010, approximately one-third of the individuals who felt they had been identified as a source of a report of wrongdoing also perceived either threats or acts of reprisal, or both" (US MSPB 2011, transmittal letter).

Qui Tam

Laws may offer financial gain as an inducement for private individuals to expose fraud and cheating against the government. The federal False Claims Act of 1863, revised in 1986, authorizes *qui tam* (pronounced "kwee tam") actions against federal contractors and other private entities that are paid or funded by the government. *Qui tam* is short for "qui tam pro rege quam pro sic ipso in hoc parte sequitur," which means "who as well as for the king as for himself sues in this matter" (USLegal, n.d.).

In modern terms, *qui tam* actions empower a whistle-blower to try to recover public funds by suing a person or organization that has allegedly defrauded the government. Because a *qui tam* plaintiff, called a "relator," sues on behalf of the government, he or she is not required to show a personal injury, as is usually necessary to gain standing to litigate. If the suit is successful, the relator will share the funds recovered with the government.

Under the False Claims Act, the Department of Justice has the option of joining the suit. As amended in 1986, the act enables successful whistle-blowers to receive up to 25 to 30 percent of the recovery in the absence of the department's intervention and 15 to 25 percent with it. Defendants are prohibited from taking adverse actions against their whistle-blowing employees and may be required to reinstate them with double back pay and other compensation. From 1986 through 2006, the federal government recovered over $18 billion through *qui tam* suits, and whistle-blowers received about $1.8 billion. Cases involved Medicare and Medicaid fraud, defective products, and false billing, among other matters (Chang 2009; LawyerShop.com, n.d.; The Qui Tam Online Network, n.d.).

Conclusion: An Opaque Fishbowl?

Here is a snippet from a brief conversation I had with a *USA Today* reporter in the mid-1990s when "reinventing government" was a hot topic:

REPORTER: "Can government operate like a business?"
ME: "Which one? Tobacco? Silicone implants?"
REPORTER: "What?"
ME: "Did you ever try to 'FOIA' Philip Morris or Dow Corning?"

The reporter laughed. Of course, she might have had the same response if asked whether she had ever tried to FOIA the CIA for its budget numbers. Many contend that public administrators operate in a fishbowl; many others say government has a strong penchant for secrecy. For some, the water in the fishbowl is too clear; for others, it is too murky. And many feel quite passionately about how open government should be. But as one of the twentieth century's leading public administrative thinkers, Dwight Waldo, was fond of asking, "Compared to what?"

If the comparison is to the private sector, many executives with experience in both government and business would undoubtedly agree that "governmental management tends to be exposed to public scrutiny and to be more open, while private business management is more private and its processes more internal and less exposed to public review" (Allison 1994 [1979], 136). If the comparison is to public administration before and after the development of regulations for transparency, there would be broad agreement that freedom of information, sunshine, and whistle-blower protection have advanced, though not fully achieved, their purposes.

It is worth keeping Waldo's question in mind when assessing transparency policy. If criticism alone could make for perfection, freedom of information in particular might be among the most perfect of all public policies. The job of improving and fine-tuning transparency policy is more difficult than diagnosing what is wrong; it requires prescribing what will be better. As noted in the chapter's discussion of *United States v. Richardson*, open government necessarily involves trade-offs and balances among competing concerns of fundamental importance to US democratic constitutionalism. The exemptions in FOIA and open meetings laws, exceptions in the Privacy Act, crafting of whistle-blower protection, and judicial decisions dealing with transparency inescapably provide an ever-evolving, applied political theory of openness in contemporary US government. The tensions among openness, security, administrative effectiveness and efficiency, access, privacy, confidentiality, the public's sovereignty, and workable constitutional democracy may be irresolvable yet manageable through continual adjustments to transparency policy. And clearly, the long-term trend has been toward better implementation of FOIA and other transparency provisions.

Additional Reading

Foerstel, Herbert N. *Freedom of Information and the Right to Know*. Westport, CT: Greenwood Press, 1999.

Peltz-Steele, Richard. *The Law of Access to Government*. Durham, NC: Carolina Academic Press, 2012.

Piotrowski, Suzanne J., ed. *Transparency and Secrecy: A Reader Linking Literature and Contemporary Debate.* Lanham, MD: Lexington Books, 2010.

Discussion Questions

1. Do you agree with the Supreme Court's decision regarding FOIA exemption 7(C) in the *Favish* case? Why or why not?

2. Is there any exemption in FOIA that you would eliminate? How about exemption 5, the gist of which does not apply to open meetings and presidential records?

3. The Civil Service Reform Act of 1978 contains significant whistleblower protections; yet even after these were strengthened in 1989, the Merit System Protection Board reports that reprisals against whistleblowers are still common. Why do you think this is the case? What, if anything, can be done to reduce reprisals?

4. Do you think the Privacy Act and FOIA exemptions 6 and 7 adequately protect Americans' personal privacy from government incursions? If not, what might be done to provide greater protection?

6

Judicial and Legislative Review of Administrative Action

Introduction: The Drug Companies' Acetaminophen, Salicylic Acid, and Caffeine Headache

In 1962, Congress amended the Food, Drug, and Cosmetic Act of 1938 to require pharmaceutical companies to print a drug's generic name "prominently and in type at least half as large" when using the drug's trade name on labels and advertising. The point was to familiarize doctors and the public with the availability of identical generic versions of many proprietary drugs—identical, that is, in everything but price.

The Food and Drug Administration (FDA) commissioner undertook notice and comment rulemaking to develop rules for efficient enforcement of the amendment. The final regulations mandated that the labels and advertisements for prescription drugs include the generic name every time the trade name appeared. Thirty-seven individual drug companies and the Pharmaceutical Manufacturers Association found the commissioner's action hard to swallow. To them, the rules were a prescription for lower profits. They brought suit to block enforcement on the grounds that the 1962 amendment did not authorize the every-time requirement.

When *Abbott Laboratories v. Gardner* (1967) reached the Supreme Court, the issue was whether the drug companies were entitled to preenforcement review of the legality of the FDA commissioner's final rules. The Court split 5–3 in favor of such review (one justice did not participate).

The majority reasoned that precedent and the Administrative Procedure Act (APA) of 1946 created a strong presumption in favor of judicial review for anyone legally wronged, adversely affected, or aggrieved by agency action. In their view, the regulations clearly put the drug companies in an aggravating bind: "If [they] wish to comply they must change all their labels, advertisements, and promotional materials; they must destroy stocks of printed matter; and they must invest heavily in new printing type and new supplies. The alternative to compliance—continued use of the material which they believe in good faith meets the statutory requirements, but which clearly does not meet the regulation of the Commissioner—may be even more costly. That course would risk serious criminal and civil penalties for the unlawful distribution of 'misbranded' drugs." Moreover, enforcement could harm the companies' public image even if it ultimately turned out the commissioner, not they, had acted illegally. So, better for the courts to review the regulations before the commissioner enforced them.

Sensible? Not according to the three dissenters. They argued that "established principles of jurisprudence, solidly rooted in the constitutional structure of our Government, require that the courts should not intervene in the administrative process at this stage, under these facts and in this gross, shotgun fashion." In litigious America, a precedent favoring preenforcement review would insidiously "threaten programs of vast importance to the public welfare" in order to assuage "the cries of anguish and distress" raised by regulated industries. A potential flood of litigation would forestall the implementation of untold congressional mandates. The dissenters adamantly warned against accepting "the invitation to abandon the traditional insistence of the courts upon specific, concrete facts, and instead entertain this massive onslaught in which it will be utterly impossible to make the kind of discrete judgments which are within judicial competence." Preenforcement judicial review would "permit the administration of a law of the Congress to be disrupted by [a] nonadjudicable mass assault" (*Abbott Laboratories v. Gardner* 1967, 152–153, 175–176, 200–201).

Sensible as well. These opinions speak to the large questions of judicial review of administrative action. Under what conditions should the courts rule on the legality or constitutionality of administrative action? What are the consequences of taking a case too soon or too late? Should the courts entertain cases only after a concrete factual record has been developed through an agency's enforcement of a regulation? Should the courts decide matters, as in *Abbott Labs*, when there are genuine legal issues and either preenforcement compliance or noncompliance would be expensive? What are the effects of such choices on the relationships between courts and agencies? How might they affect the role of the courts in an institutional sense? The doctrines and case law regarding judicial review address these and related questions. They focus on determining what is judicially reviewable as well as the timing and scope of review.

Legislative review of agency action raises a companion set of issues. Who is in a better position than Congress to determine whether the commissioner's every-time regulation was in keeping with legislative intent? Justice Tom Clark joined the dissenters in *Abbott Labs* but also added a few choice words of his own: "I hope that the Congress will not delay in amending the Act to close this judicial exition [*sic*] that the Court has unwisely opened up for the pharmaceutical companies." Why? Well, in nonjudicious language, the companies have "deceitfully and exorbitantly extorted high prices . . . from the sick and the infirm. Indeed, I was so gouged myself just recently when I purchased some ordinary eyewash drops and later learned that I paid 10 times the price the drops should have cost." "Rather than crying over the plight that the laboratories have brought on themselves, the Court should think more of the poor ailing folks who suffer" because the drug companies "mislead the public by passing off ordinary medicines as fancy cures." According to Clark, because the Court's majority got it wrong, Congress should step in and make it right (*Abbott Laboratories v. Gardner* 1967, 201).

Sensible? Of course, but thousands of federal rules are promulgated annually. How can Congress deal with them all? What if the sentiment of a legislature changes faster than an agency can write a rule? What form should congressional action take, if and when it occurs? More generally, how can a legislature ensure that administrators' exercise of delegated legislative authority is in keeping with its intent?

Judicial Review of Administrative Action

The courts are generally viewed as essential to subordinating administrative action to the rule of law. They provide a check against abuse of administrative discretion and unconstitutional, illegal, irrational, or procedurally irregular decisionmaking and enforcement. They are a full-fledged part of public administration and often considered partners, or, more likely, senior partners, with administrators (Bazelon 1976).

However, the precise shape that the partnership should take is inherently debatable. As suggested by the colliding opinions in *Abbott Labs*, the key questions are what should be reviewable, when, and how deeply. Over the years, the courts have developed complex—some might say convoluted—legal doctrines in an effort to supply answers. Judicial review of administrative action is an area of the law in which there are exceptions to everything—including, no doubt, this statement. One can even read a law review article titled "Judicial Review of Non-reviewable Administrative Action" (Morris 1977). This chapter provides an overview of the main principles and considerations that define contemporary judicial review of public administration. It then focuses on the tools for legislative review of agency activity.

The Court System

Judicial review takes place within federal and state court systems. These generally have a well-defined division of labor among trial courts, appellate courts, and specialized courts. The federal court system is illustrative.

The district courts are the workhorses of the federal judiciary. There are eighty-nine district courts in the United States (one to four per state, depending on size), plus one each in the District of Columbia, Commonwealth of Puerto Rico, Virgin Islands, Guam, and Northern Mariana Islands. They are trial courts and hear criminal as well as civil cases. Litigation at this stage of the process is aimed at establishing the relevant facts, applying the law to them, and resolving disputed legal issues. The judge determines matters of law; the jury, if one is sitting, determines the facts. In bench trials, there is no jury; the judge decides whether the plaintiff's or the defendant's version of the facts is more credible, as well as the legal outcome. When there is no factual dispute, the case may be decided efficiently by summary judgment, in which the judge rules on the legal questions presented. A single judge presides over most district court cases, though sometimes a three-judge panel is used. The district courts are usually the first judicial level to deal with administrative law cases, as in *Abbott Labs* and *Nova Scotia* (discussed in Chapter 3).

The district courts can resolve administrative law cases in several ways. They can rule that an administrative action is legal (e.g., that the FDA commissioner had legal authority to write the every-time rule and properly promulgated it). Alternatively, they can find that the administrative action was illegal or unconstitutional. When ruling against the government, the district courts can block further enforcement of an administrative rule or order. They can also remand cases (send them back) to the agency for further rulemaking, clarification, or adjudication. Short of resolution, the courts can also issue temporary restraining orders to prohibit the continuation of a challenged activity while a trial is held or a final decision reached. They can also dismiss a suit because it fails to constitute a case or controversy within the meaning of Article III of the Constitution, lacks a substantial federal legal question, or is otherwise not suitable for judicial resolution (as discussed below in this chapter).

Judges explain the legal and logical basis for their decisions in written opinions. Though these are not necessarily published or widely circulated, written opinions are central to judicial accountability and the evolution of US legal doctrines. Future cases are decided by weighing the applicability, reasoning, and conclusions of past decisions—that is, precedents—to them. Precedents can be modified or even discarded, but they are rarely disregarded altogether. Most federal cases, including administrative law cases, begin and end in the district courts (Warren 1996, 42).

Appeals from district court decisions usually go to a court of appeals, though decisions in a three-judge case may be appealed directly to the Supreme Court. The courts of appeals are organized by circuit. There are eleven numbered territorial circuits, such as the Second Circuit (Vermont, Connecticut, New York) and the Seventh Circuit (Indiana, Illinois, Wisconsin), as well as a District of Columbia Circuit. There is also a Court of Appeals for the Federal Circuit, which has nationwide geographic jurisdiction but specialized legal jurisdiction involving patents, federal contracts, trade, veterans' claims, and some administrative actions by the Merit Systems Protection Board, the Department of Veterans Affairs, and other agencies. Appeals court cases are usually heard by three judges. Sometimes all the judges in a circuit will sit as a full panel, which is called a hearing en banc.

Appeals courts serve as a check on the district courts. Even though only a limited proportion of cases are appealed, the possibility of review probably enhances the quality of district court decisions. Appeals overwhelmingly deal with matters of law. The appellate courts ordinarily accept the factual record as it comes from the district court. In nonjury cases, the lower court's factual findings may be rejected if they are clearly erroneous. In jury cases a more difficult standard is applied: essentially the evidence or the inferences drawn from it must be so faulty that the jury's verdict is completely implausible (Strauss et al. 1995, 522–523).

As with the district courts, appeals court decisions are written in the form of opinions. They can create a number of outcomes. The district court's decision may be affirmed or reversed or, occasionally, affirmed in part and reversed in part (in other words, an appellate ruling may agree or disagree with separate parts of the lower court's opinion). The appeals court may remand the case to the district court for further proceedings. A district court's decision may also be vacated—that is, entirely voided, as when the appeals court finds that the district court misconstrued the legal matter at issue. A vacated civil action may be relitigated if the dispute is not resolved in some other way unless the appeals court instructs that it be dismissed. In addition, sometimes a specific legal question is sent by a district court to an appeals court for certification, that is, to be answered one way or another so that the lower court can proceed. Appeals court decisions apply directly only within their particular circuits. Consequently, an agency that loses a case in one territorial circuit is not required to change its practices in the others. When two or more circuits are at odds with one another, agency operations must comport with the law governing the geographic area where they take place. As a result, the administration of a single federal program may vary significantly from circuit to circuit unless or until the Supreme Court definitively resolves the issues involved.

Judge Patricia Wald of the Court of Appeals for the District of Columbia Circuit described what may be a fairly typical array of appeals court outcomes in cases involving administrative rules:

> Between July 1, 1992, and July 1, 1993, panels of our circuit sat on thirty-five cases involving . . . rules (plus one en banc proceeding).
> . . .
>
> Out of the thirty-six cases, the agency's judgment was upheld in its entirety nineteen times or more than fifty percent. In the remaining seventeen cases, a portion of the rule or rules was remanded; although in most of those cases the key portions of the rule survived. In four of these cases parts of the rule went back for failure to provide the required APA notice and comment, the agency having unsuccessfully argued in court that they were only "clarifications" not "amendments" of existing rules, or that there was "good cause" for waiving notice and comment. The court sent the rule or parts thereof back for failure of the agency adequately to explain its rationale in six cases; in seven cases, it thought the agency had interpreted the statute in a way that contradicted the clear intent of Congress; in a few cases it was a combination of these two reasons that doomed the rules. It must also be noted that in many of these cases the rule was left in place [rather than nullified] while on remand. (Wald 1994, 632, 636–638; quoted in Strauss et al. 1995, 650–651)

The Supreme Court sits at the top of the federal court system. Its most important jurisdiction is appellate—that is, it hears cases brought from the lower federal courts, primarily the appeals courts, and from the state supreme courts or their equivalents (which may be called courts of appeals, as in New York and Maryland, or have other names). It possesses *original jurisdiction* to act as a trial court only in a limited range of cases, such as controversies between two or more states (e.g., over disputed boundaries).

The Court has very broad discretion to pick and choose among the roughly 7,000 petitions for review it receives annually. Nowadays, it will end up writing full decisions in approximately eighty cases each year. Most cases come to the Supreme Court via writ of certiorari (i.e., review); cases are accepted when four or more justices favor granting review. Administrative law cases are not typically a large part of the Court's docket. The justices are likely to take them in order to resolve significant differences among the circuits or because they raise issues of national importance. Cases involving some federally protected civil rights and voting rights, antitrust issues, and a few other matters may be brought on appeal, rather than via certiorari, which increases the likelihood that the Court will give them full attention.

Original jurisdiction aside, Supreme Court case outcomes parallel those of the appeals courts. The Court can affirm or reverse the lower court, vacate judgments, remand for further action, and certify legal questions. Its decisions are by majority vote of the justices who hear a case, which is usually the full body of nine. When a majority of those voting subscribe to a single written opinion, it becomes the opinion of the Court. If a majority of the justices agree on the specific holding (e.g., to affirm) but not the reasons for doing so, there is a judgment—but no opinion—of the Court. In such instances, the written opinion supported by the largest number of justices favoring the judgment is called a plurality opinion. When the chief justice is in the majority, then he (or a future she) assigns the task of writing the Court's opinion to himself or another justice in the majority. When the chief justice is in the minority, the most senior justice in the majority determines who will write the majority opinion. Any justice is free to write a separate concurring or dissenting opinion. In future decisions, concurrences and dissents are given whatever weight their reasoning commands. Only opinions of the Court are true precedents, which generally serve as significant—though not necessarily binding—guides to resolving subsequent cases.

The federal court system also includes a number of specialized courts and functionaries that do not fit neatly into the three tiers described above. These include the Court of Federal Claims (hearing money claims against the United States), the Court of Appeals for the Armed Forces, the Tax Court, the Court of Appeals for Veterans Claims, Foreign Intelligence Surveillance Court (for issuing surveillance warrants in connection with national security), and the Court of International Trade (dealing with import transactions). There are also special courts and judges for bankruptcy cases, as well as federal magistrates who are supervised by district courts and preside over some civil and misdemeanor trials.

Supreme Court, district, and appeals court judges are appointed by the president with the advice and consent of the Senate. They hold office during good behavior and are removable only through impeachment and conviction. These are called Article III judges because their authority and appointments are governed directly by the Constitution's third article, dealing with the federal judiciary. This is true even though the district and appeals courts are established by legislation rather than the Constitution itself. The district courts in Guam, the Northern Mariana Islands, and the Virgin Islands are an exception because they are established by statute under Article IV dealing with US territories. Their judges hold ten-year terms. Article I courts (e.g., the US Court of Federal Claims and the US Tax Court), which are also established by law, have limited subject matter jurisdiction and authority rather than Article III's full judicial power. The terms of Article I judges are also fixed by law. As noted earlier, state court systems more or less parallel the federal model, though many state judges are elected.

The federal courts are a powerful component of government and a major institutional force in administrative law. Chapter 2 explained how federal court decisions have brought the Constitution to bear directly on administrators' relationships with clients, customers, fellow government workers, contractors, and individuals involved in street-level regulatory encounters, as well as on the management of prisoners and individuals confined to public mental health facilities. Agency rulemaking, adjudication, and transparency have also been substantially affected by court decisions. Yet, like all US political institutions, the judiciary operates within a system of checks and balances.

One obvious limitation on judicial power is that court decisions are not necessarily self-enforcing. Many a judge has become frustrated at the slow pace of court-ordered public school desegregation, prison reform, and other changes in government operations. Judges can use writs and powers, such as holding individuals in contempt of court, in an effort to compel compliance. In the end, though, as Alexander Hamilton pointed out more than two centuries ago, the judiciary "may truly be said to have neither FORCE nor WILL but merely judgment; and must ultimately depend upon the aid of the executive arm even for the efficacy of its judgments" (1961 [1788], 465).

Another institutional limitation is the judiciary's inability to reach out to initiate cases. Courts can decide only matters that are brought to them in appropriate form. Under Article III, the federal judiciary's power is limited to deciding *cases and controversies* arising under the Constitution or federal laws or involving diplomats, admiralty, the United States, or, in some situations, one or more of the states as a party. Not every dispute, even when framed in legal terms, qualifies as a case or controversy within the Constitution's meaning. This is the matter of reviewability.

Reviewability

Judicial review in the United States has at least two meanings. One is the power to declare governmental actions unconstitutional (and therefore null and void). For instance, a federal court can declare the whole or part of an act of Congress, treaty, presidential executive order, lower court action, or agency rule, practice, or decision, as well as their equivalents at the state or local levels, unconstitutional. State courts exercise similar powers within their jurisdictions. Judicial review in this sense is not found in the text of the US Constitution. It was established for the federal courts by the Supreme Court's decision in *Marbury v. Madison* (1803). It is generally well accepted as necessary if the Constitution is to remain the supreme law of the land, though as noted in Chapter 3, unitary executive branch theory maintains that the president's executive powers include the authority to independently assess the constitutionality of federal laws, including those that he (or a future she) has signed.

Another meaning of judicial review concerns what it is that the courts will review, when, and how. Article III courts cannot give advisory opinions because, constitutionally, their power is confined to resolving legal cases and controversies. These are genuine only when the parties have an adversarial relationship with some substantial concrete interest at stake, such as liberty or property. The adversary legal system functions best when there are true adversaries working hard to adduce evidence and legal argument that may convince a court of the correctness of their own claims and the weaknesses of their opponent's. In part, the dissenters in *Abbott Labs* did not want to grant preenforcement review because the full parameters of the adversarial relationship between the FDA commissioner and the pharmaceutical interests had yet to be established.

Over the years, the courts have developed several tests to determine whether a dispute is judicially reviewable—that is, whether it is a case or controversy suitable for judicial resolution. Reviewability in this context is known as *justiciability*. It is rooted in (1) the limits Article III places on judicial authority in the context of the constitutional separation of powers, and (2) "the prudential limits" that embody "judicially self-imposed limits on the exercise of federal jurisdiction" that are "essentially matters of judicial self-governance" "designed to protect the courts from 'decid[ing] abstract questions of wide public significance even [when] other governmental institutions may be more competent to address the questions and even though judicial intervention may be unnecessary to protect individual rights'" (*United States v. Windsor* 2013, 2685–2686). The main components of justiciability follow.

Standing to Sue. Having *standing to sue* means that one has a sufficient stake to bring a case against another party to court. Perhaps Supreme Court Justice Antonin Scalia explained Article III standing most succinctly:

> Over the years, our cases have established that the irreducible constitutional minimum of standing contains three elements. First, the plaintiff must have suffered an "injury in fact"—an invasion of a legally protected interest which is (a) concrete and particularized, . . . and (b) "actual or imminent, not 'conjectural' or 'hypothetical.'" Second, there must be a causal connection between the injury and the conduct complained of— the injury has to be "fairly . . . trace[able] to the challenged action of the defendant, and not . . . th[e] result [of] the independent action of some third party not before the court." . . . Third, it must be "likely," as opposed to merely "speculative," that the injury will be "redressed by a favorable decision." (*Lujan v. Defenders of Wildlife* 1992, 560–561)

Each of these components has been defined through litigation integrating them with prudential limits that the courts have fashioned with respect to standing.

"Injury" is treated broadly as a "zone of interest" that may include economic, aesthetic, conservational, recreational, and other such cognizable concerns, as well as harm to one's constitutional or legal rights or status. Under the APA an injury includes "suffering legal wrong" or being "adversely affected or aggrieved" by agency action (sec. 702). "In fact" creates a strong presumption that the party seeking standing is personally among those injured. Generally, the injured is an individual, entity, or group directly regulated by governmental action. However, sometimes the injury will be to an adversely affected third party. For example, in *Craig v. Boren* (1976), a licensed vendor of 3.2 percent "nonintoxicating" beer had standing to bring an equal protection challenge against an Oklahoma statute allowing females to purchase the brew upon reaching age eighteen but males only at twenty-one. The beer seller had an injury in fact because she "must obey the statutory provisions and incur economic injury or disobey the statute and suffer sanctions" (*Craig v. Boren* 1976, 190). An association or organization meets the "in fact" requirement when its members would individually have standing, it seeks to protect interests of importance to its purpose, and the nature of the suit does not require personal participation by its members (Strauss et al. 1995, 1144).

The injury must also be "concrete and particularized." It is easier to say what is not such an injury than what is. The grievance a citizen feels when he or she believes a statute or agency rule is unconstitutional, illegal, or bad public policy is neither concrete nor particularized. It is a generalized complaint that may be shared with many other citizens. Consequently, at the federal level, citizens do not have standing as citizens per se to sue the government. This was William Richardson's problem in *United States v. Richardson* (1974), discussed in Chapter 5. In most instances, being a taxpayer is also insufficient to create standing to bring cases in federal court. The effect of a national public policy on one's income tax bill is a generalized injury that is widely shared with other individuals (*Frothingham v. Mellon* 1923). An exception occurs when a taxpayer is challenging the federal taxing and spending power to fund a policy that is specifically forbidden by the Constitution, such as government spending that establishes religion (*Flast v. Cohen* 1968).

The requirement that the injury be "actual or imminent" rather than "conjectural" or "hypothetical" is also central to the adversary process. The courts prefer that "the legal questions presented . . . will be resolved, not in the rarefied atmosphere of a debating society, but in a concrete factual context conducive to a realistic appreciation of the consequences of judicial action" (*Valley Forge Christian College v. Americans United for Separation of Church and State, Inc.* 1982, 472). When the harm is actual, the courts and parties to the case can evaluate it and weigh the government's countervailing interests. When it is imminent, its character and scope can be assessed. But when it is merely conjectural or hypothetical, the adversary process operates uncomfortably like legislative decisionmaking. The courts are not well positioned, relative to elected legislatures and expert administrators, to deal with the speculative costs and benefits of one policy option over another.

The requirement that the plaintiff demonstrate that the injury was fairly traceable to a governmental action may be easily met, as when one is directly regulated by an agency rule. However, sometimes it will be alleged that a policy creates an injury in the zone of interest of a third party who is not directly regulated but more like an innocent bystander who incidentally suffers harm. An obvious chain of causality, as in *Craig v. Boren*, satisfies the traceability requirement. Some cases are more difficult. In *Allen v. Wright* (1984), the parents of African American public school students challenged the US Internal Revenue Service's lax enforcement of a legal provision disallowing tax-exempt status to racially discriminatory private schools. The parents argued that the racially discriminatory schools were using tax-deductible contributions to expand their attractiveness to white students, which frustrated efforts to racially desegregate the public schools. The Supreme Court found the alleged causal chain far too weak to convey standing. The more speculative, tenuous, or convoluted the purported connection between cause and effect, the less likely traceability is to be accepted.

The final standing requirement is that the injury will likely be redressed by a favorable court decision. All other components of standing being met, good lawyering should prevent this from being an issue. Before filing suit, one ought to know whether victory will appropriately remedy injuries. Remedies can be complex, as in prison reform and public school desegregation cases, or straightforward, as when a rule is nullified, a practice stopped, a new hearing held, a plaintiff compensated, and so on. But they should be clearly connected to the injury.

The main problem regarding redressability arises when there is an uncertain relationship between the requested relief and the course of action a defendant or third party may take if the plaintiff prevails. For instance, in 1969 the Internal Revenue Service dropped a ruling allowing charitable nonprofit hospitals to receive beneficial tax status by providing services to indigents below cost. A welfare rights organization sued to have the ruling reinstated. It argued that the inducement of favorable tax treatment was necessary to encourage the hospitals to care for indigents. The Supreme Court found it insufficiently likely that the relief sought would redress the injury. The Court thought that the hospitals might just as plausibly forfeit their tax status as bear the costs of treating indigents (*Simon v. Eastern Kentucky Welfare Rights Organization* 1976). In a later case, an obviously frustrated Supreme Court found the requested relief "worthless" not only to the plaintiffs but "seemingly worthless to all the world" (*Steel Co. v. Citizens for a Better Environment* 1998, 106).

Mootness.   A case is not reviewable if it is *moot*, meaning that a judicial decision will have no practical effect because the specific legal dispute has disappeared or already been resolved in some other way. For instance, in *Craig v. Boren*, one of the plaintiffs, Curtis Craig, had sought prospective relief—to be legally eligible to buy 3.2 beer at age eighteen. By the time the case was decided, he was twenty-one, and the Court's ruling could have no effect on his purchase of beer. His case was moot. The suit proceeded because the other plaintiff, the beer seller, was suffering an ongoing injury. In another example, a condemned prisoner's challenge to electrocution as cruel and unusual punishment was mooted when the state offered death row inmates a choice between lethal injection and the electric chair (*Bryan v. Moore* 2000).

An exception to mootness may occur when the issue is "capable of repetition and yet evading review" (Barron and Dienes 1999, 51). *Roe v. Wade* (1973), which protected the right to have an abortion, is a classic example. It would be next to impossible for a pregnant woman to have such a case decided with finality by the Supreme Court within nine months. Yet at any given time, millions of women are pregnant, and at the time of *Roe*, abortion was widely prohibited by state laws. There are two ways around this type of problem. Most simply, the case can proceed if the plaintiff is capable of repeating the behavior: Jane Roe (Norma Leah McCorvey) could have conceived again and sought an abortion. The other is to file the suit as a class action representing a substantial number of parties in the same situation.

Another exception is that a case will not necessarily be moot because one of the parties voluntarily changes his, her, or its behavior. For instance, after the city of Erie, Pennsylvania, made it an offense to "knowingly or intentionally appear in public in a 'state of nudity,'" Pap's A.M., a corporation operating the nude dancing establishment Kandyland, challenged the ordinance as a violation of freedom of expression under the First and Fourteenth amendments. The city lost at the trial level, won on appeal, lost in the Pennsylvania Supreme Court, and then petitioned the US Supreme Court for review. In the meantime, Pap's stopped the nudity at Kandyland and operated no other business falling under Erie's prohibition. Pap's wanted the Supreme Court to dismiss the case as moot. The Court refused because Erie was still bound by the Pennsylvania high court decision and therefore could not enforce its ordinance. Pap's might also go nude again in the future and would be free to do so if the Pennsylvania court's ruling stood. Finding Pap's apparent strategy in pleading for mootness too transparent, the US Supreme Court noted that its own prudential "interest in preventing litigants from attempting to manipulate the Court's jurisdiction to insulate a favorable decision from review further counsels against a finding of mootness" (*City of Erie v. Pap's A.M.* 2000, 277, 278). The Court went on to reverse the Pennsylvania Supreme Court.

Ripeness.　*Ripeness* focuses on whether the matters involved in a case have developed sufficiently to make it ready for judicial review. As explained in *Abbott Laboratories v. Gardner*, the basic rationale for demanding that a case be ripe "is to prevent the courts, through avoidance of premature adjudication, from entangling themselves in abstract disagreements over

administrative policies and also to protect the agencies from judicial interference until an administrative decision has been formalized and its effects
felt in a concrete way by the challenging parties. The problem is best seen
in a two-fold aspect, requiring us to evaluate both the fitness of the issues
for judicial decision and the hardship to the parties of withholding court
consideration" (1967, 148–149). *Abbott Labs* was a difficult ripeness case
that split the Court. The majority found the issues sufficiently clear and the
potential harm to the drug companies great enough to warrant preenforcement review. The minority argued that the case was not ripe and would
not be until enforcement occurred or perhaps was imminent.

The Supreme Court's decision in a companion case to *Abbott Labs* illustrates how ripeness analysis works. *Toilet Goods Association, Inc. v. Gardner*
(1967) dealt with coloring additives in cosmetics, which are regulated by
the Food and Drug Administration. In order to facilitate enforcement, the
FDA commissioner issued a regulation authorizing immediate suspension
of FDA certification service to anyone who denied the agency's employees
access "to all manufacturing facilities, processes, and formulae involved
in the manufacture of color additives." The Toilet Goods Association's
members were manufacturers whose products accounted for 90 percent
of all domestic cosmetic sales annually. It challenged the regulation as
exceeding the commissioner's authority under the relevant statutes. The
association viewed the commissioner's action as a circumvention of legislative intent, noting that the FDA had long asked Congress to authorize
the kind of access the commissioner sought and that Congress had always
refused, except with respect to prescription drugs. The cosmetic manufacturers were particularly concerned that free access could compromise
valuable trade secrets.

The Supreme Court reasoned that *Toilet Goods*, unlike *Abbott Labs*, was
not ripe for judicial resolution. On the one hand, the issues were speculative. Until the commissioner implemented the regulation, the courts could
not understand what kind of enforcement problems the FDA faced and
how these might be resolved within the agency's statutory authority with
appropriate attention to safeguarding trade secrets. On the other hand,
refusal to decide the case at this stage placed minimal hardships on the
cosmetic companies. In the Court's words, "a refusal to admit an inspector here would at most lead only to suspension of certification services to
the particular party, a determination that can then be promptly challenged
through an administrative procedure, which in turn is reviewable by a
court" (*Toilet Goods Association, Inc. v. Gardner* 1967, 161, 165). Although
ripeness is subjective, the contrast between *Abbott Labs* and *Toilet Goods*
well illustrates how the underlying theory is applied.

Political Questions. Political questions are not justiciable. These are defined by three considerations: (1) the matter is committed by the Constitution's text to the legislature or executive branch or both, (2) the courts would lack "discoverable and manageable standards for resolving" the issues, and (3) no other provision of the Constitution would be defeated by the judiciary's refusal to adjudicate the issues (*Nixon v. United States* 1993, 224–225). *Nixon v. United States* (1993) may be the best illustration. Walter L. Nixon Jr. was convicted of federal crimes and sentenced to prison. He was also chief judge of a federal district court, holding tenure during good behavior and drawing pay. He was impeached by the House of Representatives. A Senate committee took testimony from him and reported to the whole Senate, which voted to convict. Nixon claimed that the Senate's action violated the Constitution's Impeachment Clause, which provides that the "Senate shall have the sole Power to try all Impeachments" (Art. I, sec. 3, cl. 6).

Did the Senate try Nixon? The Supreme Court held that the question was political rather than legal and therefore not justiciable. First, the Constitution's text unarguably commits impeachment trials to the Senate. Second, the word "try" is too vague in this context to yield standards that would be judicially manageable on review. Nixon's protection against arbitrary decisionmaking lay primarily in the requirement that conviction be by a two-thirds majority vote. Finally, failure to review would have no effect on the constitutional system.

Nixon has some relevance to administrative law because the Court's decision would apply to the impeachment of executive officers as well. However, political questions are likely to arise far less frequently in the administrative context than concerns about standing, mootness, and ripeness.

Timing

Reviewability analysis is infused with constitutional considerations and prudential interests driven by the scope of judicial authority under Article III and the separation of powers. Timing concerns are primarily prudential policy decisions about when judicial review of administrative action should take place. These are embodied in the principles of primary jurisdiction, exhaustion, and finality and doctrines regarding federal judicial deference to state courts.

Primary Jurisdiction. Primary jurisdiction is relevant when a case is brought to court that could also be decided, at least initially, by an administrative agency. The court may essentially tell the parties to take the case to the agency for resolution. The agency may have greater expertise in the subject matter than the court. A decision at the administrative level, where regulations are enforced, may also promote the application of uniform standards. A decision that an agency has primary jurisdiction also helps lighten the courts' heavy dockets.

In fact, from an administrative law standpoint, there seem to be only three good reasons why a court should not place primary jurisdiction with an agency. First, the question may involve a matter of law in which the agency has no special expertise. One of the more remarkable illustrations grew out of Allegheny Airlines' incredibly bad judgment in bumping consumer advocate Ralph Nader from a flight. Nader charged that the airline's overbooking practices amounted to fraudulent misrepresentation. Looking for a friendly forum, the airline argued that the Civil Aeronautics Board (CAB) should have primary jurisdiction because it regulated unfair and deceptive practices in the industry. Ultimately, the Supreme Court ruled for Nader on the basis that the courts, rather than the CAB, have special expertise in the law of fraudulent misrepresentation (*Nader v. Allegheny Airlines, Inc.* 1976).

A court may also avoid placing primary jurisdiction with an agency when a challenged regulation, decision, or action appears completely unreasonable. In such circumstances, there is no point in prolonging the matter. Finally, the agency may have already ruled on the matter in a case involving other parties. If so, the court is not likely to learn much from another agency decision along the same lines. These exceptions notwithstanding, the basic premise with respect to the division of labor between courts and agencies is that the agencies should generally have primary jurisdiction (Warren 1996, 437).

Exhaustion of Administrative Remedies. As a rule, parties are required to exhaust their administrative remedies before turning to the courts for relief. From a jurisprudential policy perspective, exhaustion takes advantage of agency expertise, allows agencies to learn where their operations are causing problems and correct them, if possible, and reduces the judiciary's caseload. However, as suggested in Chapter 4, from the perspective of a nongovernmental party, such as Cinderella, exhaustion may seem just that—exhaustion of time, energy, spirit, and resources. An individual, firm, or other entity may be required to deal with the issue, and perhaps an appeal, at the agency level in what may appear to be a futile effort at winning justice.

Not surprisingly, exhaustion is porous. The courts can often relieve parties of it at their discretion. This is most likely when (1) the issue is purely legal, with no factual dispute; (2) the agency lacks the wherewithal to provide the remedy sought or any meaningful one; (3) the agency has clearly exceeded or misused its authority; (4) violations of constitutional procedural due process inhere in the agency's procedures; (5) the agency is responsible for unreasonable delays; or (6) the only step not exhausted in the agency's process is an optional one (Warren 1996, 439–440; Gellhorn and Levin 1997, 372–373).

Finality.   Finality concerns are similar to those for exhaustion. The courts and agencies have strong interests in avoiding premature judicial review. The APA provides for review of "final agency action" but does not define the phrase (sec. 704). When an agency issues a final rule or order, finality is clear enough. But what if it makes a policy decision that appears final but is not communicated as such? For instance, an agency might consider regulating something but ultimately decide not to do so without making any formal announcement. Under some circumstances, such inaction can be construed as final. Alternatively, an agency may take an interim or temporary step that burdens some as it proceeds toward its final action. Challenging such preliminary action may not be barred by the finality principle. An agency may also offer an interim step that is insufficient to prevent its action from being considered final. For example, in *Sackett v. Environmental Protection Agency* (2012), the Sacketts faced fines of $75,000 per day for not obeying an Environmental Protection Agency (EPA) compliance order based on alleged violations of the Clean Water Act, which they disputed. The EPA denied them a hearing, though the compliance order did invite them to "'engage in informal discussion of the terms and requirements' of the order with the EPA and to inform the agency of 'any allegations [t]herein which [they] believe[d] to be inaccurate.'" Notwithstanding this invitation, the Supreme Court held that the EPA's action was final and subject to judicial review under the APA. It noted that the invitation "confers no entitlement to further agency review. The mere possibility that an agency might reconsider in light of 'informal discussion' and invited contentions of inaccuracy does not suffice to make an otherwise final agency action nonfinal" (*Sackett v. Environmental Protection Agency* 2012, 1372). Perhaps the best generalization is that when finality is unclear, judicial analysis will be highly fact specific (Gellhorn and Levin 1997, 378).

Deference to State Courts.   Federal judicial deference to state courts is embodied in two main doctrines. First, under the doctrine of adequate and independent state grounds, the US Supreme Court will not exercise jurisdiction over a case appealed from a state supreme court (or its equivalent) if the state court was able to decide it on the basis of state law, independently of whatever federal question may have been involved. For example, a state may afford individuals greater civil rights and liberties in some contexts than they would have under the US Constitution or federal statutes. In such circumstances, a state court ruling in favor of an individual could be based on adequate and independent state grounds, without reference to the parallel federal provisions. Second, under the doctrine of abstention, the federal courts will temporarily abstain from hearing a constitutional claim when the case turns on an unsettled matter of state law. The doctrine also limits federal court involvement in state criminal proceedings and, sometimes, in administrative and civil proceedings when there is an important state interest at stake. It does not prevent a state losing in its own highest court from appealing to the US Supreme Court (e.g., *Delaware v. Prouse* 1979; *New Jersey v. T.L.O.* 1985).

The Scope of Judicial Review

The *scope* of judicial review refers to the depth of the courts' probe of administrative action. It establishes the extent of judicial deference to administrators' expertise and their need for flexibility. It also defines the quality of the partnership between courts and agencies. The more deferential judges are, the greater discretion agencies have in formulating and implementing their policies and programs. A limited scope of review discourages litigation and reduces the judiciary's role in public administration.

Administrative law scholars are divided on the question of how deeply the courts should review various administrative activities. At times, the discussion was posed in terms of whether the courts should be passive or active in reviewing agencies' actions. Passive judges were seen as essentially conservative, adhering to the letter of the Constitution's text and the framers' original intent. Activist judges were considered to be results oriented in their jurisprudence—that is, prone to legal interpretation that promoted their own policy preferences (which were usually liberal). However, the Rehnquist Court (1986–2005) drastically altered the terms of the debate. Its Commerce Clause and Tenth and Eleventh Amendment decisions clearly demonstrated that a court can be both activist and politically conservative at once (see Chapter 2). Regardless of the judiciary's political leanings, today the federal courts as a whole are far more active in reviewing administrative action than in the 1950s and 1960s. Arguments against judicial involvement (i.e., meddling) in administration may now be more common in law review articles than in court decisions (see Warren 1996, 421–426; Tushnet 2004).

To some extent, the debate over passive versus active jurisprudence obscured the reality that the scope of review has always been variable. As discussed in Chapter 2, in constitutional law cases the scope of review varies from strict scrutiny to reasonableness to rational basis analysis depending on the specific rights and legal questions involved. It also varies in administrative law, though the terminology is different. Scrutiny is frequently conceived in terms of "looks," ranging from a most probing "hard look" through a "soft" one to essentially "no look"[1] at all. These "looks" are really degrees of deference to the agencies. Which look the courts apply is guided by the APA's language, but the matter also depends heavily on judicial doctrines, practices, and discretion. It is best to think of the relationship between the scope of review and specific administrative activities as one of tendencies rather than inflexible rules. In a litigious nation with one-twentieth of the world's population and two-thirds of its lawyers, there are ample exceptions (Warren 1996, 420).

Agency Rules. The substance of agency rules and their underlying logic tend to receive a hard look. Ever since the 1970s, the courts have shown strong interest in evaluating the legal basis and rationale for challenged rules. All rules must be in accordance with constitutional and statutory law. Under the APA, final rules made through formal rulemaking must be supported by "substantial evidence" (sec. 706[2][E]). Although this may sound like a high threshold, "substantial" basically means "reasonable" in this context (Warren 2011, 398–400). Rules produced by informal rulemaking are subject to review under a standard requiring that they not be "arbitrary, capricious, an abuse of discretion, or otherwise not in accordance with law" (sec. 706[2][A]). In nuance, this standard is weaker. But the difference may be no greater than saying formally made rules must be supported by reasonable evidence, whereas informally promulgated rules must not be unreasonable. Arcane distinctions between the substantial evidence and arbitrary and capricious tests notwithstanding, in practice the federal courts are apt to apply a hard look to substantive rules. This is well illustrated by two Supreme Court decisions that helped define the hard look.

Industrial Union Department, AFL-CIO v. American Petroleum Institute (1980) involved Occupational Safety and Health Administration (OSHA) standards for reducing benzene from ten parts per million to one part per

---

1. This is the author's term.

million in the ambient atmosphere in a number of industries. The Occupational Safety and Health Act of 1970 directs OSHA to "set the standard [for toxic materials or harmful physical agents] which most adequately assures, to the extent feasible, on the basis of the best available evidence, that no employee will suffer material impairment of health or functional capacity." OSHA's policy was to assume that carcinogens like benzene had no safe limit and to regulate accordingly. It established the benzene standard after notice and comment, along with public hearings. There is no doubt that inhaling benzene can do awful damage to one's health. And there was also no doubt that the standard was expensive. The first-year costs per employee would be $82,000 in the petroleum industry, $39,675 in petrochemicals, and $1,390 in manufacturing rubber.

Using a hard look, the court of appeals held that the standard was invalid because it was not supported by the administrative record. The court "concluded that OSHA had exceeded its standard-setting authority because it had not been shown that the 1 ppm [part per million] exposure limit was 'reasonably necessary or appropriate to provide safe and healthful employment' . . . and that [the Occupational Safety and Health Act] did not give OSHA the unbridled discretion to adopt standards designed to create absolutely risk-free workplaces regardless of cost."

The Supreme Court was badly splintered. Five justices voted to affirm the lower court's invalidation of the rule. Three argued that "the [statutory] burden was on OSHA to show, on the basis of substantial evidence, that it is at least more likely than not that long-term exposure to 10 ppm of benzene presents a significant risk of material health impairment. Here, OSHA did not even attempt to carry such burden of proof." One justice believed that under the act OSHA was obliged to explain "the method by which it determined that the benefits justified the costs and their economic effects." Justice William Rehnquist would have invalidated the standard on the basis that the section of the act involved was an unconstitutional delegation of legislative authority. In his view, it provided a "legislative mirage" rather than a constitutionally required "intelligible principle" to guide the agency and reviewing court. He also argued that Congress, not OSHA, should make the important social policy choice of what is feasible in terms of costs and benefits.

Four justices dissented. They contended that review of OSHA standards should be more deferential than the plurality's opinion claimed because (1) judges are not trained or experienced in the highly complex technical issues linking toxic substances to diseases, (2) the factual issues in making such links sometimes defy definitive resolution, and (3) "the ultimate decision must necessarily be based on considerations of policy as well as empirically verifiable facts," which is a job for an agency rather than a court. These are good reasons to give a softer look. The fact that they did not convince the other five justices suggested that the hard look approach, taken primarily by the lower courts in the late 1960s and 1970s, had become dominant (*Industrial Union Department, AFL-CIO v. American Petroleum Institute* 1980, 607–610, 681, 685–686, 705–706).

If there had been any doubt about the ascendance of the hard look, it was dispelled three years later in *Motor Vehicle Manufacturers Association of the United States, Inc. v. State Farm Mutual Automobile Insurance Co.* (1983). The case concerned the "complex and convoluted history" of the National Highway Traffic Safety Administration's (NHTSA) rules regarding safety restraints in automobiles. Between 1967 and 1982, the agency issued approximately sixty rulemaking notices leading to the imposing, amending, rescinding, reimposing, and re-rescinding of various requirements. At issue was the agency's decision to rescind a passive restraint rule requiring automobiles to be equipped with either automatic seatbelts or air bags. When NHTSA adopted the rule, it assumed automatic seatbelts would be installed in 40 percent of new cars and airbags in the other 60 percent. By 1981, it was clear that 99 percent of new cars would have automatic seatbelts and only 1 percent would be equipped with airbags. Armed with this new information, the agency viewed the passive restraint rule as pointless. Conventional seatbelts were already standard equipment, and the large number of recalcitrant drivers and passengers who refused to buckle them would simply detach the automatic ones.

The Supreme Court ruled that the rescission was subject to the same arbitrary and capricious standard of review as would be used in dealing with a new rule. It then applied a hard look and concluded that NHTSA could not pass the test. First, the agency was mixing its apples and oranges: "The . . . most obvious reason for finding the rescission arbitrary and capricious is that NHTSA apparently gave no consideration whatever to modifying the Standard to require that air bag technology be utilized." Second, "the agency's explanation for rescission of the passive restraint requirement is not sufficient to enable us to conclude that the rescission was the product of reasoned decisionmaking." In sum, "the scope of review under the 'arbitrary and capricious' standard is narrow and a court is not to substitute its judgment for that of the agency. Nevertheless, the agency must examine the relevant data and articulate a satisfactory explanation for its action. . . . In reviewing that explanation, we must 'consider whether the decision was based on a consideration of the relevant factors and whether there has been a clear error of judgment'" (*Motor Vehicle Manufacturers Association of the United States, Inc. v. State Farm Mutual Automobile Insurance Co.* 1983, 43, 46, 52).

In *Federal Communications Commission v. Fox Television Stations* the Supreme Court clarified the application of *Motor Vehicle Manufacturers* and the hard look to agency policy changes:

> To be sure, the requirement that an agency provide reasoned explanation for its action would ordinarily demand that it display awareness that it *is* changing position. An agency may not, for example, depart from a prior policy *sub silentio* or simply disregard rules that are still on the books. . . . And of course the agency must show that there are good reasons for the new policy. But it need not demonstrate to a court's satisfaction that the reasons for the new policy are *better* than the reasons for the old one; it suffices that the new policy is permissible under the statute, that there are good reasons for it, and that the agency *believes* it to be better, which the conscious change of course adequately indicates. This means that the agency need not always provide a more detailed justification than what would suffice for a new policy created on a blank slate. Sometimes it must—when, for example, its new policy rests upon factual findings that contradict those which underlay its prior policy; or when its prior policy has engendered serious reliance interests that must be taken into account. . . . It would be arbitrary or capricious to ignore such matters. In such cases it is not that further justification is demanded by the mere fact of policy change; but that a reasoned explanation is needed for disregarding facts and circumstances that underlay or were engendered by the prior policy. (2009, 515–516 [emphasis in the original])

In practice, under some circumstances this construction may lead to a "hard look lite," that is, a somewhat less probing judicial review of agency policy changes.

FOIA Requests. Denials of freedom of information requests receive a hard look. Under the Freedom of Information Act (1966, as amended), the agency has the burden of persuasion in showing that an exemption or other legal provision permits or requires it to withhold requested information. In deciding cases, courts should not be deferential to the agency.

Rulemaking Procedures. Rulemaking procedures receive a soft look insofar as they meet the minimum APA or other applicable statutory requirements. This was established in *Vermont Yankee Nuclear Power Corp. v. Natural*

Resources Defense Council, Inc. (1978). After the Atomic Energy Commission (AEC), which was succeeded by the Nuclear Regulatory Commission in 1975, issued a license to Vermont Yankee and a permit to Consumers Power Company to operate and construct nuclear power plants, the Court of Appeals for the District of Columbia Circuit imposed more substantial rulemaking procedures ("hybrid rulemaking") on the agency to consider the environmental impacts potentially associated with nuclear waste and to examine conservation as an alternative to the generation of electricity. On review, the Supreme Court unanimously upheld the AEC, noting that informal rulemaking does not require the agency to hold hearings and that, in drafting the APA, "Congress intended that the discretion of the *agencies* and not that of the courts be exercised in determining when extra procedural devices should be employed."

The Supreme Court concluded that a soft look was necessary for three reasons. First, "if courts continually review agency proceedings to determine whether the agency employed procedures which were, in the court's opinion, perfectly tailored to reach what the court perceives to be the 'best' or 'correct' result, judicial review would be totally unpredictable." In self-defense, the agencies would have to hold full formal hearings, despite the fact that Congress deliberately avoided making them the only vehicle for rulemaking.

Second, the lower court "reviewed the agency's choice of procedures on the basis of the record actually produced at the hearing . . . and not on the basis of the information available to the agency when it made the decision to structure the proceedings in a certain way." Allowing hindsight to determine what agencies might have done better would, again, virtually compel them "to conduct all rulemaking proceedings with the full panoply of procedural devices normally associated only with adjudicatory hearings."

Third, "and perhaps most importantly" in terms of the soft look, the lower court's decision "fundamentally misconceives the nature of the standard for judicial review of an agency rule." In informal rulemaking, the adequacy of the record depends on whether the agency has followed the APA or other relevant statutes, not on how much opportunity is given to interested parties to participate in the proceedings (*Vermont Yankee Nuclear Power Corp. v. Natural Resources Defense Council, Inc.* 1978, 546–547; Justices Harry Blackmun and Lewis Powell did not participate).

Agencies' Statutory Interpretations. An agency's reasoned interpretation of the statutes it administers also receives a soft look. *Chevron U.S.A., Inc. v. Natural Resources Defense Council, Inc.* (1984) tested the EPA's authority to define "stationary sources" of air pollution in two very different ways in different programs and also differently in the same program at different times. One definition was that such sources could be individual machines or pieces of equipment; the other was that they were entire plants or industrial groupings. The Supreme Court's landmark decision framed the application of a soft look for statutory interpretation as follows: (1) if Congress has directly spoken to the precise issue and its intent is clear, the agency has to implement the statute accordingly; (2) if the court determines that Congress has not clearly addressed the issue, then "the question for the court is whether the agency's [interpretation] is based on a permissible construction of the statute"; and (3) the agency's statutory interpretations will be permissible "unless they are arbitrary, capricious, or manifestly contrary to the statute." In short, the courts should be deferential to agencies' statutory interpretation. They should also recognize that "an initial agency interpretation is not instantly carved in stone" but rather is flexible and subject to reasonable change. Two different definitions of the same two words in a single statute are permissible as long as both definitions are reasonable (*Chevron U.S.A., Inc. v. Natural Resources Defense Council, Inc.* 1984, 843, 844, 863).

Chevron provides the agencies with great flexibility in defining the terms of vague delegations of legislative authority. However, the Supreme Court applied an important caveat in *United States v. Mead Corp.* (2001). *Chevron* deference applies when "Congress delegated authority to the agency generally to make rules carrying the force of law, and . . . the agency interpretation claiming deference was promulgated in the exercise of that authority." But where an agency issues a number of ruling letters that do not have the force of law, such as a Customs Service classification of day planners as dutiable diaries (as in *Mead*), weaker deference is granted to its statutory interpretation (*United States v. Mead Corp.* 2001, 2166). This is called *Skidmore* deference, which treats the agency's action with respect or courtesy but requires a harder look than under *Chevron* (*Skidmore v. Swift & Co.* 1944).

Although the extent to which federal courts actually adhere to "*Chevron* deference" is debatable, the Supreme Court extended it to agencies' statutory interpretation of the scope of their authority (i.e., jurisdiction) in *City of Arlington, Texas v. Federal Communications Commission* (2013) (Warren 2011, 375–377). In the Court's view, "judges should not waste their time in the mental acrobatics needed to decide whether an agency's interpretation of a statutory provision is 'jurisdictional' or 'nonjurisdictional'":

Those who assert that applying *Chevron* to "jurisdictional" interpretations "leaves the fox in charge of the henhouse" overlook the reality that a separate category of "jurisdictional" interpretations does not exist. The fox-in-the-henhouse syndrome is to be avoided not by establishing an arbitrary and undefinable category of agency decisionmaking that is accorded no deference, but by taking seriously, and applying rigorously, in all cases, statutory limits on agencies' authority. Where Congress has established a clear line, the agency cannot go beyond it; and where Congress has established an ambiguous line, the agency can go no further than the ambiguity will fairly allow. But in rigorously applying the latter rule, a court need not pause to puzzle over whether the interpretive question presented is "jurisdictional." If "the agency's answer is based on a permissible construction of the statute," that is the end of the matter. (*City of Arlington, Texas v. Federal Communications Commission* 2013, 1870, 1874–1875)

Agency Nonenforcement. An agency's discretion not to undertake an enforcement action, within constitutional and statutory limits, essentially receives no look—or at least there is a very strong presumption against judicial review under the APA. In *Heckler v. Chaney* (1985), death row prisoners challenged the FDA's failure either to approve the drugs used in lethal injection as "'safe and effective' for human execution" or to prohibit their use for that purpose.

The Supreme Court noted that under the APA judicial review is not available when another statute precludes it or if the agency action "is committed to agency discretion by law" (sec. 701[a][1][2]). The Court reasoned that these provisions were based on sound jurisprudential policy. Decisions not to take enforcement steps are generally unsuitable for judicial review for several reasons, as stated in *Heckler v. Chaney*:

> First, an agency decision not to enforce often involves a complicated balancing of a number of factors which are peculiarly within its expertise. Thus, the agency must not only assess whether a violation has occurred, but whether agency resources are best spent on this violation or another, whether the agency is likely to succeed if it acts, whether the particular enforcement action requested best fits the agency's overall policies, and, indeed, whether the agency has enough resources to undertake the action at all. An agency generally cannot act against each technical violation of the statute it is charged with enforcing. The agency is far better equipped than the courts to deal with the many variables involved in the proper ordering of its priorities. Similar concerns animate the principles of administrative law that courts generally will defer to an agency's construction of the statute it is charged with implementing, and to the procedures it adopts for implementing that statute. . . .
>
> In addition to these administrative concerns, we note that when an agency refuses to act it generally does not exercise its *coercive* power over

an individual's liberty or property rights, and thus does not infringe upon areas that courts are often called upon to protect. Similarly, when an agency *does* act to enforce, that action itself provides a focus for judicial review, inasmuch as the agency must have exercised its power in some manner.

The Court went on to compare agency decisions not to enforce to those of prosecutors, whose discretion not to seek indictment is regarded as part of the executive's constitutional responsibility to "take Care that the Laws be faithfully executed."

The Court's sweeping language triggered a concurring opinion by Justice William Brennan, who cautioned that the presumption of nonreviewability did not apply where an agency (1) claims that it lacks enforcement authority, (2) "engages in a pattern of nonenforcement of clear statutory language," (3) refuses "to enforce a regulation lawfully promulgated and still in effect," and (4) violates constitutional rights through its nonenforcement (*Heckler v. Chaney* 1985, 831–832, 839).

In *Massachusetts v. Environmental Protection Agency* (2007), the Supreme Court differentiated between nonenforcement in situations like *Heckler v. Chaney* and those in which an agency is petitioned by a proper party to engage in rulemaking and, in declining to do so, fails to follow a statutory requirement. The Court explained,

> There are key differences between a denial of a petition for rulemaking and an agency's decision not to initiate an enforcement action. . . . In contrast to nonenforcement decisions, agency refusals to initiate rulemaking "are less frequent, more apt to involve legal as opposed to factual analysis, and subject to special formalities, including a public explanation." . . . They moreover arise out of denials of petitions for rulemaking which (at least in the circumstances here) the affected party had an undoubted procedural right to file in the first instance. Refusals to promulgate rules are thus susceptible to judicial review, though such review is "extremely limited" and "highly deferential."

The Court went on to hold that "under the clear terms of the Clean Air Act, EPA can avoid taking further action only if it determines that greenhouse gases do not contribute to climate change or if it provides some reasonable explanation as to why it cannot or will not exercise its discretion to determine whether they do." Otherwise the EPA's inaction violates the APA's stricture against action that is "arbitrary, capricious, . . . or . . . not in accordance with law" (*Massachusetts v. Environmental Protection Agency* 2007, 527, 533, 534).

To date the Court's decision in *Massachusetts v. Environmental Protection Agency* does not appear to threaten the general no look approach to nonenforcement. Rather it seems to carve out a narrow exception or perhaps a deviation from it.

Discretionary Actions. By contrast, discretionary actions on substantial matters tend to receive a hard look. These are a residual catchall of agency activities, other than nonenforcement, that are not precluded from judicial review by the APA or another statute and do not fall into some regulated category of agency action, such as rulemaking, adjudication, or freedom of information. In *Citizens to Preserve Overton Park, Inc. v. Volpe* (1971), the Supreme Court held that judicially reviewable administrative discretion should be assessed under a somewhat generalized APA standard, which requires "the reviewing court to engage in a substantial inquiry." This includes attention to whether (1) the administrator acted within the scope of his or her authority, (2) the decision was within the range of options allowed by the applicable statutes, (3) the relevant factors were considered, (4) the administrator made "a clear error of judgment," and (5) the necessary procedures were followed. None of this was particularly new, but more followed.

Overton Park dealt with federal highway statutes instructing the secretary of the Department of Transportation to withhold approval of highway projects using land in public parks, recreation areas, wildlife and waterfowl refuges, or historic sites unless there was "no feasible and prudent alternative." The statutory provisions also required minimizing the harm to such areas when roads were built through them. Transportation Secretary John Volpe approved a six-lane interstate highway project that would have severed Overton Park, a 342-acre city park in Memphis, Tennessee.

Volpe provided no formal statement of factual findings indicating why there was no feasible and prudent alternative or why the design could not be changed to reduce harm to the park. Instead, he offered "'post hoc' rationalizations." These did not constitute a whole record—or even an adequate record—for review. The Supreme Court remanded the case to the district court for full review of the administrative record on which Volpe had made his decision. It noted that the lower court might require Volpe and other officials who participated in the decision to explain their action (*Citizens to Preserve Overton Park, Inc. v. Volpe* 1971, 411, 415–416, 419).

The district court eventually held that Volpe either never made an analysis of alternative routes or made it incorrectly. The case was then remanded back to Volpe for a new decision based on the statutory criteria. In the end, Volpe found that Interstate 40 could not legally be built through Overton

Park. The effect of *Overton Park* is to prompt agencies to keep formal records explaining their discretionary actions, especially if they are likely to provoke significant litigation. The case also encouraged agencies to keep more copious records when engaging in informal rulemaking.

Adjudication. Formal adjudication is subject to substantial evidence review and can also be challenged for procedural irregularity. The APA specifically provides that an agency's adjudicatory decision may be reversed if it is "unwarranted by the facts to the extent that the facts are subject to trial de novo [anew] by the reviewing court" (sec. 706[2][F]). These provisions encourage a hard look. The reviewing court will consider the whole record to determine whether the facts, in the context of the governing statutes or rules, reasonably support the agency's decision. This approach has been a staple of federal administrative law at least since 1951, when the Supreme Court outlined it in *Universal Camera Corp. v. National Labor Relations Board.*

Legislative Review of Administration

Judicial review of public administration in the United States is episodic. It takes place in distinct cases. Individual judicial decisions eventually aggregate into the legal and constitutional doctrines that govern administrative practice. Legislative review is more continuous and diffuse. It takes place whenever a legislature is in session and deals with the entire range of administrative concerns—budgets, human resources, implementation, organizational design, use of technology, strategic planning, policy choices, reporting, and even the architecture and location of agency buildings, offices, and other facilities.

At the federal level, the constitutional basis for congressional review of administrative activity is crystal clear. The agencies implement legislative mandates with congressionally appropriated funds, often exercising delegated legislative authority. Therefore, Congress has a legitimate role in ensuring that agency actions are in keeping with legislative intent. It is well established that "keeping a watchful eye on the administration of the laws it has enacted is [an] important function of our National Legislature" (La Follette 1946, 45). The more difficult issue is how Congress can exercise oversight of the agencies without undue micromanagement, causing needless inefficiency, or interfering with principled administrative decision-making. The following are the main mechanisms for congressional review of federal administration.

Oversight by Committees and Subcommittees

The Legislative Reorganization Act of 1946 charged the standing commit-tees in the House of Representatives and Senate with exercising "continu-ous watchfulness" of the administrative execution of the laws under their jurisdictions (sec. 136). In 1970, this language was strengthened to require the committees to "review and study" agency implementation "on a con-tinuing basis" (Legislative Reorganization Act 1970, sec. 118). This mandate is broad enough to support informal contacts between committee members or their staffs and agency personnel as well as formal legislative hearings on administrative performance.

A leading empirical study of committee review of agency activity yielded the following conclusions: (1) communication levels between congressio-nal staff and administrators is "very extensive"; (2) slightly over half the committees engage in active or intermediate monitoring of the agencies, the remainder being reactive; (3) "the nature of congressional oversight is rather impressive"; and (4) "congressional oversight probably improves policy at the margins" (Aberbach 1990, 85, 95, 198). Additionally, the study found that almost all the committees had intermediately or well-developed networks for obtaining information from and about the agencies (Aber-bach 1990, 88).

Reporting Requirements

Congressional review of administration relies on agency reports, often heavily, as Vice President Al Gore's National Performance Review made clear in 1993:

> Today the annual calendar is jammed with report deadlines. On August 31 of each year, the Chief Financial Officers (CFO) Act requires that agen-cies file a 5-year financial plan and a CFO annual report. On September 1, budget exhibits for financial management activities and high risk ar-eas are due. November 30, IG [inspector general] reports are expected, along with reports required by the Prompt Payment Act. On January 31, reports under the Federal Civil Penalties Inflation Report Adjustment Act of 1990 come due. On March 31, financial statements are due, and on May 1 annual single-audit reports must be filed. On May 31 another round of IG reports are due. At the end of July and December, "high risk" reports are filed. On August 31, it all begins again. And these are just major reports!

> In fiscal year 1993, Congress required executive branch agencies to pre-
> pare 5,348 reports. (Gore 1993, 34)

In fact there are so many required reports, that in the Government Performance and Results Act Modernization Act of 2010 (GPRA Modernization Act), Congress called on the agencies to "compile a list that identifies all plans and reports the agency produces for Congress, in accordance with statutory requirements or as directed in congressional reports" and, in consultation with appropriate congressional committees to identify those that are "outdated or duplicative." The act required that in the first year of implementation at least 10 percent of all required plans and reports be identified as outdated or duplicative (sec. 11[b][a] [1–3][b][1]).

One can easily conclude from the GPRA Modernization Act that Congress itself believes that the agency reporting it requires is somewhat dysfunctional. However, chances are that even material that goes unread gets a good agency write. Just knowing that such reports must be filed may influence agency behavior.

Research, Evaluation, Audit, and Investigation

Congressional review is assisted by a number of legislative agencies and functionaries. The Government Accountability Office (GAO), Congressional Research Service (CRS), and Congressional Budget Office (CBO) all play a role in assessing agency performance. In particular, the GAO engages in investigations, broad program reviews, and evaluations of administrative activity. The CRS supplies Congress with policy and legal analyses, which often bear upon federal administration. The CBO is mainly concerned with federal budget matters, but it also undertakes program analyses of federal spending at the request of congressional committees.

In addition, Congress learns about administration from the inspectors general (IGs) and chief financial officers within the agencies. The IGs are sometimes considered "congressional 'moles,'" or the eyes and ears of Congress, within the agencies (Moore and Gates 1986, 10; Gore 1993, 31). They are employed by the agencies to audit, investigate, and report maladministration both to Congress and the agency heads. The CFOs oversee the financial management of administrative operations. Their annual reports are an invaluable source of financial information.

Sunset Legislation

Congressional and state legislation is sometimes subject to sunset provisions. These specify that the programs or administrative operations a law authorizes will terminate after a number of years—often five—unless reauthorized by statute. Such provisions are intended to force legislatures periodically to engage in probing evaluations of the administrative implementation and efficacy of the laws they enact. Sunsetting by Congress guards against the continuation of programs and agencies that have outlived their usefulness. It seeks to reverse the effect of legislative inertia by attaching specific consequences to inaction. The threat of sunset also places agencies on notice that inadequate performance may lead to the demise of the agency itself or some of its programs.

Although once viewed as a promising approach to legislative review of public administrative operations, in practice sunset legislation has had mixed results. In a sense, sunset laws are redundant. Congress and the state legislatures evaluate agencies and programs in conjunction with passing budgets, generally on an annual or biennial basis. Budget hearings ought to reveal what is not working as intended. Consequently, requiring the reauthorization of agencies and their programs at fixed times, even when there is no sign of trouble, may involve an unnecessary investment of legislative effort and expense. Even when sunset provisions prompt legislative review of administrative operations that usually go largely unnoticed, they may not be cost-effective. In any case, most programs under sunset legislation are apparently reauthorized, and several states have lost interest in this form of legislative review (Warren 2011, 140–142).

Casework

Casework, or constituency service, is another means of congressional review, albeit a haphazard one. It runs the gamut from helping constituents arrange visits to Washington, DC, to intervening in administrative processes to resolve their problems with federal agencies. Through their staff, senators and representatives routinely send letters to the agencies on behalf of constituents. The agencies generally refer to these as "congressionals" and expedite attention to the matters involved. Casework is taxing on the congressional offices, but the public expects it, members of Congress may solicit it, and it helps members get reelected. The volume is huge. In 1984, it exceeded 5,000 to 10,000 requests per year in many congressional offices—a number that has no doubt grown exponentially with the increasing popularity and ease of e-mail (Vogler 1988, 219).

Much casework has no significant impact on federal administration, but sometimes it prompts agencies to recognize "problems occurring at the middle and lower levels of the bureaucracy . . . and even search for patterns behind the complaints" (Dodd and Schott 1979, 269). It may also reveal such ineptitude, abuse, or other ills that Congress will revamp an agency's authority, organization, processes, or leadership. Casework helped alert Congress to the abuses and poor administration addressed by the Taxpayer Bill of Rights legislation in 1986 and the Internal Revenue Service Restructuring and Reform Act of 1998 (Burnham 1989, 305; Roth and Nixon 1999).

Strategic Planning and Performance Reports

The Government Performance and Results Act of 1993 was a congressional initiative aimed at substantially upgrading legislative review. It was premised partly on the finding that "congressional policymaking, spending decisions and program oversight are seriously handicapped by insufficient attention to [administrative] program performance and results" (sec. 2[a][3]). It was superseded by the GPRA Modernization Act, which coordinates agency strategic planning with the presidential term of office and places a heavy emphasis on establishing performance goals and performance reporting. The act specifically requires agencies to consult with Congress "when developing or making adjustments to a strategic plan" (sec. 306[d]). It makes agency chief operating officers responsible for "improving . . . management and performance" and provides for the position of "performance improvement officer" within the agencies (sec. 8[a–b]; sec. 9[a][1–2]). Whether these officers will be forward-looking in terms of innovation and the adoption of best practices and new technologies or highly focused on meeting strategic goals and performance reporting is an open question (Rosenbloom 2013b).

The GPRA Modernization Act's future effectiveness is uncertain, though potentially it remains a powerful tool for congressional review and direction of the agencies. Most notably, Congress's participation in the development of agency strategic plans can strengthen administrative understanding of legislative intent and improve implementation.

Congressional Review Act

Title II of the Small Business Regulatory Enforcement Fairness Act of 1996 includes a subtitle known as the Congressional Review Act. It requires the agencies to submit all covered final or interim rules to Congress and the GAO before they can take effect. Coverage extends to interpretive and procedural rules but excludes rules on a variety of subjects and those exempted from notice and comment for good cause under APA provisions.

The act provides for two levels of review, depending on whether a rule is *major* or *ordinary*. Major rules are those expected to have an annual economic impact of at least $100 million or to have a substantial effect on key economic concerns such as costs, prices, employment, and productivity. With some exceptions, major rules are subject to a sixty-day review period in Congress during which it can pass a joint resolution of disapproval. The resolution is subject to presidential veto and legislative override. Rules can be published simultaneously in the *Federal Register* and, if not disapproved, take effect as indicated therein.

Ordinary rules are also subject to congressional disapproval but not the sixty-day review period. They can be published as final after being submitted to Congress and the GAO. No rule that is disapproved can be reissued in identical or similar form unless the agency receives specific statutory authorization to do so. The act specifically provides that congressional failure to disapprove a rule should not be taken by the courts or agencies as tacitly inferring any legislative intent.

Legislative review of agency rules is not a new idea. It was discussed in the 1940s in connection with drafting the APA. Michigan adopted it in 1944, and by 1970 Kansas, Nebraska, Virginia, and Wisconsin had followed suit (US Senate 1970, 1293). At least twenty-two states currently provide for review of rules by legislative committees of one kind or another. Joint committees are frequently used, as in Alabama, Illinois, Kansas, Maryland, Michigan, Ohio, Vermont, Washington, and Wisconsin (Bonfield 1986, 482–483; Bonfield 1993, 184–185). Although some forty resolutions of disapproval have been introduced in Congress, only one—the OSHA ergonomics rule in 2001—has been disapproved (Dewar 2001; US GAO, n.d.). The fact that OSHA had taken about a decade or so to write the rule suggests that agencies can be blindsided by political change unless they remain responsive to key committee members in Congress. Past legislative intent will not bind current congressional review.

Conclusion: Checks, Balances, and Federal Administration

During debate on an administrative law bill in 1940, a senator rose to contend that "the bureaucrats are drunk with power" and "believe that their ipse dixit [say-so] should settle all questions" (US Congress 1940, 7176; Senator Henry Ashurst [D-AZ]). Times have changed! Today's administrators are more apt to be frustrated by a lack of power and multiplicity of challenges to their expertise. Judicial and legislative review have brought a substantial measure of checks and balances to bear on federal administrative processes. Although this encumbers administration, the expansion of both types of review was fully predictable. US constitutional government has been likened to "a machine that would go of itself," and as early as 1939, when the full-fledged administrative state was new, it was clear that "under our system of divided powers, the executive branch of the national government is not exclusively controlled by the President, by the Congress, or by the courts. All three have a hand in controlling it, each from a different angle and each in a different way" (Kamen 1987; Meriam 1939, 131). It just took the judicial and legislative branches time to catch up with the strong "imperial presidency" that developed out of the New Deal, World War II, and the Cold War (Schlesinger 1973). Some criticize judicial and congressional review for gridlocking administration. Others see it as part of the normal messiness of the constitutional separation of powers. Almost everybody agrees that when the constitutional machine moves significantly in one direction or another, administrative law is sure to follow.

Additional Reading

Carp, Robert, Ronald Stidham, and Kenneth Manning. *Judicial Process in America*. 8th ed. Washington, DC: CQ Press, 2011.

Discussion Questions

1. Does the application of the "hard look" and "soft look" as described in the chapter seem arbitrary or sensible to you? Why?

2. In *Massachusetts v. Environmental Protection Agency*, the Supreme Court required the EPA to take action to comply with the Clean Air Act. Is this a proper role for the courts, or should forcing action be left to Congress, which delegated its legislative authority to the EPA under the act and has control over the agency's authority and budget? The EPA, like the FDA, is headed by a presidential appointee. Should the presidential administration have unbridled discretion not to enforce laws? Is nonenforcement essentially a "political question" even though the Supreme Court did not treat it as one?

3. Congress appears to have ample constitutional authority and means to oversee federal administration; yet the Government Performance and Results Act of 1993 and GPRA Modernization Act suggest that it is not satisfied with agency performance. If you were called upon to make recommendations to Congress for exercising better oversight and stronger influence over the agencies, what would you suggest?

7

Staying Current

This book has described and analyzed the core premises, processes, and principles of administrative law in the United States, mostly with respect to the federal level. It should continue to have a long shelf life. The Administrative Procedure Act (APA) of 1946 still provides the federal government's basic administrative law framework. It has been able to accommodate substantial amendment because its fundamental principles have endured. Congress's key point in enacting it was that public administration should incorporate the democratic-constitutional values of representation, participation, transparency, fairness, accountability, and limited government intrusion on private activity. Major subsequent administrative law initiatives—including negotiated rulemaking, freedom of information, alternative dispute resolution, paperwork reduction, and legislative review—have been intended to advance these values. If folding them into administrative law and practice is sometimes bumpy, it is not because they run counter to the APA's initial purposes—in fact, national security policy aside, it is difficult to think of a single post-1946 administrative law statute that undercuts the APA's intent. Similarly, cases like *Nova Scotia* and *Cinderella*, decided decades ago, remain good law because they are firmly rooted in principles on which the APA is based (*United States v. Nova Scotia Food Products Corp.* 1977; *Cinderella Career and Finishing Schools, Inc. v. Federal Trade Commission* 1970).

Public managers can reasonably expect stability in the larger purposes of administrative law. However, they can also expect change in the particulars. Today, rulemaking, adjudication, transparency, and judicial review are not the same as in 1946. The constitutional law affecting public administration is radically different. How can public managers stay current? There are at least three relatively easy steps and one harder one. The easy ones are to (1) always keep the primary function of American administrative law in mind, (2) frequently consult administrative law publications and websites, and (3) talk to agency colleagues and attorneys about new administrative law developments. The more difficult and expensive step is to have experts conduct periodic administrative law audits to ensure compliance with newer requirements.

The Primary Function of US Administrative Law

In some fields of study, a couple of underlying principles go a long way in organizing thinking, research, and application. In economics, these are supply and demand; in sociology, stratification and mobility. In administrative law, the tension between constitutional contractarianism and public administrative instrumentalism is the defining element. The primary function of administrative law is to funnel constitutional contractarian values into administrative practice in order to harmonize public administration with constitutional democracy. The simple secret of the APA's remarkable durability is that by focusing on procedure rather than substantive policy criteria (e.g., cost-benefit, environmental justice), it acts as such a funnel.

Constitutional Contractarianism

Constitutional contractarianism is based on natural rights theory. Its basic assumptions are that individuals are born with fundamental rights and that they form governments to protect those rights. Rights are not created by government; they preexist it. Government is a mechanism for preventing others from encroaching on our rights and for achieving common purposes. Perhaps nowhere are these principles more succinctly stated than in the Declaration of Independence and the Preamble of the US Constitution.

In the Declaration's famous words, "We hold these Truths to be self-evident, that all Men are created equal, that they are endowed by their Creator with certain unalienable Rights, that among these are Life, Liberty, and the Pursuit of Happiness—That to secure these Rights, Governments are instituted among Men, deriving their just Powers from the Consent of the Governed." The Preamble is a compact between "We the People" that aims, as one of its prime objectives, to "secure the Blessings of Liberty to ourselves and our Posterity."

Contractarianism pervades the Constitution's Bill of Rights. It identifies spheres of personal freedom, such as religion and speech, in which the government may tread only under extraordinary circumstances. It affords a wide variety of protections for persons accused of crimes. The Eighth Amendment's ban on cruel and unusual punishments protects those convicted as well. Here is one court's contractarian interpretation: "Inadequate resources can *never* be an adequate justification for the state's depriving *any* person of his constitutional rights. If the state cannot obtain the resources to detain persons awaiting trial in accordance with minimum constitutional standards, then the state simply will not be permitted to detain such persons" (*Hamilton v. Love* 1971, 1194 [emphasis added]). This sounds radical, but the identical premise is written into the Fifth Amendment's Takings Clause: government can take private property only for "public use" and with "just compensation." If the state is unable to pay for someone's land, then it cannot have it—no matter how beneficial to a community or the nation a highway, bridge, dam, or other piece of infrastructure might be.[1] Contractarian premises that may raise the cost of administration in the process of protecting individual rights are also reflected in the construction of strict scrutiny in constitutional law. As applied to equal protection and substantive rights, strict scrutiny requires government to show a compelling interest for its action and to narrowly tailor the infringement or to make the means of achieving its interest that approach which is least restrictive of those rights (see Chapter 2). Paralleling other contractarian decisions, the Supreme Court has made it clear that "administrative challenges [do] not render constitutional an otherwise problematic system" (*Gratz v. Bollinger* 2003, 275).

Contractarianism in the sense of privileging rights over administrative costs and convenience is incorporated into several aspects of contemporary administrative law. For instance, the absence of standing requirements gives everyone a right to comment on proposed rules in informal rulemaking and to file freedom of information requests. The procedural due process protection provided in adjudications is another example. Executive orders seeking to protect specific values in federal rulemaking, such as environmental justice and vibrant federalism, also embody contractarianism.

Public Administrative Instrumentalism

Public administration in the United States is instrumental, rather than contractarian, in its outlook. It pervasively emphasizes cost-effectiveness in

---

1. Regulatory takings of "noxious" or injurious property are more complicated. See *Lucas v. South Carolina Costal Council* (1992).

achieving results. It sometimes considers benefit-cost ratios, though not necessarily (or perhaps even generally) with full attention to their distribution (Stone 2002). From the field's founding in Woodrow Wilson's day in the 1880s through former vice president Al Gore's National Performance Review in the 1990s and continuing up to the present, the grand public administrative purpose has been to make government "work better and cost less" (Wilson [1887] 1987; Gore 1993). This basic posture is captured in a classic statement on public budgeting that contrasts sharply with the Eighth Amendment interpretation quoted above:

> Budget decisions must be made on the basis of relative values. There is no absolute standard of value. It is not enough to say that an expenditure for a particular purpose is desirable or worthwhile. The results must be more valuable than they would be if the money were used for any other purpose.
>
> . . .
>
> Costs must be judged in relation to the results and the results must be worth their cost in terms of alternative results that are foregone or displaced. (Lewis [1952] 1987, 213–214, 215)

Is the best possible use of public money really to reduce jail crowding? To the contractarian judge, the question is irrelevant; to administrative budgeters and much budget reform since the 1940s, it is central.

It is an uncomfortable reality that public administration's instrumentalism sometimes leads to a remarkably callous disregard for individual rights (Rosenbloom, O'Leary, and Chanin 2010). This is one reason why Congress considered the APA necessary in the 1940s and the federal courts began building constitutional rights into individuals' encounters with public administration in the 1950s. As late as 1993, a federal circuit court of appeals had the following to say in response to a prison warden's manual for search procedures, which literally compelled male guards to sexually abuse female prisoners:

> A bland American civil servant can be as much of a beast as a ferocious concentration camp guard if he does not think about what his actions are doing. . . . Half the cruelties of human history have been inflicted by conscientious servants of the state. The mildest of bureaucrats can be a brute if he does not raise his eyes from his task and consider the human beings on whom he is having an impact. . . .
>
> How did a civilized country and a civilized state like Washington get into this fix where it takes federal judges to tell a responsible state official

to stop his approval of indecency because he is violating the Constitution? (*Jordan v. Gardner* 1993, 1544)

A major function of US administrative law is to ensure that administrators do raise their eyes to the broad contractarian values that underlie constitutional democracy—at the very least when legally or constitutionally required to do so.

The tension between contractarianism and instrumentalism necessarily results in compromises. Instrumental public administration also has roots in the Preamble, which calls for promoting the common defense and general welfare. Cost-effectiveness is not irrelevant to public policy, and cost-benefit is often central to it. The constitutional law regarding procedural due process in administrative contexts recognizes this. The cost of more elaborate procedural protections is balanced with the individual's interest and the relative efficacy of the procedures in place. Consequently, in the metaphor of administrative law as a funnel, the funnel has a filter. Pure contractarianism is not feasible. A government cannot really release potentially dangerous persons indicted for predatory crimes because it cannot afford constitutional jails. Rulemaking by unelected administrators is far less democratic than legislation by elected representatives; administrative evidentiary adjudication affords individuals less protection than judicial trials in terms of procedure, quality of evidence, burden or persuasion of proof, and availability of juries; transparency has exemptions and exceptions.

Administrative law's compromises between contractarianism and instrumentalism cannot satisfy everyone all the time. Some critics will want more contractarianism; others, more instrumentalism. If the debate did not begin with the framing of the Constitution, it certainly goes back that far. In *The Federalist* (1787–1788), James Madison argued for checks and balances as "auxiliary precautions" necessary to ensure that the government would "control itself." Alexander Hamilton maintained that a strong, independent executive was required to prevent "bad execution," for "a government ill-executed, whatever it may be in theory, must be, in practice, a bad government" (Publius 1961 [1787–1788], No. 51, 322; No. 70, 423). In the 1990s, the Hamiltonians favored reinventing government to make it results rather than procedure oriented. They condemned the one-size-fits-all approach that administrative law promotes (Gore 1993, 1–9). Madisonians might have responded in the words of Senator Pat McCarran (D-NV), a leading sponsor of the APA in 1946: "It is sometimes said that . . . the substantive and procedural law applicable to an administrative agency should be prescribed piecemeal, for that agency alone. . . . Diversity merely feeds confusion, which is a great vice in any form of government and operates to defeat the very purposes of good government" (1946, 829).

Since the September 11, 2001, terrorist attacks on the United States, debate over constitutional contractarianism and administrative instrumentalism has focused more sharply on a putative conflict between government transparency and individual personal privacy on one side and national security on the other. Keeping the tension between the contractarian and instrumental outlooks in mind usually makes it easier to understand such controversies and to assimilate change in administrative law.

Periodicals and Websites

For the reader of this book, continuing self-education in administrative law should be straightforward. It ought to be relatively easy to follow and understand any general administrative law discussion, principle, or development. Technical court decisions and statutory provisions may present more difficulty, but few should be impenetrable. The following sources are worth consulting periodically:

1. The American Bar Association's Section of Administrative Law and Regulatory Practice publishes an invaluable quarterly newsletter, *Administrative and Regulatory Law News*. It contains reviews of major court cases and developments in state administrative law as well as discussions of leading law review articles. It is available at http://www.americanbar.org/groups/administrative_law/publications/administrativeandregulatorylawnews.html.

2. The *Administrative Law Review* contains highly readable articles on the entire range of administrative law topics, including frequent analyses of recent developments in specific areas, such as paperwork reduction and sunshine. Careful attention to its contents is an excellent way of staying current. For information, consult http://www.administrativelawreview.org.

3. Federal district and appellate court decisions, the *Federal Register*, the Code of Federal Regulations, the US Code, and a variety of other federal government publications and documents can be accessed at http://www.gpo.gov/fdsys.

4. Periodically consulting the Department of Justice's *Guide to the Freedom of Information Act* is a convenient way of keeping up with the latest Supreme Court decisions and other developments. See http://www.justice.gov/oip/foia_guide09.htm.

5. Supreme Court cases can be accessed at http://www.supremecourt
   .gov/opinions/opinions.aspx. These, in addition to federal appeals
   court and some federal special court decisions as well as state materials, can be found at http://www.findlaw.com/casecode. OpenJu-
   rist (http://openjurist.org) is another site on which Supreme Court
   decisions can be readily accessed. It also has US Courts of Appeals
   decisions from 1790 to the present, as well as the Declaration of Independence and the Constitution.
6. Presidential executive orders issued from 1937 to the present are accessible at the National Archives and Records Administration website at http://www.archives.gov/federal-register/executive-orders/
   disposition.html.
7. The Office of Information and Regulatory Affairs makes "Current
   Regulatory Plan and the Unified Agenda of Regulatory and Deregulatory Actions" available at http://www.reginfo.gov/public/do/
   eAgendaMain.
8. Regulations.gov is a portal for submitting comments on proposed
   federal regulations and viewing final regulations, notices, scientific
   and technical findings, agency guidance, adjudications, comments
   submitted by others, and the *Unified Agenda and Regulatory Plan.* See
   http://www.regulations.gov/#!home.
9. Federal budget information is available from the US Office of Management and Budget (OMB) at http://www.whitehouse.gov/omb.
10. Agency performance plans are available on their individual websites
    and can be found through search engines. An interesting use of OMB
    scorecards for assessing agency performance on Executive Order
    13,514, "Federal Sustainability," is available at http://sustainability
    .performance.gov.

This list only scratches the surface of what is available on the Internet,
which can also be used to access law review and other scholarly articles,
books, commentary, and an amazing amount of information related to administrative law in the United States and abroad. We are getting very close
to the time when the Internet will almost completely replace traditional
law libraries.

Talk Administrative Law Talk

A well-known article titled "Stories Managers Tell: Why They Are as Valid
as Science" noted that "managers first and foremost communicate through

stories that constitute or construct their world" (Hummel 1991, 39). Public managers talk about human resources management, budgeting, organizational design, program evaluation, and other administrative practices. They learn a great deal through such talk. Talking about administrative law will solidify and expand one's understanding and knowledge. Today administrative law is too central to administrative practice to be considered a technical specialty best left to the lawyers. Typically it is public managers, not legal staff, who are called on to integrate administrative law into day-to-day administrative operations. As noted in Chapter 2, they are also the ones who may end up being sued personally for violation of someone's clearly established constitutional or statutory rights.

Administrative Law Audits

The vast judicial intervention in prison administration during the last quarter of the twentieth century spawned "an emerging new specialty in the corrections field, which, according to some proponents of the idea, trains and designates officials to perform 'constitutional audits' of facilities and procedures in order to reduce legal liabilities" (though protecting the prisoners' constitutional rights would be reason enough) (Feeley and Hanson 1990, 26). In 2000, the US Department of Agriculture contracted out for civil rights audits. Administrative law audits can also be of great value. Many agencies lack systematic processes for learning about new court decisions on administrative law and integrating them into their operations. Over time, personnel and other procedural manuals can become dated and standard practices out of sync with the latest legal developments. Even where legal staffs copiously attempt to adjust agency operations to new administrative law requirements, there may be gaps in what reaches frontline personnel. Periodic administrative law audits would systematically focus attention on practices that need updating. They could also serve as an educational tool for agency personnel. Financial audits (instrumental) are common; are administrative law audits (contractarian) less important?

The Next Level

This book aims to equip public managers with the essentials to understand, follow, and integrate administrative law into their daily practice. It also provides a knowledge base for those who want to study administrative law further or dig more deeply into any of its major areas. Several books can take public administrators to the next level. The classic work emphasizing state-level administrative law is Michael Asimow, Arthur Bonfield, and Ronald Levin, *State and Federal Administrative Law* (4th ed., 2013). A good next step for those primarily interested in federal-level law would be Kenneth Warren's encyclopedic *Administrative Law in the Political System* (5th ed., 2011), parts of which have already been listed under "Additional Reading" in Chapters 1 and 4. Kenneth Culp Davis's older but still thought provoking *Administrative Law and Government* (1975) is a classic in the field. Following either of these, one cannot go wrong with Peter Strauss et al.'s massive *Gellhorn and Byse's Administrative Law: Cases and Comments* (11th ed., 2011). Administrative law is a key part of the hard work of modern democracy. One can never learn too much about it.

Discussion Questions

1. Do you think posing a tension between constitutional contractarianism and public administrative instrumentalism correctly explains how administrative law fits into contemporary US constitutional government? Why or why not?

2. Having read the book, if you could change any three aspects of contemporary constitutional law, including judicial decisions and judicial review, what would they be and why?

References

Abbott Laboratories v. Gardner. 1967. 387 US 136.

Aberbach, Joel. 1990. *Keeping a Watchful Eye.* Washington, DC: Brookings Institution.

Aberbach, Joel, and Bert Rockman. 2000. *The Web of Politics.* Washington, DC: Brookings Institution.

Abood v. Detroit Board of Education. 1977. 431 US 265.

Adarand Constructors v. Pena. 1995. 515 US 200.

Administrative Dispute Resolution Act. 1990. PL 101-552. 104 Stat. 2736. 5 USC 571.

Administrative Procedure Act. 1946. PL 79–404. 60 Stat. 237. 5 USC 551.

Allen v. Wright. 1984. 468 US 737.

Allen, Mike, and George Lardner Jr. 2001. "Veto over Presidential Papers." *Washington Post,* November 2, A1.

Allison, Graham. 1994 [1979]. "Public and Private Management: Are They Fundamentally Alike in All Unimportant Respects?" In *Contemporary Public Administration,* edited by David Rosenbloom, Deborah Goldman, and Patricia Ingraham, 151–171. New York: McGraw-Hill.

American Bar Association. 1934. "Report of the Special Committee on Administrative Law." In US Congress, Senate, Committee on the Judiciary, Subcommittee on Separation of Powers. *Separation of Powers and the Independent Agencies: Cases and Selected Readings.* 91st Cong., 1st sess. Document 91–49, 214–239. Washington, DC: US Government Printing Office, 1970.

American Federation of Government Employees, Local 32 v. Federal Labor Relations Authority. 1985. 774 F.2d 498.

American Historical Association v. National Archives and Records Administration. 2007. US District Court for the District of Columbia, Civil Action No. 01–2447.

Asimow, Michael, Arthur Bonfield, and Ronald Levin. 1998. *State and Federal Administrative Law.* 2nd ed. St. Paul, MN: West Group.

Assessment of Federal Regulations and Policies on Families Act. 1998. PL 105–277. 112 Stat. 2681. 5 USC 601.

Associated Press. 2011. "Obama: If Congress Won't Act I Will." *Newsday,* October 31. http://www.newsday.com/news/nation/obama-if-congress-won-t-act-i-will-1.3287261.

Association of American Physicians and Surgeons, Inc. v. Hillary Rodham Clinton. 1993. 997 F.2d 898.

Atwater v. City of Lago Vista. 2001. 532 US 318.

Automotive Parts & Accessories Association v. Boyd. 1968. 407 F.2d 330.

Baker v. City of St. Petersburg. 1968. 400 F.2d 294.

Ball, Howard. 1986. "Downwind from the Bomb." *New York Times Magazine,* February 9, 33ff.

Ball, James. 2012. "Obama Administration Struggles to Live Up to Its Transparency Promise, Post Analysis Shows." *Washington Post,* August 3. http://www.washingtonpost.com/world/national-security/obama-adminis tration-struggles-to-live-up-to-its-transparency-promise-post-analysis -shows/2012/08/03/71172462-dcae-11e1-9974-5c975ae4810f_story.html.

Bardach, Eugene, and Robert Kagan. 1982. *Going by the Book.* Philadelphia: Temple University Press.

Barger, Harold. 1984. *The Impossible Presidency.* Glenview, IL: Scott Foresman.

Barr, Stephen. 2000. "Some Pessimism on 'Reinvention.'" *Washington Post,* March 31, 427.

Barron, Jerome, and C. Thomas Dienes. 1999. *Constitutional Law in a Nutshell.* St. Paul, MN: West Group.

Bazelon, David. 1976. "The Impact of the Courts on Public Administration." *Indiana Law Journal* 52, no. 1: 101–110.

Bernstein, Marver. 1955. *Regulating Business by Independent Commission.* Princeton, NJ: Princeton University Press.

Bi-metallic Investment Co. v. State Board of Equalization of Colorado. 1915. 239 US 441.

Board of County Commissioners, Wabaunsee County v. Umbehr. 1996. 518 US 668.

Board of Curators of the University of Missouri v. Horowitz. 1978. 435 US 78.

Board of Education of Independent School District No. 92 of Pottawatomie County v. Earls. 2002. 536 US 822.

Board of Trustees of the University of Alabama v. Garrett. 2001. 121 S.Ct. 955; 531 US 356.

Bonfield, Arthur. 1986. *State Administrative Rule Making.* Boston: Little, Brown.

——. 1993. *State Administrative Rule Making: Supplement.* Boston: Little, Brown.

Bonfield, Arthur, and Michael Asimow. 1989. *State and Federal Administrative Law.* St. Paul, MN: West Publishing.

Brentwood Academy v. Tennessee Secondary School Athletic Association et al. 2001. 531 US 288.

Bryan v. Moore. 2000. 528 US 1133.

Buckley v. American Constitutional Law Foundation. 1999. 525 US 182.

Bureau of National Affairs, Inc. v. U.S. Department of Justice. 1984. 742 F.2d 1484.

Burnham, David. 1989. *A Law unto Itself.* New York: Random House.

C & A Carbone, Inc. v. Town of Clarkstown. 1994. 511 US 383.

Carter v. Carter Coal Co. 1936. 298 US 238.

Center for Effective Government. 2014. "Federal Advisory Committees." Center for Effective Government's Regulatory Resource Center. http://www.foreffec tivegov.org/node/3471.

Central Intelligence Act. 1949. PL 81-110. 63 Stat. 208. 50 USC 403a.

Chamber of Commerce of the United States et al. v. Reich. 1996. 74 F.3d 1322.

Chang, Y. 2009. *The Importance of the False Claims Act in the Middle Age of NPM and Reinventing Government Stream.* Saarbrucken, Germany: VDM Verlag Dr. Muller.

Cheney v. District Court. 2004. 542 US 367.

Chevron U.S.A., Inc. v. Natural Resources Defense Council, Inc. 1984. 467 US 837.

Chicago Teachers Union v. Hudson. 1986. 475 US 292.

Cinderella Career and Finishing Schools, Inc. v. Federal Trade Commission. 1970. 425 F.2d 583.

Citizens to Preserve Overton Park, Inc. v. Volpe. 1971. 401 US 402.

City of Arlington, Texas v. Federal Communications Commission. 2013. 133 S.Ct. 1863.

City of Canton v. Harris. 1989. 489 US 378.

City of Erie v. Pap's A.M. 2000. 529 US 277.

City of Ontario, California v. Quon. 2010. 130 S.Ct. 2619; 560 US 746.

Civil Service Reform Act. 1978. PL 95–454. 92 Stat. 1111. 5 USC 1101.

Clark, Charles. 2013. "Is the Obama Administration Really Breaking Red Tape Records?" *Government Executive*. May 21. http://www.govexec.com/manage ment/2013/05/obama-administration-really-breaking-red-tape-records/63398.

Cleveland Board of Education v. La Fleur. 1974. 414 US 632.

Cleveland Board of Education v. Loudermill. 1985. 470 US 532.

Coglianese, Cary. 1997. "Assessing Consensus: The Promise and Performance of Negotiated Rulemaking." *Duke Law Journal* 46, no. 6: 1255–1349.

Cohen, David. 1996. "Amateur Government: When Political Appointees Manage the Federal Bureaucracy." DPM Working Paper 96–1. Washington, DC: Brookings Institution. http://www.brookings.edu/~/media/research/files /papers/1996/2/bureaucracy%20cohen/amateur.pdf.

Congressional Review Act. 1996. PL 104–12. 110 Stat. 868. 5 US Code 801.

Coyle, Marcia. 1995. "Agencies Ask for Less Sunshine." *National Law Journal*, September 25, A12.

Craig v. Boren. 1976. 429 US 190.

Crews, Clyde Wayne, Jr. 2013. *Ten Thousand Commandments: An Annual Snapshot of the Federal Regulatory State*. Washington, DC: Competitive Enterprise Institute.

Data Quality Act. 2000. PL 106–554. 114 Stat. 2763A (sec. 515).

Davis, Kenneth Culp. 1975. *Administrative Law and Government*. St. Paul, MN: West Publishing.

Delaware v. Prouse. 1979. 440 US 648.

Department of the Air Force v. Rose. 1976. 425 US 352.

Dewar, Helen. 2001. "Ergonomics Repeal Prompts Look Back." *Washington Post*, March 9, A16.

Dodd, Lawrence, and Richard Schott. 1979. *Congress and the Administrative State*. New York: Wiley.

Dolan v. City of Tigard. 1994. 512 US 374.

Edwards, George, III, and Stephen Wayne. 1985. *Presidential Leadership*. New York: St. Martin's Press.

Ehrenfreund, Max. 2013. "CIA Is Largest US Spy Agency, According to Black Budget Leaked by Edward Snowden." *Washington Post*, August 29. http://www .washingtonpost.com/world/national-security/cia-is-largest-us-spy-agency -according-to-black-budget-leaked-by-edward-snowden/2013/08/29/ d8d6d5de-10ec-11e3-bdf6-e4fc677d94a1_story.html.

Engquist v. Oregon Department of Agriculture. 2008. 553 US 591.

Executive Order 8,802. 1941. 6 *US Federal Register* 3109.

Executive Order 12,044. 1978. 43 *US Federal Register* 12661.

Executive Order 12,291. 1981. 46 *US Federal Register* 13193.

Executive Order 12,498. 1985. 50 *US Federal Register* 1036.

Executive Order 12,600. 1987. 52 *US Federal Register* 23781.

Executive Order 12,606. 1987. 52 *US Federal Register* 34188.

Executive Order 12,612. 1987. 52 *US Federal Register* 41685.

Executive Order 12,866. 1993. 58 *US Federal Register* 190.

Executive Order 12,898. 1994. 59 *US Federal Register* 32.

Executive Order 12,954. 1995. 60 *US Federal Register* 13023.

Executive Order 13,233. 2001. 66 *US Federal Register* 56025.

Executive Order 13,422. 2007. 72 *US Federal Register* 2763.

Executive Order 13,489. 2009. 74 *US Federal Register* 4669.

Executive Order 13,514. 2009. 74 *US Federal Register* 52117.

Executive Order 13,526. 2009. 75 *US Federal Register* 707.

Executive Order 13,563. 2011. 76 *US Federal Register* 3821.

False Claims Act. 1863. 12 Stat. 696. 31 USC 3729.

Federal Advisory Committee Act. 1972. PL 92–463. 86 Stat. 770. 5 USC Appendix 2.

Federal Aviation Administration v. Cooper. 2012. 132 S.Ct. 1441.

Federal Communications Commission v. AT&T. 2011. 131 S.Ct. 1177.

Federal Communications Commission v. Fox Television Stations. 2009. 556 US 502.

Federal Maritime Commission v. South Carolina State Ports Authority. 2002. 535 US 743.

Federal Trade Commission v. Cement Institute. 1948. 333 US 683.

Federal Trade Commission v. Ruberoid. 1952. 343 US 470.

Federal Trade Secrets Act. 1948. PL 80–772. 62 Stat. 791. 18 USC 1905.

Feeley, Malcolm, and Roger Hanson. 1990. "The Impact of Judicial Intervention on Prisons and Jails." In *Courts, Corrections, and the Constitution,* edited by John DiIulio Jr., 12–46. New York: Oxford University Press.

Ferguson v. City of Charleston. 2001. 121 S.Ct. 1281; 532 US 67.

Filarsky v. Delia. 2012. 132 S.Ct. 1657.

Fiorina, Morris. 1977. *Congress: Keystone of the Washington Establishment.* New Haven, CT: Yale University Press.

Fisher v. University of Texas at Austin. 2013. 133 S.Ct. 2411.

Flast v. Cohen. 1968. 392 US 83.

Foerstel, Herbert N. *Freedom of Information and the Right to Know.* Westport, CT: Greenwood Press, 1999.

FOIA.gov. N.d. http://www.foia.gov.

Ford Motor Company v. Federal Trade Commission. 1981. 673 F.2d 1008.

Fox, Tom. 2013. "Dealing with Poor Performers in Government." *Washington Post,* April 19. http://www.washingtonpost.com/business/on-leadership/deal ing-with-poor-performers-in-government/2013/04/19/77d58398-a92c-11e2 -a8e2-5b98cb59187f_story.html.

Fox, William, Jr. 2000. *Understanding Administrative Law.* New York: Lexis Publishing.

Free Enterprise Fund v. Public Company Accounting Oversight Board. 2010. 130 S.Ct. 3138.

Freedom of Information Act. 1966. PL 89–487. 80 Stat. 250. 5 USC 552.

Frothingham v. Mellon (Commonwealth of Massachusetts v. Mellon). 1923. 262 US 447.

Funk, William. 1987. "When Smoke Gets in Your Eyes: Regulatory Negotiation and the Public Interest—EPA's Woodstove Standards." *Environmental Law* 18 (fall): 55–98.

Funk, William, and Richard Seamon. 2012. *Administrative Law.* 4th ed. New York: Wolters Kluwer Law and Business.

Funk, William, Jeffrey Lubbers, and Charles Pou, eds. 2000. *Federal Administrative Procedure Sourcebook.* 3rd ed. Chicago: American Bar Association.

Funk, William, Sidney Shapiro, and Russell Weaver. 1997. *Administrative Procedure and Practice.* St. Paul, MN: West Group.

Gagnon v. Scarpelli. 1973. 411 US 778.

Garcetti v. Ceballos. 2006. 547 US 410.

Garcia v. San Antonio Metropolitan Transit Authority. 1985. 469 US 528.

Gellhorn, Ernest, and Ronald Levin. 1997. *Administrative Law and Process in a Nutshell.* 4th ed. St. Paul, MN: West Group.

———. 2006. *Administrative Law and Process in a Nutshell.* 5th ed. St. Paul, MN: Thomson/West.

Gellman, Barton, and Greg Miller. 2013. "U.S. Spy Network's Successes, Failures and Objectives Detailed in 'Black Budget' Summary." *Washington Post,* August 29. http://www.washingtonpost.com/world/national-security /black-budget-summary-details-us-spy-networks-successes-failures-and -objectives/2013/08/29/7e57bb78-10ab-11e3-8cdd-bcdc09410972_story.html.

Gilbert v. Homar. 1997. 520 US 924.

Goldberg v. Kelly. 1970. 397 US 254.

Golden, Marissa Martino. 1998. "Interest Groups in the Rulemaking Process: Who Participates?" *Journal of Public Administration Research and Theory* 8 (April): 245–270 (proquestmail@bellhowell.infolearning.com version).

Goldstein, Amy. 2001. "'Last Minute' Spin on Regulatory Rite." *Washington Post,* June 9, A1ff.

Gonzales v. Raich. 2005. 545 US 1.

Gore, Al. 1993. *From Red Tape to Results: Creating a Government That Works Better and Costs Less.* Washington, DC: US Government Printing Office.

———. 1995. *Common Sense Government Works Better and Costs Less.* Washington, DC: US Government Printing Office.

Goss v. Lopez. 1975. 419 US 565.

Government in the Sunshine Act. 1976. PL 94–409. 90 Stat. 1241. 5 USC 552b.

Government Performance and Results Act. 1993. PL 103–62. 107 Stat. 285. 31 USC 1101.

Government Performance and Results Act Modernization Act of 2010. 2011. PL 111–352. 124 Stat. 3866. 31 USC 1101. January 4.

Graham, John. 2002. "Open Reviews, Better Data Improve Regulations." *Federal Times,* January 7, 15.

Gratz v. Bollinger. 2003. 539 US 244.

Griggs v. Duke Power Co. 1971. 401 US 424.

Grunwald, Michael. 2001. "Business Lobbyists Asked to Discuss Onerous Rules." *Washington Post,* December 4, A3.

Grutter v. Bollinger. 2003. 539 US 306.

Hamilton, Alexander. 1961 [1788]. "Federalist Paper No. 78." In *The Federalist Papers,* edited by Clinton Rossiter, 464–472. New York: Mentor.

Hamilton v. Love 1971. 328 F. Supp. 1182.

Harlow v. Fitzgerald. 1982. 457 US 800.

Hawes, Leonard, and Richard Rieke. 1998. "Alternative Dispute Resolution." In *International Encyclopedia of Public Policy and Administration,* edited by Jay Shafritz, 104–107. Boulder, CO: Westview Press.

Heckler v. Campbell. 1983. 461 US 458.

Heckler v. Chaney. 1985. 470 US 821.

Heclo, Hugh. 1977. *A Government of Strangers.* Washington, DC: Brookings Institution.

———. 1978. "Issue Networks and the Executive Establishment." In *The New American Political System,* edited by Anthony King, 87–124. Washington, DC: American Enterprise Institute.

Hood, Christopher. 1991. "A Public Management for All Seasons." *Public Administration* 69 (spring): 3–19.

Hope v. Pelzer. 2002. 536 US 730.

Housing Study Group v. Kemp. 1990. 736 F.Supp. 321.

Hummel, Ralph. 1991. "Stories Managers Tell: Why They Are as Valid as Science." *Public Administration Review* 51 (January/February): 31–41.

Humphrey's Executor v. United States. 1935. 295 US 602.

Implementing Recommendations of the 9/11 Commission Act. 2007. PL 110–53. 121 Stat. 266. 6 USC 101.

In re Cheney. 2005. 406 F.3d 723.

Industrial Union Department, AFL-CIO v. American Petroleum Institute. 1980. 448 US 607.

J. W. Hampton, Jr. & Co. v. United States. 1928. 276 US 394.

Jordan v. Gardner. 1993. 986 F.2d 1521.

Kamen, Michael. 1987. *A Machine That Would Go of Itself.* New York: Knopf.

Kelley v. Johnson. 1976. 425 US 238.

Kendall v. United States. 1838. 37 US 524.

Kerwin, Cornelius. 1999. *Rulemaking.* 2nd ed. Washington, DC: CQ Press.

Kerwin, Cornelius, and Scott Furlong. 1992. "Time and Rulemaking: An Empirical Test of Theory." *Journal of Public Administration Research and Theory* 2 (April): 113–138.

La Follette, Robert, Jr. 1946. "Congress Wins a Victory over Congress." *New York Times Magazine,* August 4, 11ff.

Lardner, George, Jr. 2001. "Bush Urged to Rescind Order on Presidential Materials." *Washington Post,* November 7, A27.

Larrabee, Jennifer. 1997. "'DWB (Driving While Black)' and Equal Protection: The Realities of an Unconstitutional Police Practice." *Journal of Law and Policy* 6, no. 1: 291–328.

LawyerShop. N.d. "Qui Tam Case Examples." LawyerShop. http://www.lawyershop.com/practice-areas/criminal-law/white-collar-crimes/qui-tamcase-examples.

Leahy, Patrick. 1976. *A Report on Advisory Committees in the Department of Agriculture and Department of Defense.* Washington, DC: Office of US Senator Leahy.

Legislative Reorganization Act. 1946. PL 79–601. 60 Stat. 812.

Legislative Reorganization Act. 1970. PL 91–510. 84 Stat. 1140.

Lewis, Vern. (1952) 1987. "Toward a Theory of Budgeting." In *Classics of Public Administration,* edited by Jay Shafritz and Albert Hyde, 213–229. 2nd ed. Chicago: Dorsey Press.

Light, Paul. 1995. *Thickening Government.* Washington, DC: Brookings Institution.

Lipsky, Michael. 1980. *Street-Level Bureaucracy.* New York: Russell Sage Foundation.

Local 2677, American Federation of Government Employees v. Phillips. 1973. 358 F.Supp. 60.

Lowi, Theodore. 1969. *The End of Liberalism*. New York: Norton.

Lubbers, Jeffrey. 1994. "Management of Federal Agency Adjudication." In *Handbook of Regulation and Administrative Law*, edited by David Rosenbloom and Richard Schwartz, 287–323. New York: Marcel Dekker.

———. 1997. "Paperwork Redux: The (Stronger) Paperwork Reduction Act of 1995." *Administrative Law Review* 49 (winter): 111–121.

Lucas v. South Carolina Costal Council. 1992. 505 US 1003.

Lujan v. Defenders of Wildlife. 1992. 504 US 555.

Madison, James. 1999. *James Madison: Writings*. Compiled and annotated by Jack Rakove. New York: Library of America.

Marbury v. Madison. 1803. 5 US 137.

Marks, Josh. 2013. "Obama: If Congress Doesn't Act on Climate Change, 'I Will.'" *National Memo*, February 13. http://www.nationalmemo.com/obama-if-congress-doesnt-act-on-climate-change-i-will.

Marshall v. Barlow's, Inc. 1978. 436 US 307.

Mashaw, Jerry, Richard Merrill, and Peter Shane. 1992. *Administrative Law*. 3rd ed. St. Paul, MN: West Publishing.

Massachusetts v. Environmental Protection Agency. 2007. 549 US 497.

Mathews v. Eldridge. 1976. 424 US 319.

May, Randolph. 1997. "Reforming the Sunshine Act: Report and Recommendation by the Special Committee to Review the Government in the Sunshine Act." *Administrative Law Review* 49 (spring): 415–428.

Maynard-Moody, Steven, and Michael Musheno. 2003. *Cops, Teachers, Counselors*. Ann Arbor: University of Michigan Press.

McCarran, Pat. 1946. "Improving 'Administrative Justice.'" *American Bar Association Journal* 32: 827ff.

McMillian v. Monroe County, Alabama 1997. 520 US 781.

Memphis Light, Gas & Water Division v. Craft. 1978. 436 US 1.

Meriam, Lewis. 1939. *Reorganization of the National Government, Part I: An Analysis of the Problem*. Washington, DC: Brookings Institution.

Michigan v. Tyler. 1978. 436 US 499.

Milbank, Dana. 2002. "GAO Sues Administration for Task Force Records." *Washington Post*, February 23, A7.

Miller, Bill. 2001. "Records Order Spurs Lawsuit." *Washington Post*, November 29, A31.

———. 2002. "$37.7 Billion for Homeland Defense Is a Start, Bush Says." *Washington Post*, January 25, A15.

Minneci v. Pollard. 2012. 132 S. Ct. 617.

Missouri v. Jenkins. 1995. 515 US 70.

Model State Administrative Procedure Act. 1981. *Selected Federal and State Administrative and Regulatory Laws*, edited by William Funk, Sidney Shapiro, and Russell Weaver, 299–353. St. Paul, MN: West Group.

Moore, Mark, and Margaret Gates. 1986. *The Inspectors-General*. New York: Russell Sage.

Moreno, Angel. 1994. "Presidential Coordination of the Independent Regulatory Process." *Administrative Law Journal of the American University* 8 (fall): 461–516.

Morgan v. United States. 1936. 298 US 468.

Morgan v. United States. 1938. 304 US 1.

Morris, Kim. 1977. "Judicial Review of Non-reviewable Administrative Action." *Administrative Law Review* 29 (winter): 65–86.

Morrison v. Olson. 1988. 487 US 654.

Motor Vehicle Manufacturers Association of the United States, Inc. v. State Farm Mutual Automobile Insurance Co. 1983. 463 US 29.

Nader v. Allegheny Airlines, Inc. 1976. 426 US 290.

Naff, Katherine, Norma Riccucci, and Siegrun Fox Freyss. 2014. *Personnel Management in Government.* 7th ed. Boca Raton, FL: CRC/Taylor and Francis.

Nakashima, Ellen. 2001. "Environmental Group Sues for Records of Energy Task Force." *Washington Post,* December 12, A33.

National Archives. 2012. 2012 Executive Orders Disposition Tables. National Archives. http://www.archives.gov/federal-register/executive-orders/2012.html.

———. 2013. 2013 Executive Orders Disposition Tables. National Archives. http://www.archives.gov/federal-register/executive-orders/2013.html.

National Archives and Records Administration v. Favish. 2004. 541 US 157.

National Association of Government Employees v. Federal Labor Relations Authority. 1985. 770 F.2d 1223.

National Conference of State Legislatures (NCSL). 2010. "State Whistleblower Laws." NCSL. http://www.ncsl.org/research/labor-and-employment/state-whistleblower-laws.aspx.

National Environmental Policy Act of 1969. 1970. PL 91–190. 83 Stat. 852. 42 USC 4321 et seq.

National Federation of Independent Business v. Sebelius. 2012. 132 S.Ct. 2566.

National Performance Review. 1995. "Federal Regulators Did It: 16,000 Pages of Rules Cut." *Reinvention Roundtable* 2 (summer): 1–11. http://govinfo.library.unt.edu/npr/library/rtable/244e.html.

National Security Archive. 2006. "A FOIA Request Celebrates Its 17th Birthday." George Washington University. http://www2.gwu.edu/~nsarchiv/NSAEBB/NSAEBB182.

Negotiated Rulemaking Act. 1990. PL 101–648. 104 Stat. 4969. 5 USC 561.

New Jersey v. T.L.O. 1985. 469 US 325.

New York v. Burger. 1987. 482 US 691.

New York v. United States. 1992. 505 US 144.

Nixon v. Administrator of General Services. 1977. 433 US 425.

Nixon v. United States. 1993. 506 US 224.

O'Hare Truck Service, Inc. v. City of Northlake. 1996. 518 US 712.

O'Leary, Rosemary, and Susan Raines. 2001. "Lessons Learned from Two Decades of Alternative Dispute Resolution Programs and Processes at the U.S. Environmental Protection Agency." *Public Administration Review* 61 (November/December): 682–692.

Office of Information and Privacy. 2001. "FOIA Post." US Department of Justice. http://www.usdoj.gov/oip/foiapost/2001/foiapost19.html.

Office of Information and Regulatory Affairs. N.d. "How to Use the Unified Agenda." Reginfo.gov. http://www.reginfo.gov/public/jsp/eAgenda/Static Content/UA_HowTo.jsp.

Office of Public Affairs. 2009. "Justice News." US Department of Justice. March 19. http://www.justice.gov/opa/pr/2009/March/09-ag-253.html.

Office of the Federal Register. 1999. *The United States Government Manual, 1999/2000.* Washington, DC: US Government Printing Office.

Olson, William, and Alan Woll. 1999. "Executive Orders and National Emergencies: How Presidents Have Come to 'Run the Country' by Usurping Legislative Power." *Policy Analysis,* No. 358. Washington, DC: Cato Institute, October 28.

OMBwatch. 2001. http://www.ombwatch.org/info/2001/access.html.

Openness Promotes Effectiveness in Our National Government Act. 2007. PL 110–175. 121 Stat. 2524. 5 US C. 552.

Osborne, David, and Ted Gaebler. 1992. *Reinventing Government.* Reading, MA: Addison-Wesley.

Owen v. City of Independence. 1980. 445 US 622.

Paperwork Reduction Act. 1980. PL 96–511. 94 Stat. 2812. 44 USC 3501.

Paperwork Reduction Act. 1995. PL 104–13. 109 Stat. 163. 44 USC 3501.

Pear, Robert. 2007. "Bush Directive Increases Sway on Regulation." *New York Times,* January 30. http://www.nytimes.com/2007/01/30/washington/30rules.html?ex=1171688400&en=758eb5cf26328a60&ei=5070.

Pembaur v. City of Cincinnati. 1986. 475 US 469.

Pfiffner, James. N.d. "Presidential Appointments and Managing the Executive Branch." Political Appointee Project, National Academy of Public Administration, Washington, DC. http://www.politicalappointeeproject.org/commentary/appointments-and-managing-executive-branch.

Phillippi v. CIA. 1976. 546 F.2d 1009.

Pike v. Bruce Church, Inc. 1970. 397 US 137.

Piotrowski, Suzanne, and David Rosenbloom. 2002. "The Problem of Nonmission-Based Values in Results-Oriented Public Management: The Case of Freedom of Information." *Public Administration Review* 62 (November/December): 643–657.

Presidential Records Act. 1978. PL 95–591. 92 Stat. 2523. 44 USC 101, 2201.

Printz v. United States. 1997. 521 US 898.

Pritchett, C. Herman. 1977. *The American Constitution.* New York: McGraw-Hill.

Privacy Act. 1974. PL 93–579. 88 Stat. 1896. 5 USC 552a.

Professional Airways Systems Specialists, MEBA, AFL-CIO v. Federal Labor Relations Authority. 1987. 809 F.2d 855.

Publius. 1961 [1787–1788]. *The Federalist Papers,* edited by Clinton Rossiter. New York: Mentor Books.

Qui Tam Online Network. N.d. "Common Types of Qui Tam Fraud." Qui Tam Online Network. http://www.quitamonline.com/fraud.html.

Quirk, Paul. 1980. "Food and Drug Administration." In *The Politics of Regulation,* edited by James Q. Wilson, 191–235. New York: Basic Books.

Rankin v. McPherson. 1987. 483 US 378.

Regulatory Flexibility Act. 1980. PL 96–354. 94 Stat. 1164. 5 USC 601.

Reich, Charles. 1964. "The New Property." *Yale Law Journal* 73 (April): 733–787.

Richardson v. McKnight. 1997. 521 US 399.

Richardson v. Perales. 1971. 402 US 389.

Rivenbark, Leigh. 1998. "Cases Swamp EEOC." *Federal Times,* August 10, 3.

Roe v. Wade. 1973. 410 US 113.

Rohr, John. 1989. *Ethics for Bureaucrats.* 2nd ed. New York: Marcel Dekker.

Rosenbloom, David. 1971. *Federal Service and the Constitution*. Ithaca, NY: Cornell University Press.

———. 1992. "The Federal Labor Relations Authority." In *The Promise and Paradox of Civil Service Reform*, edited by Patricia Ingraham and David Rosenbloom, 141–156. Pittsburgh: University of Pittsburgh Press.

———. 2000. *Building a Legislative-Centered Public Administration: Congress and the Administrative State, 1946–1999*. Tuscaloosa: University of Alabama Press.

———. 2010. "Reevaluating Executive Centered Public Administration." In *Oxford Handbook of American Bureaucracy*, edited by Robert Durant, 101–127. New York: Oxford University Press.

———. 2013a. "Federal Law Against Age and Disability Discrimination Meets the Dignity of the States: The Supreme Court, States' Sovereign Immunity, and Judicial Review." *Review of Public Personnel Administration* (October 31): doi: 10.1177/0734371X13506623.

———. 2013b. "Silo Busting: Effective Strategies for Government Reorganization." Testimony, US Senate, Committee on the Budget, Task Force on Government Performance, May 16.

Rosenbloom, David, and Robert Kravchuk. 2002. *Public Administration: Understanding Management, Politics, and Law in the Public Sector*. 5th ed. New York: McGraw-Hill.

Rosenbloom, David H., James Carroll, and Jonathan Carroll. 2000. *Constitutional Competence for Public Managers: Cases and Commentary*. Itasca, IL: F. E. Peacock.

Rosenbloom, David, Rosemary O'Leary, and Joshua Chanin. 2010. *Public Administration and Law*. 3rd ed. Boca Raton, FL: CRC/Taylor and Francis.

Roth, William, Jr., and William Nixon. 1999. *The Power to Destroy*. New York: Atlantic Monthly Press.

Rourke, Francis. 1993. "Whose Bureaucracy Is This, Anyway? Congress, the President, and Public Administration." *PS: Political Science and Politics* 26 (December): 687–692.

Rutan v. Republican Party of Illinois. 1990. 497 US 62.

Sackett v. Environmental Protection Agency. 2012. 132 S.Ct. 1367.

San Diego v. Roe. 2004. 543 US 77.

Sargentich, Thomas. 1997. "The Small Business Regulatory Enforcement Fairness Act." *Administrative Law Review* 49 (winter): 123–137.

Schechter Poultry Corp. v. United States. 1935. 295 US 495.

Schlesinger, Arthur, Jr. 1973. *The Imperial Presidency*. Boston: Houghton Mifflin.

Scholz, John. 1994. "Managing Regulatory Enforcement in the United States." In *Handbook of Regulation and Administrative Law*, edited by David Rosenbloom and Richard Schwartz, 423–462. New York: Marcel Dekker.

Schwartz, Bernard. 1994. "Some Crucial Issues in Administrative Law." In *Handbook of Regulation and Administrative Law*, edited by David Rosenbloom and Richard Schwartz, 207–222. New York: Marcel Dekker.

Schweiker v. Hansen. 1981. 450 US 785.

Shafritz, Jay, David Rosenbloom, Norma Riccucci, Katherine Naff, and Albert Hyde. 2001. *Personnel Management in Government*. 5th ed. New York: Marcel Dekker.

Shapiro v. Thompson. 1969. 394 US 618.

Simon v. Eastern Kentucky Welfare Rights Organization. 1976. 426 US 26.

Skidmore v. Swift & Co. 1944. 323 US 134.

Skrzycki, Cindy. 1998. "Congress: Fewer Forms or Budgets Will Suffer." *Washington Post*, August 14, G1ff.

Small Business Regulatory Enforcement Fairness Act. 1996. PL 104–121. 110 Stat. 857. 5 USC 601.

South Dakota v. Dole. 1987. 483 US 203.

Spady v. Mount Vernon. 1974. 419 US 983.

Sparrow, Malcolm. 1994. *Imposing Duties.* Westport, CT: Praeger.

Stanley v. Illinois. 1972. 405 US 645.

Steadman v. Securities and Exchange Commission. 1981. 450 US 91.

Steck, Henry. 1984. "Politics and Administration: Private Advice for Public Purpose in a Corporatist Setting." In *Politics and Administration: Woodrow Wilson and American Public Administration,* edited by Jack Rabin and James Bowman, 147–174. New York: Marcel Dekker.

Steel Co. v. Citizens for a Better Environment. 1998. 523 US 83.

Stewart, Richard. 1975. "The Reformation of American Administrative Law." *Harvard Law Review* 88 (June): 1667–1813.

Stone, Deborah. 2002. *The Policy Paradox.* New York: Norton.

Strauss, Peter, Todd Rakoff, Roy Schotland, and Cynthia Farina. 1995. *Gellhorn and Byse's Administrative Law: Cases and Comments.* 9th ed. Westbury, NY: Foundation Press.

Toilet Goods Association, Inc. v. Gardner. 1967. 387 US 158.

Tushnet, Mark. 2004. "On the Rehnquist Court, Everyone Has Been a Judicial Activist." *Chronicle of Higher Education,* November 26, B9–B10.

US Congress. 1939. *Congressional Record* 84, 76th Cong., 1st sess. Washington, DC: US Government Printing Office.

———. 1940. *Congressional Record* 86, 76th Cong., 3rd sess. Washington, DC: US Government Printing Office.

———. 1946. *Congressional Record* 92, 79th Cong., 2nd sess. Washington, DC: US Government Printing Office.

———. 1966. *Special Inquiry on Invasion of Privacy.* House Committee on Government Operations, 89th Cong., 1st. sess. Washington, DC: US Government Printing Office.

U.S. Department of Defense v. Federal Labor Relations Authority. 1994. 510 US 487.

US Department of Health and Human Services. 1978. "Residual Functional Capacity: Maximum Sustained Work Capability Limited to Light and Medium Work as a Result of Severe Medically Determinable Impairment(s)." *Federal Register* 43 (November 28): 55369–55370.

US Department of Justice. 2010. *FOIA Reference Guide.* US Department of Justice. http://www.justice.gov/oip/04_3.html.

US Equal Employment Opportunity Commission (EEOC). N.d. "Annual Report of the Federal Work Force Part I: EEO Complaints Processing Fiscal Year 2011." EEOC. http://www.eeoc.gov/federal/reports/fsp2011/index.cfm#I.

US Food and Drug Administration (FDA). Periodic. "Defect Levels Handbook." FDA. http://www.fda.gov/food/guidanceregulation/guidancedocuments regulatoryinformation/sanitationtransportation/ucm056174.htm.

US General Accounting Office. 1998. *Federal Rulemaking: Agencies Often Published Final Actions Without Proposed Rules.* Washington, DC: US General Accounting Office.

US Government Accountability Office (GAO). N.d. "Congressional Review Act (CRA) FAQs." GAO. http://www.gao.gov/legal/congressact/cra_faq.html#9.

US House of Representatives. 2001. *Oversight Hearing on Presidential Records Act.* Subcommittee on Government Efficiency, Financial Management and Intergovernmental Relations. November 6. http://www.house.gov/reform /gefmir/hearings/1106_presidential_records/1106.

US Merit Systems Protection Board. 1995. *Sexual Harassment in the Federal Workplace.* Washington, DC: US Merit Systems Protection Board.

———. 1997. *Adherence to Merit Principles in the Workplace: Federal Employees' Views.* Washington, DC: US Merit Systems Protection Board.

———. 1998. *Issues of Merit.* Washington, DC: US Merit Systems Protection Board, February.

———. 2002a. *Issues of Merit.* Washington, DC: US Merit Systems Protection Board, January.

———. 2002b. *Issues of Merit.* Washington, DC: US Merit Systems Protection Board, April.

———. 2010. *Whistleblower Protections for Federal Employees.* Washington, DC: US Merit Systems Protection Board, September. http://www.mspb.gov/netsearch/view docs.aspx?docnumber=557972&version=559604&application=ACROBAT.

———. 2011. *Blowing the Whistle: Barriers to Federal Employees Making Disclosures.* Washington, DC: US Merit Systems Protection Board, November. http://www .mspb.gov/netsearch/viewdocs.aspx?docnumber=662503&version=664475.

———. 2013. *Preserving the Integrity of the Federal Merit Systems: Understanding and Addressing Perceptions of Favoritism.* Washington, DC: US Merit Systems Protection Board, December. http://www.mspb.gov/netsearch/viewdocs .aspx?docnumber=945850&version=949626&application=ACROBAT.

US Office of Personnel Management. 2008. *Federal Human Capital Survey 2008.* Washington, DC: US Office of Personnel Management. http://www.fedview.opm .gov/2008FILES/2008_Govtwide_Report.pdf.

US Senate. 1970. *Separation of Powers and the Independent Agencies: Cases and Selected Readings.* Committee on the Judiciary, Subcommittee on Administrative Practice and Procedures. 93rd Cong., 2nd sess. Washington, DC: US Government Printing Office.

———. 1974. *Freedom of Information Act Source Book.* Committee on the Judiciary, Subcommittee on Administrative Practice and Procedure, 93rd Cong., 2nd sess. Washington, DC: US Government Printing Office.

———. 1978. *Federal Advisory Committee Act (Public Law 92–463): Source Book: Legislative History, Texts, and Other Documents.* Committee on Governmental Affairs, Subcommittee on Energy, Nuclear Proliferation, and Federal Services. 95th Cong., 2nd sess. Washington, DC: US Government Printing Office.

———. 1989. *Negotiated Rulemaking Act of 1989: Report.* Committee on Governmental Affairs, 101st Cong., 1st sess. Report 101–97 (August 1). Washington, DC: US Government Printing Office.

United States Department of Justice v. Reporters Committee for Freedom of Press. 1989. 489 US 749.

United States v. Florida East Coast Railway Co. 1973. 410 US 224.

United States v. International Boxing Club of New York, Inc. 1955. 348 US 236.

United States v. Lopez. 1995. 514 US 549.

United States v. Mead Corp. 2001. 121 S.Ct. 2164; 533 US 218.

United States v. Morrison. 2000. 529 US 598.

United States v. National Treasury Employees Union. 1995. 513 US 454.

United States v. Nixon. 1974. 418 US 683.

United States v. Nova Scotia Food Products Corp. 1977. 568 F.2d 240.

United States v. Richardson. 1974. 418 US 166.

United States v. Virginia. 1996. 518 US 515.

United States v. Windsor. 2013. 133 S.Ct. 2675.

Universal Camera Corp. v. National Labor Relations Board. 1951. 340 US 474.

USLegal. N.d. "Definitions: Qui Tam and Law and Legal Definition." USLegal. http://definitions.uslegal.com/q/qui-tam.

Vaughn, Robert. 1992. "The US Merit Systems Protection Board and the Office of Special Counsel." In *The Promise and Paradox of Civil Service Reform,* edited by Patricia Ingraham and David Rosenbloom, 121–140. Pittsburgh, PA: University of Pittsburgh Press.

Vermont Yankee Nuclear Power Corp. v. Natural Resources Defense Council, Inc. 1978. 435 US 519.

Vernonia School District 47J v. Acton. 1995. 515 US 646.

Village of Willowbrook v. Olech. 2000. 528 US 562.

Vogler, David. 1988. *The Politics of Congress.* 5th ed. Boston, MA: Allyn and Bacon.

Wald, Patricia. 1994. "Regulation at Risk: Are the Courts Part of the Solution or Most of the Problem?" *Southern California Law Review* 67 (March): 621–657.

Warren, Kenneth. 1996. *Administrative Law in the Political System.* 3rd ed. Upper Saddle River, NJ: Prentice Hall.

———. 2011. *Administrative Law in the Political System.* 5th ed. Boulder, CO: Westview.

Weinberg, Steven. 2000. "Author's Research on John Lennon Is a Textbook on How to Use the Freedom of Information Act." *St. Louis Post-Dispatch,* February 13, F11.

West v. Atkins. 1988. 487 US 42.

Westin, Alan. 1967. *Privacy and Freedom.* New York: Antheneum.

Wharton, Dale. 1995. "Blank Check." University of Texas Department of Economics. http://www.eco.utexas.edu/~archive/chiapas95/1995.05/msg00201.html.

Whistleblower Protection Act. 1989. PL 101–12. 103 Stat. 16. 5 USC 1201.

White House. 2012. "2012 Annual Report to Congress on White House Staff." White House. http://www.whitehouse.gov/briefing-room/disclosures/annual -records/2012.

Whren v. United States. 1996. 517 US 806.

Wickard v. Filburn. 1942. 317 US 111.

Willoughby, W. F. 1927. *Principles of Public Administration.* Washington, DC: Brookings Institution.

———. 1934. *Principles of Legislative Organization and Administration.* Washington, DC: Brookings Institution.

Wilson, Woodrow. (1887) 1987. "The Study of Administration." In *Classics of Public Administration,* edited by Jay Shafritz and Albert Hyde, 1–25. 2nd ed. Chicago: Dorsey Press.

Woll, Peter. 1977. *American Bureaucracy.* 2nd ed. New York: W. W. Norton.

Wood, B. Dan, and Richard Waterman. 1994. *Bureaucratic Dynamics.* Boulder, CO: Westview Press.

Wyatt v. Stickney. 1971. 325 F.Supp. 781; 334 F.Supp. 1341.

Wyman v. James. 1971. 400 US 309.

Youngstown Sheet & Tube Co. v. Sawyer. 1952. 343 US 579.

Zajac, Andrew. 2012. "As Number of Regulators Rises, Their Overseer's Staff Shrinks." *Washington Post,* June 25.

Ziegler, Molly. 2003. "Agencies Fail to Rein Paperwork Burden on Public." *Federal Times,* April 21.

Zifcak, Spencer. 1998. "Freedom of Information." In *International Encyclopedia of Public Policy and Administration,* edited by Jay Shafritz, 941–944. Boulder, CO: Westview Press.

Index

Abbott Laboratories v. Gardner, 151–152, 153, 154, 159, 163–164

Abortion, 163

Abstention, doctrine of, 168

Accountability, 4, 13, 68, 137, 155, 185

ADA. *See* Americans with Disabilities Act of 1990

Adjudication, 9, 32, 47, 66, 154, 158, 185
  criticisms of, 93–98
  formal, 92, 120, 178
  hearings, 108–113
  reasons for agencies' use of, 99–108 (*see also* Agencies: agency adjudication)
  reforms, 120–121
  See also Evidentiary administrative adjudication

Administrative and Regulatory Law News (American Bar Association), 190

Administrative Dispute Resolution Act (ADRA), 14, 77, 115–117, 120–121

Administrative inspections, 56–57. *See also* Inspections

Administrative law, 6, 67, 155, 184
  administrative law judges (ALJs), 11, 94, 95, 103, 104, 105, 109, 110–113, 114, 115, 120, 121 (*see also* Judges)
  and appearance of bias, 111
  audits, 186, 192
  books about, 192–193
  changes in, 185–186
  defined, 1
  as funnel, 189
  importance of, 1–4

periodicals and websites about, 190–191 (*see also* Websites)
  primary function of, 186–191
  talking about, 191–192
  and transparent government, 125–126

Administrative Law and Government (Davis), 193

Administrative Law in the Political System (Warren), 193

Administrative Law Review, 190

Administrative Procedure Act (APA) of 1946, 8, 12–13, 64, 70, 113, 118, 133, 139, 152, 167, 169, 173, 175, 177, 178, 183, 188
  and adjudications, 92, 94, 102, 106, 108–109, 111, 114, 115, 120
  as focusing on procedure, 186
  importance of, 185
  and public reporting, 126
  and rulemaking processes, 71–75, 76, 81, 82

Administrative state, 12, 34

ADR. *See* Alternative dispute resolution

ADRA. *See* Administrative Dispute Resolution Act

Adverse action system, 98

Advertising, 9, 66, 89, 90, 93, 102, 119, 151

Advisory committees, 144

AEC. *See* Atomic Energy Commission

Affirmative action, 44, 45–46

Afghanistan, 125

African Americans, 96, 161–162

Agencies, 1, 8, 9, 11, 13, 17, 21, 24, 25, 32, 54, 59, 64, 65, 69, 72, 75, 76–77, 78, 79, 80, 84, 85, 92, 111, 115, 116, 117, 118, 121, 122
  agency adjudication, 89–91, 94, 95, 99–108, 120 (*see also* Adjudication; Evidentiary administrative adjudication)
  agency nonenforcement, 175–177
  agency reports, 179–180, 182
  agency rules, 14, 15, 23, 68, 94, 169, 183
  core missions, 99
  exhaustion of remedies by, 166–167
  and Freedom of Information Act, 129, 130, 132, 133, 136, 137, 140
  inadequate performance of, 181
  and internal appellate review, 114
  and jurisdiction issues, 165–166, 174–175
  and law of estoppel, 108
  mission statements of, 127
  partnership between courts and agencies, 168, 169
  policy changes of, 172
  publishing in *Federal Register*, 126
  reversal of adjudicatory decisions of, 178
  and rules of evidence, 113
  single-headed/multiheaded, 114
  statutory interpretations of, 173–175
  strategic plans of, 182
  as threat to Congress, 12
  website concerning agency performance, 191
  See also Adjudication: reasons for agencies' use of; Congress: delegation of legislative authority to administrative agencies
Agriculture Department, 192
Air bags, 171
Air Force Academy, 133
Alaska, 147
ALJs. *See* Administrative law: administrative law judges
Allegheny Airlines, 166
Allen v. Wright, 161–162

Alternative dispute resolution (ADR), 95–96, 120, 185
American Bar Association, 70, 190
American Federation of Government Employees, 96
American Historical Association, 138
American Political Science Association, 138
American Psychiatric Association, 55
Americans with Disabilities Act (ADA) of 1990, 20, 42–43
APA. *See* Administrative Procedure Act of 1946
Appeals, 113–114, 115, 155. *See also* Courts: appeals courts
Appointment calendars, 133
Arbitration, 116
Archivist of the United States, 138
Arizona, 40
Arrests, 57
Ashcroft, John, 132
Ashurst, Henry, 183
Asian Pacific Americans, 96
Asimow, Michael, 192
Assessment of Federal Regulations and Policies on Families Act (1998), 14, 80
Association of American Physicians and Surgeons, Inc. v. Hillary Rodham Clinton, 144
Association of Smoked Fish Processors, Inc., 63, 69
Atomic Energy Commission (AEC), 173
Audits, 56. *See also under* Administrative law
Automobiles, 171

Bankruptcy cases, 157
Benefits, 10, 46, 61, 66, 71, 91, 102–103, 106, 147
  means-tested, 46, 47, 107
  retroactive, 108
  veteran claims, 113
  See also Disability benefits
Benzene, 169–170
Bias, 111, 112. *See also* Impartiality
Bonfield, Arthur, 192
Botanic Garden, 127, 128

Botulism, 63, 64, 92
Brandeis, Louis, 142
Brennan, William, 105, 108, 176
Budget issues, 30, 123–125, 136, 178, 179, 181, 188, 191
Building permits, 48
Bureau of National Affairs, Inc. v. U.S. Department of Justice, 132, 133
Bush, George H. W., 83, 138
Bush, George W., 30, 82, 83–84, 144–145
executive orders of, 80, 138–139

CAB. *See* Civil Aeronautics Board
Campbell, Carmen, 103, 104–105
Carcinogens, 170
Card, Andrew, Jr., 83
Carter, Jimmy, 24
executive orders of, 82–83
Casework, 181–182
Caveat Estoppel, 107–108
Central Intelligence Agency (CIA), 123–125, 130, 140, 144, 149
Central Intelligence Agency Act of 1949, 123
Checks and balances, 5, 6, 158, 184, 189
Cheney, Dick, 23–24, 144
Chevron U.S.A., Inc. v. Natural Resources Defense Council, Inc., 173–174
Chicago River, 77
Chief Financial Officers Act, 179, 180
Children, 11
CIA. *See* Central Intelligence Agency
Cinderella Career College and Finishing Schools, Inc., 89–91, 92, 115, 166
Cinderella Career College and Finishing Schools, Inc. v. Federal Trade Commission, 90, 91, 93, 99, 102, 106, 111–112, 114, 185
Citizens to Preserve Overton Park, Inc., v. Volpe, 177
City of Arlington, Texas v. Federal Communications Commission, 174–175
City of Ontario, California v. Quon, 101
Civil Aeronautics Board (CAB), 166
Civil rights, 157, 168, 192
Civil Rights Act of 1964, 32, 37, 66

Civil service, 11, 24, 31, 51, 68, 85, 106
Civil Service Reform Act (1978), 146
Clapper, James R., Jr., 125
Clark, Tom, 153
Classification issues, 43–46, 52, 53, 57, 58, 174
Clean Air Act (1977), 7, 176
Clean Water Act, 167
Climate change, 24
Clinton, Bill, 20–21, 25–26, 31, 83, 84, 142
executive orders of, 69, 70, 80
Reinventing Government initiative by, 24, 120
Clinton, Hillary, 144, 145
Coal mining, 36
Coast Guard, 77
Code of Federal Regulations, 190
Cold War, 125, 184
Colorado, 147
Common Cause, 143
Compassion. *See* Equity and compassion
Competence, 92, 95, 97, 98, 110, 112, 115, 120, 121
Compromises, 10, 100
Congress, 3, 4, 11–12, 22–23, 24, 36, 74, 75, 78, 79, 111, 115, 117, 170, 174, 175, 181
and adjudicatory ordermaking, 95
administrative agencies as threat to, 12
and agencies' strategic plans, 182
delegation of legislative authority to administrative agencies, 4–7, 12, 29, 31, 70, 82, 83, 153, 178
grants to states, 41, 43
House of Representatives, 165, 179
legislative review of administration, 153, 178–184, 185
and presidential vetoes, 125
Senate Judiciary Committee, 13
volume of lawmaking per year, 65
Congressional Budget Office, 23, 180
Congressional Research Service (CRS), 180
Congressional Review Act (1996), 23, 182–183

Constitution, 6, 12, 19, 60, 123, 126, 159, 191
   Appointment Clause, 27
   Article I, 35, 36–40, 41, 158
   Article II, 24, 25, 31, 33
   Article III, 154, 158, 159, 160, 165
   Article IV, 158
   Bill of Rights, 35, 125, 187
   Commerce Clause, 168
   constitutional contractarianism, 186–187 (*see also* Contractarianism)
   constitutionalism, 8, 16, 149
   constitutional law, 4, 9, 10, 21, 34, 35, 43, 48, 50, 54, 58, 59, 60, 66, 146, 169, 186, 187, 189
   constitutional rights, 11, 21, 33, 34, 42, 43–58, 59, 60, 188 (*see also* Rights)
   Impeachment Clause, 165
   liability for constitutional torts, 58–60
   original intent of framers, 168
   Preamble, 186, 189
   state constitutions, 11, 22
   unconstitutional conditions doctrine, 47–48, 53
   See also individual amendments
Consultants, 144
Consumers Power Company, 173
Contractarianism, 186–187, 188, 189
Contractors/contracts, 26, 53–54, 92–93, 130, 146, 148
Controlled Substance Act, 38
Corporations, 9
Corruption, 142
Cosmetics, 164
Costs, 2, 26, 117, 181, 187
   of advisory committees, 79
   of benzene reduction in atmosphere, 170
   cost-benefit analysis, 9, 15, 68, 82, 83, 86, 99, 161, 170, 188, 189
   concerning rulemaking, 65
Council on Competiveness, 83
Courts 12, 22, 26, 42, 48, 49, 56, 74, 75, 76, 86, 97–98, 136, 139
   appeals courts, 90–91, 104, 105, 146, 155–156, 157, 158, 170, 173, 188, 190, 191 (*see also* Appeals)

Court of Appeals for the District of Columbia Circuit, 90–91, 156, 173
Court of Appeals for the Federal Circuit, 32, 146, 155
   district courts, 154, 155, 156, 158, 165, 177, 190
   division of labor between courts and agencies, 166
   federal court system, 154–159
   partnership between courts and agencies, 168
   specialized courts, 157
   state courts, 159, 165, 167–168
   See also Judiciary
Craig v. Boren, 160, 161, 162
Criminal conduct, 36, 38, 45, 114, 118, 131, 141, 165, 168, 187, 189
CRS. *See* Congressional Research Service
Customs Service, 119, 174

Daily agendas, 132
Data Quality Act (2000), 14, 64
Davis, Kenneth Culp, 193
Death row, 163, 175
Decisionmaking, 3, 4, 8–10, 58, 60, 78, 91, 97, 102, 106, 110, 112, 129, 142, 153, 161, 166, 171
   adjudicatory decisions, 47, 94–95, 100, 111, 113–114
   formal/informal, 9
   predecisional information/ discussions, 134, 143
   procedural and substantive reviews of, 10–12
   rationality and lawfulness in, 8, 10
   retrospective/prospective/present tense decisions, 9–10
   tentative decisions, 113
Declaration of Independence, 186, 191
Defense Department, 141
Dell, Virginia, 142
Deportations, 106
Depositions, 110
Desegregation of public schools, 33–34, 162. *See also* Segregation
Disability benefits, 47, 49, 103–105, 112

Discretion in formulating standards and policies, 7–8
Discrimination, 32, 37–38, 45, 51, 53, 95, 96–97, 162
Dixon, Paul Rand, 90, 91, 99, 111–112
Douglas, William O., 124, 125
Drones, 124, 125
Drug companies, 151–152, 153, 159, 164
Drug testing, 51
Dual sovereignty, 40. *See also* Sovereignty
Due process, 10, 13, 22, 34, 35, 44, 67, 90, 91, 92, 94, 99, 167
   Due Process Clause, 46, 52, 106
   procedural, 46–47, 51–52, 55, 102, 106–107, 113, 187, 189
   substantive, 52–53

Economics, 186
EEO. *See* Equal employment opportunity
EEOC. *See* Equal Employment Opportunity Commission
Efficiency, 21, 26, 28, 31, 48, 50, 69, 74, 92, 95, 97, 98, 105, 110, 112, 115, 120, 121, 129, 146
Eighth Amendment, 54, 55, 187, 188
Eleventh Amendment, 21, 35, 41–43, 168
Emergency situations, 119
Employment, 32, 37, 66, 103–105, 106. *See also* Public employees
Energy issues, 127
Enforcement issues, 3, 7, 9, 12, 13, 33, 40, 41, 66, 68, 69, 85, 111, 117–120, 136, 146, 152, 153, 154, 164, 166
   agency nonenforcement, 175–177
   biased enforcement, 112
   enforcement clauses, 42
   enforcement of Regulatory Flexibility Act, 79–80
   flexibility in enforcing policy, 99
   See also Law enforcement
Environment, 9, 11, 39, 64, 68, 76, 79, 81, 127, 169–170, 173, 187. *See also* Environmental Protection Agency; Water

Environmental Protection Agency (EPA), 4, 5, 11, 39, 65, 80, 117, 167, 176
   authority to define sources of air pollution, 173–174
   Farmworker Protection Standards, 77
EOP. *See* Executive branch: Executive Office of the President
EPA. *See* Environmental Protection Agency
Equal employment opportunity (EEO), 95, 96, 97, 98
Equal Employment Opportunity Commission (EEOC), 66, 95
Equal protection, 10, 34, 35, 41, 43–46, 48, 49, 52, 160, 187
   constraints, 57–58
   Equal Protection Clause, 42, 56, 58
   three-tiered structure of, 43–44
Equity and compassion, 99, 102–105
Ethics in Government Act of 1978, 26
Ethnicity, 44, 45, 52, 53, 57
Evidentiary administrative adjudication, 98, 113, 189
   alternative dispute resolution, 115–117
   conduct and application cases, 101–102
   formalization of, 120–121
   objectives of, 92
   review boards, 114
   use of, 91–92
   See also Adjudication
Executions, 175
Executive branch, 5, 11, 12, 184, 189
   Executive Office of the President (EOP), 29–30, 130, 139
   executive privilege, 134, 138, 139, 144
   and federal agency rulemaking, 82–85
   federal contracts, 26 (*see also* Contractors/contracts)
   federal employees, 22 (*see also* Federal employees; Public employees)
   Senior Executive Service, 31
   unitary executive branch theory, 83, 159

Executive branch (*continued*)
  vice presidents, 138, 139
  White House Office, 29, 30, 31
  See also Presidents
Executive orders, 191. *See also under*
  Presidents
Ex parte communications, 110
Expertise, 5, 10, 67, 78, 115, 166, 168

FACA. *See* Federal Advisory Committee
  Act
Facilitators, 115
Fact-finding, 115
Fairness, 22, 69, 91, 92, 93, 95, 96, 97,
  98, 101, 102, 106, 110, 111, 115, 120,
  121, 141, 185
False Claims Act of 1863, 148
Families, 52, 68, 99
Favish, Allan, 135
FCC. *See* Federal Communications
  Commission
FDA. *See* Food and Drug
  Administration
Feasibility requirement, 7, 64
Federal Advisory Committee Act
  (FACA) (1972), 14, 75, 78–79, 81,
  142, 143–144
Federal Aviation Administration, 66
Federal Bureau of Investigation, 128,
  130
Federal Civil Penalties Inflation Report
  Adjustment Act of 1990, 179
Federal Communications Commission
  (FCC), 7, 80, 100, 111, 172
Federal Communications Commission v.
  Fox Television Stations, 172
Federal employees, 22, 24, 59, 65, 79,
  96–98, 110, 113, 144, 146. *See also*
  Public employees
Federal Food, Drug, and Cosmetic Act
  of 1938, 74, 151
Federalism, 9, 21, 35–43, 60, 99, 187
Federalist, The, 189
Federal Labor Relations Authority
  (FLRA), 95, 97–98, 140–141
"Federal Leadership in Environmental,
  Energy, and Economic

Performance" (executive order),
  127
Federal Register, 71, 72, 73, 74, 77, 79, 80,
  84, 99, 126, 140, 143, 183, 190
Federal Reserve System, 144
Federal Trade Commission (FTC), 27,
  80, 89–91, 99, 111
Federal Trade Secrets Act (1948), 129
Fees, 107, 128, 129, 130, 136
Ferguson, Homer, 85–86
Fifteenth Amendment, 36, 42
Fifth Amendment, 46, 48, 52, 92, 106,
  118, 187
First Amendment, 35, 44, 48, 49–51, 52,
  163. *See also* Freedom of speech
Flexibility in rulemaking/adjudication,
  67–68, 79, 100, 109
Florida, 111
FLRA. *See* Federal Labor Relations
  Authority
FOIA. *See* Freedom of Information Act
  of 1966
Food and Drug Administration (FDA),
  63–64, 66, 68, 69, 73, 74, 84, 151,
  159, 164, 175
  product testing, 119
  regulation of impurities in food, 1–4,
  5
Food industry representatives, 3
Ford, Gerald, 82
Foster, Vincent, 135
Fourteenth Amendment, 35, 41, 42, 45,
  46, 52, 54, 92, 106, 118, 163
Fourth Amendment, 49, 51, 52, 101,
  118–119, 119–120
  constraints, 56–57
Frankfurter, Felix, 100
Fraud, 148, 166
Freedom of association, 48, 49, 50–51
Freedom of expression, 163
Freedom of information, 126, 142,
  149, 172, 185. *See also* Freedom of
  Information Act (1966)
Freedom of Information Act of 1966
  (FOIA), 14, 32, 75, 128–139, 148,
  172, 190
  amendments to, 128, 130
  enforcement of, 136, 137

exemptions concerning, 129, 130–132, 133–135, 135, 138, 139, 143, 149
FOIA Reference Guide, 129
government spending on requests concerning, 137
and Privacy Act, 140–141
Freedom of speech, 21, 48–49, 53, 187
limitations on, 49–50, 145–146
FTC. *See* Federal Trade Commission

Gagnon v. Scarpelli, 107
GAO. *See* Government Accountability (Accounting) Office
Garcetti v. Ceballos, 145
Garrett, Patricia, 20, 21, 42
Gellhorn and Byse's Administrative Law: Cases and Comments (Strauss et al.), 193
Gender, 45–46, 52, 53, 57, 96
General Accounting Office (GAO), 23, 72, 145, 180, 182, 183. *See also* Government Accountability Office.
General Services Administration, 24
Glomar denial, 133
Goldberg v. Kelly, 106–107
Gonzales v. Raich, 38–39
Gore, Al, 24, 84, 179, 188
Goss v. Lopez, 107
Government Accountability Office (GAO), 23, 72, 126–127, 180, 182, 183
Government in the Sunshine Act (1976), 14, 75, 142–143
Government Performance and Results Act (1993), 14, 20, 23, 182
Government Performance and Results Act Modernization Act of 2010 (GPRA Modernization Act), 15, 23, 127, 180, 182
Grant of immunity, 118
Grants, 41, 43, 71
Gratzianna, John, 20, 21, 53
Great Depression, 36
Grid regulations (grid-regs), 103, 104, 105
Groundwater, 39. *See also* Water
Guam, 158

Guide to the Freedom of Information Act (Department of Justice), 190
Gun control, 38, 41

Hamilton, Alexander, 158, 189
Hansen, Ann, 107–108
Hate groups, 50
Health and Human Services, Department of, 127–128
Health issues, 2, 3, 5, 7, 10, 33, 39, 49, 64, 103, 127–128
health workers, 56
hospital patients, 57
public mental health patients, 54–55, 158
Heckler v. Campbell, 103
Heckler v. Cheney, 175–176
Herald-Traveler newspaper, 100
Hispanics, 96
Holder, Eric, 132
Homeland Security, Department of, 30
Homelessness, 55
Hope v. Pelzer, 59
Hospitals, 57, 162
Humphrey's Executor v. United States, 27

IGs. *See* Inspector generals
Impact statements, 9
Impartiality, 50, 109, 110, 111. *See also* Bias
Impeachments, 165
Incrementalism, 99, 100–101
Independent counsels, 19–20, 26, 27
Indigents, 162
Industrialization 12
Industrial Union Department, AFL-CIO v. American Petroleum Institute, 169–171
Inspections, 56–57, 109, 118–119, 120, 126
Inspectors general (IGs), 145, 179, 180
Instrumentalism, 187–190
Interest groups, 75, 76, 86
Interior, Department of, 24
Internal Revenue Service, 80, 161, 162
Internal Revenue Service Restructuring and Reform Act of 1998, 182
Internet, 126. *See also* Websites

Interstate commerce, 36, 37, 39–40
Interstate Commerce Commission, 70, 75
Iraq War, 125
Iron triangle, 75, 76
Issue networks, 76

Jackson, Robert, 12, 28–29
Judges, 154, 155, 158, 165, 174
  contractarian, 188
  passive/activist, 168, 169
  See also Administrative law: administrative law judges
Judicial review, 11, 13, 15, 44, 73, 81, 109, 112, 114, 152, 153, 183–184, 185
  of administrative action, 153–183
  and discretionary actions, 177–178
  and hard/soft "looks," 169, 171, 172, 173, 174, 177, 178
  and mootness, 162–163, 165
  nonreviewability, 176
  preenforcement review, 152, 159, 164
  premature, 167
  reviewability, 159–165
  and ripeness, 163–165
  scope of, 168–178
  timing of, 165–168
Judiciary, 32–34, 48, 49, 55, 60, 101
  appearance of bias in, 111, 112
  limitations on judicial power, 158–159
  "real 'invisible' judiciary," 113
  See also Courts; Judges; Judicial Review; Strict scrutiny; Supreme Court
Juries, 45, 154, 155, 189
Jurisdiction issues, 165–166
Justice Department, 8, 26, 118, 128, 132, 148, 190

Korean War, 19

Labor, Department of, 110
Labor practices, 9, 36, 39, 91, 93, 95, 101, 102, 141
Labor unions, 50, 93, 116, 141
Law enforcement, 51, 58, 128, 129, 131, 134, 139, 140

law enforcement searches, 56–57 (*see also* Searches)
  See also Justice Department; Police
Law of estoppel, 107–108
Legal education, 16
Legislative Reorganization Act of 1946, 179
Levin, Ronald, 193
Lewinsky, Monica, 142
Licensing, 10, 46, 47, 91, 102, 103, 106, 113, 117
Litigation, 32, 41, 42, 58–60, 71, 104, 116–117, 123, 127, 132, 138–139, 141, 142, 143, 146, 152, 154, 168
  standing to litigate, 124, 148, 160–162, 165
Louisiana, 147

McCarran, Pat, 189–190
McCorvey, Norma Leah, 163
Madison, James, 125, 137, 189
Marbury v. Madison, 159
Marijuana, 38
Marriage, 52, 55
Marshall, Thurgood, 105, 108
Massachusetts v. Environmental Protection Agency, 176–177
Media, 3, 5, 111, 127, 130, 138, 145
Mediation, 115, 116
Medicare/Medicaid, 148
Merit systems, 95, 98
Merit Systems Protection Board (MSPB), 96, 98, 110, 111, 112–113, 117, 121, 136, 146, 147–148, 155
Minitrials, 116
Minorities, 44, 45, 68, 96
  business set-asides for, 53
  See also African Americans; Asian Pacific Americans; Hispanics; Native Americans
Mission statements, 127
Miss USA/Miss Universe, 89
Mock trials, 117
Model State Administrative Procedure Act (1961, 1981), 15, 74, 82
Morrison v. Olson, 26, 27
Motor Vehicle Manufacturers Association of the United States v. State Farm

Mutual Automobile Insurance Co., 171–172
MSPB. *See* Merit Systems Protection Board
Municipal utilities, 106

Nader, Ralph, 166
NARA. *See* National Archives and Records Administration
Narrow tailoring, 44
National Archives and Records Administration (NARA), 135, 139
website for, 191
National Archives and Records Administration v. Favish, 134–135
National defense, 131. *See also* National security
National Energy Policy Development Group, 144
National Environmental Policy Act of 1969, 80
National Federation of Independent Business v. Sebelius, 39
National Highway Traffic Safety Administration (NHTSA), 66, 171
National Labor Relations Act of 1935, 20, 26
National Labor Relations Board (NLRB), 93, 101, 110
National Performance Review, 84, 179, 188
National security, 51, 124, 129, 133, 139, 190
National Security Archive, 138
Native Americans, 96
Natural Resources Defense Council, 145
Nebraska, 147
Negotiated Rulemaking Act (1990), 14, 77
New Deal, 12, 29, 36, 37, 40, 184
New Jersey, 111
New property doctrine, 43, 46, 47, 48, 52
New York v. Burger, 119
NHTSA. *See* National Highway Traffic Safety Administration
9/11 Commission Act (2007), 142
Nineteenth Amendment, 36

Nixon, Richard, 19, 21, 82, 138
Nixon, Walter L., Jr., 165
Nixon v. United States, 165
NLRB. *See* National Labor Relations Board
North Dakota, 147
Northern Mariana Islands, 158
Nova Scotia Food Products Corporation, 63, 69, 71, 73. *See also United States v. Nova Scotia Food Products Corp.*
Nuclear Regulatory Commission, 101, 173
Nuclear waste, 173
Nudity, 163
Nutrition labels on food products, 2, 3, 84

Oaths, 110
Obama, Barack, 24, 31
executive orders of, 69–70, 80, 84, 132, 139
Obamacare. *See* Patient Protection and Affordable Care Act
Occupational Safety and Health Act of 1970, 6–7
Occupational Safety and Health Administration (OSHA), 57, 67, 80, 114, 169–170, 183
Occupational Safety and Health Review Commission, 114
O'Connor, Sandra Day, 39, 40
OEO. *See* Office of Economic Opportunity
Office of Economic Opportunity (OEO), 19, 21, 25
Office of Homeland Security (OHS), 30
Office of Information and Regulatory Affairs (OIRA), 11, 30, 81, 83, 84
website for, 191
Office of Management and Budget (OMB), 4, 11, 29–30, 31, 71, 79, 80, 81, 82, 83, 84, 95, 127, 130
website for, 191
Office of Personnel Management, 98, 111
Office of Policy Development, 30
Office of Special Counsel, 146, 147

OHS. *See* Office of Homeland Security
Oil industry, 135. *See also* Petroleum
OIRA. *See* Office of Information and
    Regulatory Affairs
Oklahoma, 160
Olson, Theodore, 19–20, 21, 27
OMB. *See* Office of Management and
    Budget
Ombudsmen/ombudswomen, 115
OPEN Government Act. *See* Openness
    Promotes Effectiveness in Our
    National Government Act
Open meetings, 126, 142–145, 149
Openness Promotes Effectiveness in
    Our National Government Act
    (OPEN Government Act) (2007),
    15, 128, 129, 130, 136–137
OSHA. *See* Occupational Safety and
    Health Administration

Pakistan, 125
Paperwork Reduction Acts (1980, 1995),
    14, 80–81, 86
Pap's A.M. corporation, 163
Patient Protection and Affordable Care
    Act, 39
Paxon, Reid, 20, 21
Peanut butter, 67, 68
Pennsylvania, 147, 163
Petroleum, 127, 135, 170
Pharmaceutical companies. *See* Drug
    companies
Pharmaceutical Manufacturers
    Association, 151
Phillips, Howard, 19, 25
Police, 10, 16, 33, 53, 56
Political issues, 6, 10, 22, 51, 70–71, 76,
    85, 86, 95, 111, 165, 183
    and openness in government, 149
    political appointees, 11, 27, 30–31, 50,
        82, 83
    political favoritism, 142
Powell, Lewis, 34
Precedents, 59, 80, 82, 83, 84, 100, 107,
    115, 117, 152, 155, 157
Predetermination hearings, 107
Preemption doctrine, 39

Prescription drugs, 151. *See also* Drug
    companies
Presidential Records Act of 1978, 128,
    134, 138–139
Presidents 23–32, 78
    executive orders of, 1, 9, 15, 19, 20,
        21, 25–26, 29, 31–32, 69–70, 73, 80,
        82–83, 84, 127, 134, 187, 191
    limits to presidential authority over
        legislative rulemaking, 85
    President's Task Force on National
        Health Care Reform, 144–145
    vetoes of, 82, 125
    See also Executive branch
Prisoners/prisons, 54, 55–56, 106, 125,
    158, 162–163, 165, 175, 188, 192
Privacy, 49, 51, 56, 57, 101, 119, 128, 135,
    139–142, 190
    protection against invasion of, 14,
        126, 131, 134, 136, 141
Privacy Act (1974), 14, 129, 134, 139,
    140–141, 142, 149
Private property, 187
Private sector, 149
Probable cause, 57
Procurement Act of 1949, 20, 26
Profiling, 58
Prompt Payment Act, 179
Public accommodations, 37
Public administrative instrumentalism,
    187–190
Public Citizen, 138, 143
Public Company Accounting Oversight
    Board, 20, 21, 28
Public employees, 22, 48–52, 85, 96, 106,
    145–146, 147, 164
    number of federal employees, 65
    and procedural due process, 51–52
    street-level regulatory encounters, 56
    See also Federal employees
Public housing, 46
Public interest, 7, 24, 48, 50, 59, 67, 70,
    72, 75, 101, 141
Public personnel management, 48–49.
    See also Public employees
Public reporting, 126–128

Public schools, 33–34, 46, 47, 56, 57, 77, 106, 161–162
  suspensions from, 107
Public service model, 48–50, 52

Qualified immunity, 59, 60
Questionnaires, 139–140
Qui Tam, 148

Race, 44, 45, 52, 53, 57, 162
Railroad industry, 75
Rationality, 8, 10, 13, 45, 52, 64, 68, 69, 70, 76
Reagan, Ronald, 24, 138
  deregulatory agenda of, 85
  executive orders of, 80, 83, 84, 85
Record-keeping, 118
Reforms, 24, 33, 55, 120–121, 162, 188
Regulatory Analysis Review Group, 82
Regulatory Council, 82
Regulatory Flexibility Act (1980), 14, 79–80
Rehnquist, William, 7, 168, 170
Reinventing Government initiative, 24, 120
Religion, 47, 48, 49, 50, 51, 55, 161, 187
Reno, Janet, 132
Reporters Committee for Freedom of the Press, 138
Restraining orders, 154
Richardson, William, 123–124, 136, 161
Richardson v. Perales, 113
Rights, 22, 32, 35–36, 46, 55, 102, 135, 146, 162, 192
  to an abortion, 163
  First Amendment rights, 49–51 (*see also* First Amendment)
  natural rights theory, 186
  privacy rights, 135 (*see also* Privacy)
  voting rights, 157
  See also Civil rights; Constitution: constitutional rights
Roosevelt, Franklin D., 29, 37
Roosevelt, Theodore, 24
Rubber, 170
Rulemaking, 5, 9, 11–12, 13, 32, 63, 64–77, 154, 158, 171, 172–173, 189

advisory committees for, 78–79
  as alternative to legislative process, 69
  APA's rulemaking processes, 71–75
  complaints about, 85–86
  definition and characteristics of administrative rules, 65–67
  denial of petition for, 176
  vs. evidentiary administrative adjudication, 92, 94, 95, 99, 100, 101, 103
  hybrid rulemaking, 75–76, 173
  idealized legislative model for, 70, 71, 76, 78–82
  informal/formal rulemaking, 72–75, 76, 77, 81, 113, 169, 178, 187
  limits to presidential authority over legislative rulemaking, 85
  negotiated rulemaking (Reg-Neg), 76–77, 185
  notice and comment rulemaking, 72, 73, 75, 77, 79, 92, 151, 156, 170, 183
  number of rules per year, 65
  processes, 71–77
  regulating, 67–69
  types of rules, 66, 72–73
Rule of law, 8, 13, 26, 68, 153
Rule of necessity, 112
Rules of evidence, 113–114

Sackett v. Environmental Protection Agency, 167
Safety, 2, 5, 7, 10, 33, 39, 49, 51, 64, 79, 101, 119, 131, 171
Safety net, 102–103, 105
Sanctions, 106, 117, 118, 120, 160
Sarbanes-Oxley Act (2002), 20, 21, 28
Scalia, Antonin, 27, 137, 160
Schweiker v. Hansen, 107–108
Science, 5, 9, 64, 67, 69, 73, 84, 92, 101
Searches, 9, 48, 51, 56–57, 118–119, 130
Seatbelts, 171
SEC. *See* Securities and Exchange Commission
Secrecy, 123, 124, 125, 126, 128, 149
  trade secrets, 129, 131, 133–134, 164
  See also Transparency

Securities and Exchange Commission
(SEC), 20, 21, 28, 66
Segregation, 44. *See also* Desegregation
of public schools
Separation of powers, 6, 12, 20, 21,
22–34, 60, 125, 144, 159, 165, 184
Sexual harassment/abuse, 97, 188
Small businesses, 14, 69, 71, 79, 99
Small Business Administration, 79–80
Small Business Regulatory Enforcement
Fairness Act (1996), 14, 80, 182
Snowden, Edward, 124
Social Security, 47, 103. *See also*
Disability benefits
Social Security Act, 105
Social Security Administration (SSA),
103, 107, 110, 113, 120
Social Security Appeals Council, 104,
112
Social work, 103, 119
Sociology, 186
Sovereignty, 124. *See also* States: state
sovereignty
Special interests, 142
SSA. *See* Social Security Administration
State and Federal Administrative Law
(Asimow, Bonfield, and Levin),
193
State Department, 141
States, 22, 35–36, 118, 137, 163, 181
federal judicial deference to state
courts, 167–168
grants to, 41, 43
open meeting laws of, 142
preempted by federal legislation, 39
review of rules by legislative
committees by, 183
state actors, 53–54
state constitutions, 11, 22
state courts, 159, 165, 167–168
state sovereignty, 40, 41–42, 60
and whistle-blower protection, 147
"Stories Managers Tell: Why They Are
as Valid as Science," 191–192
Strauss, Peter, 193
Strict scrutiny, 44, 52, 53, 169, 187
Strikes, 20, 25, 31
Subpoenas, 110, 118

Sunset legislation, 180
Supreme Court, 4, 6, 8, 25, 27, 36–37, 39,
40, 42, 52, 53, 58, 59, 74, 101, 105,
107, 114, 119, 124, 133, 135–136,
145, 155, 156–157, 159, 163, 164,
167, 171–172, 174, 175, 187
number of petitions/cases, 157
packing of, 37
Rehnquist Court, 168
and relationship between FOIA and
the Privacy Act, 140–141
websites concerning, 191

Tamposi, Elizabeth, 141–142
Taxation, 33, 106, 161–162
Taxpayer Bill of Rights legislation, 182
Technology, 101, 178, 182
Telephone message slips, 132
Tenth Amendment, 35, 40–41, 168
Terrorist attacks of September 11, 2001,
125, 127, 142, 190
Thirteenth Amendment, 36, 42
Thomas, Clarence, 44(n)
Timeliness, 15, 74, 77, 92, 117, 130, 137
Toilet Goods Association, Inc. v. Gardner,
164
Transparency, 2, 3, 13, 32, 83, 142, 158,
185, 189, 190
in national security policy, 124
See also Secrecy
Transportation, 3, 12, 37, 39, 177–178
Transportation Department, 177
Treasury Department, 123
Tripp, Linda, 142
Truman, Harry, 19, 20–21, 28, 31
Twenty-First/Twenty-Fourth/Twenty-
Sixth Amendments, 36

Unemployment compensation, 47, 103
*Unified Agenda of Federal Regulatory and
Deregulatory Actions*, 65
Unions. *See* Labor unions
United Nations General Assembly, 137
United States Government Manual, 127
United States Immigration and
Customs Enforcement, 118
United States v. Lopez, 38, 39
United States v. Mead Corp., 174

United States v. Morrison, 38, 39
United States v. Nova Scotia Food Products Corp., 64, 154, 185. *See also* Nova Scotia Food Products Corporation
United States v. Richardson, 123, 124, 161
Universal Camera Corp. v. National Labor Relations Board, 178
USA Today, 148
U.S. Department of Defense v. Federal Labor Relations Authority, 140

Vaughn, Robert, 137
Vermont Yankee Nuclear Power Corp. v. Natural Resources Defense Council, Inc., 76, 172–173
Veterans Affairs, Department of, 155
Violence Against Women Act (1994), 38
Virgin Islands, 158
Volpe, John, 177–178
Voting rights, 157

Wages, 36
Wald, Patricia, 137, 156
Waldo, Dwight, 149
Warren, Kenneth, 84–85, 101, 193
Washington Post, 124
Water, 4, 5, 39, 64, 79, 81, 106, 127
Watergate, 139
Websites, 127, 186, 190–191
Welfare, 10, 45, 46, 47, 69, 102–103, 105, 106, 107
    and homes of recipients, 119
    welfare rights organizations, 162
Wheat, 37
Whistle-blowing, 49, 126, 145–148, 149
Whistleblower Protection Act of 1989, 146
Whitefish (smoked), 63–64, 92
Wickard v. Filburn, 38
Wilson, Woodrow, 19, 188
Women, 45, 53, 160, 188
World War II, 12, 184
Wyatt v. Stickney, 54, 55